T0323048

The Oriental Caravan

The
Oriental Caravan

*A Revelation of the Soul and Mind
of Asia*

Edited by
Sirdar Ikbal Ali
Shah

1984
DARF PUBLISHERS LTD
LONDON

This sublime collection of Asia's hoary wisdom is humbly dedicated to HIS MAJESTY ALA HAZRAT MOHAMED NADIR SHAH GHAZI, *the benign and sagacious monarch of the God-gifted Kingdom of Afghanistan.*

First impression   June, 1933
Second impression   Sept. 1933
New impression   1984

Printed and bound in Great Britain by
A. Wheaton & Co. Ltd., Exeter

ISBN 1 85077 015 8

$\mathcal{C}$ontents

BOOK I

RELIGIOUS LITERATURE

5

Contents

BOOK III

ROMANTIC LITERATURE

Contents

Contents

8

BOOK IV

NATIONAL LITERATURE, ESSAYS, WAR SONGS, AND MISCELLANEOUS

Introduction

$\mathcal{I}$t is presumptuous to write an introduction to most books; especially is it so in regard to a collection which has no parallel in Oriental thought, modern or ancient: but if I do so it is with such reverent feelings as may arise in the minds of men when, chanting hymns, they receive benediction from the Mighty Throne: for in all sublime and true song glimmers the Great Radiance. Is it possible then to describe that glow, that gleam?

The least of the values of this collection is that, during even a short reading of its contents, one may feel the ushering in of a fragrant calmness so necessary in the tempestuous atmosphere of modern life.

The portion dealing with the religious literature is among soulful passages as a diamond among other precious stones: because the holy passages are beyond human appraisement. For the rest, if I say that it is more beautiful than the dawn, more entrancing than the scent within the rose, I am merely praising what is beyond all praise; so let me just place this casket of Eastern jewels before you!

I most gratefully acknowledge my indebtedness to the following publishers and others for permission to quote from the works named:

T. D. Broughton, Esq.: *Popular Poetry of the Hindus*; Messrs Milford: *Rubaiyat of Omar Khyyam*; Miss L. S. Costello: *The Rose Garden of Persia*; Messrs Harper Brothers: *A Century of Indian Epigrams*; Lady Richmond: *Poems from the Divan of Hafiz*; Association Press: *Hymns from the Rigveda*; Professor Shastri: *Translations from the Gita*; Messrs Dent: *Nargas, Songs of a Sikh*; *The Modern Review*: Various Poems of Sir Rabindranath Tagore; Messrs Chapman & Hall: *Tales of Mystic Meaning*; The Royal Asiatic Society: *Lawaih of Jami*; Sir Mohammed Iqbal: Extracts from his lectures; Madrat Moulana Moha-

10 med Ali: Translation of the Holy Koran; The Golden Cockerel Press: *A Circle of Seasons* (*Kalidas*); Messrs John Murray: *Wisdom of the East* Series; Trustees of Gibb Memorial Trust: *A History of Ottoman Poetry* and *Kashf-al-Mahjub*; Cambridge University Press: Revised Version of the Holy Bible; Messrs Williams & Norgate: *Ancient Arabic Poetry*; The Jewish Historical Society: *Songs of Exile*; Messrs Wright & Brown: *Eastward to Persia*; Messrs Constable: *One hundred and Seventy Chinese Poems*; Jewish Welfare Board: *A Book of Jewish Thought*.

In conclusion, I must tender my heartfelt gratitude to C. A. Storey, Esq., the Librarian of the India Office Library, and to his Staff, who have given me the greatest possible help during the research of this work, in which I am happy to associate the names of the officers in charge of the Oriental Students' Room in the British Museum, as well as the Hon. Librarian of the Folk Lore Society.

Al Faqir,
SYED IKBAL.

LONDON,
9th *May* 1933.

BOOK I

Religious Literature

THE KORAN

The Al-Quran, the proper name of the Sacred Book of the Moslems, is believed by the followers of the Prophet Mohamed to have been vouchsafed to the Prophet through Divine agency. He was inspired to receive it in the Arabic language, in the first instance, during a night of prayer near Mecca in the year A.D. 610, when he was forty years of age.

The Book was revealed piecemeal during a period of twenty-three years, the shorter chapters generally and some of the larger ones entire and at one time, whilst the revelation of the majority of the larger chapters extended over many years. The arrangement of verses and chapters was entirely the Prophet's work.

The First Companion, Abu Bakr, made the first complete written copy by arranging the manuscripts written during the lifetime of the Prophet. The Second Companion, Omar, handed over the Book to his sister, from whom it reached the Third Companion, Usman, who had a number of duplicate copies of the original text made for the use of the faithful. At every stage of its transcription the greatest human care was exercised that not even as much as a diacritical point was altered; and therefore it is the proud boast of the Moslems that the Book which they cherish remains absolutely unchanged since it was reduced to writing from the utterance of the Prophet Mohamed thirteen centuries ago.

It is not to be inferred that the extracts from the Koran which appear in the following pages have in any way precedence over other verses, for it is not possible to select passages from any Holy Book, as the scriptures of a religion are immortal: nevertheless, what is given below are but a few fragments from the mighty mountains of Heavenly Light before which frail human intellect is bedazzled into nothingness: for, indeed, what could be a greater insolence than for a mere mortal to select passages from God's Book? The passages, however, are taken from Hadrat Moulana Mohamed Ali's English Translation of the Koran.

THE COW

Section 19.—Trials to be undergone

O you who believe! seek assistance through patience and prayer; for God is with the patient. And do not speak of those who are slain in God's way as dead; nay, (they are) alive, but you do not perceive. And We will certainly try you with somewhat of fear and hunger and loss of property and lives and fruits; and give good news to the patient, Who, when a misfortune befalls them, say: We are God's and to Him we shall return. Those are they on whom are blessings and mercy from their Lord, and those are the followers of the right course. The Safa and the Marwah are among the signs of God; so whoever makes a pilgrimage to the House or pays a visit (to it), there is no blame on him if he goes round them both; and whoever does good spontaneously, then God is Bountiful in rewarding, Knowing. Those who conceal the clear proofs and the guidance that We revealed after We made it clear in the Book for men, these it is whom God shall curse, and those who curse shall curse them (too), except those who repent and amend and make manifest (the truth); these it is to whom I turn (mercifully), and I am the Oft-returning (to mercy), the Merciful. Those who disbelieve and die while they are disbelievers, these it is on whom is the curse of God and angels and men, all: abiding in it; their chastisement shall not be lightened nor shall they be given respite. And your God is one God! there is no god but He; He is the Beneficent, the Merciful.

Section 20.—*Unity must prevail*

In the creation of the heavens and the earth and the alteration of the night and the day, and the ships that run in the sea with that which profits men, and the water that God sends down from the cloud, then gives life with it to the earth after its death and spreads in it all (kinds of) animals, and the changing of the winds and the clouds made subservient between the heaven and the earth, there are signs for a people who understand. And there are some among men who set up equals (with God) besides God—they love them as they ought to love God—and those who believe are stronger in love for God—and O that those who are unjust had seen, when they see the chastisement, that the power is wholly God's, and that

God is severe in requiting (evil). When those who were followed shall renounce those who followed (them), and they see the chastisement and their ties are cut asunder. And those who followed shall say: Had there been for us a return, then we would renounce them as they have renounced us. Thus will God show them their deeds to be intense regret to them, and they shall not come out of the fire.

Section 22.—*Retaliation and Bequests*

It is not righteousness that you turn your faces towards the East and the West, but righteousness is this that one should believe in God and the last day and the angels and the book and the prophets, and give away wealth out of love for Him to the near of kin and the orphans and the needy and the wayfarer and the beggars and for (the emancipation of) the captives, and keep up prayer and pay the poor-rate; and the performers of their promise when they make a promise, and the patient in distress and affliction and in time of conflict—these are they who are true (to themselves), and these are they who guard (against evil). O you who believe! retaliation is prescribed for you in the matter of the slain: the free for the free, and the slave for the slave, and the female for the female, but if any remission is made to any one by his (aggrieved) brother, then prosecution (for the bloodwit) should be made according to usage, and payment should be made to him in a good manner; this is an alleviation from your Lord and a mercy; so whoever exceeds the limit after this, he shall have a painful chastisement, and there is life for you in (the law of) retaliation, O men of understanding, that you may guard yourselves. Bequest is prescribed for you when death approaches one of you, if he leaves behind wealth for parents and near relatives, according to usage, a duty (incumbent) upon the righteous. Then whoever alters it after he has heard it—the sin of it is only upon those who alter it; for God is Hearing, Knowing. But he who fears an inclining to a wrong course or an act of disobedience on the part of the testator, and effects an

16 agreement between them, there is no blame on him; for God is Forgiving, Merciful.

Section 34.—*Great Power of God*

O you who believe! spend out of what We have given you before the day comes in which there is no bargaining, neither any friendship nor intercession, and the unbelievers are unjust. God is He besides Whom there is no god, the Ever-living, the Self-subsisting by whom all subsist; slumber does not overtake Him nor sleep; whatever is in the heavens and whatever is in the earth is His; who is he that can intercede with Him but by His permission? He knows what is before them and what is behind them, and they cannot comprehend anything out of His knowledge except what He pleases; His knowledge extends over the heavens and the earth, and the preservation of them both tires Him not, and He is the Most High, the Great. There is no compulsion in religion; indeed the right way has become clearly distinct from error; therefore, whoever disbelieves in the devil and believes in God, he has laid hold on the firmest handle, which shall not break off, and God is Hearing, Knowing. God is the guardian of those who believe: He brings them out of the darkness into the light; and (as to) those who disbelieve, their guardians are the devils who take them out of the light into the darkness; they are the inmates of the fire, in it they shall abide.

Section 36.—*Reward of Charity*

The parable of those who spend their property in the way of God is as the parable of a grain growing seven ears (with) a hundred grains in every ear; and God multiplies for whom He pleases; and God is Ample-giving, Knowing. (As for) those who spend their property in the way of God, then do not follow up what they have spent with reproach or injury, they shall have their reward from their Lord, and they shall have no fear nor shall they grieve. Kind speech and forgiveness is better than charity followed

by injury; and God is Self-sufficient, Forbearing. O you
who believe! do not make your charity worthless by
reproach and injury, like him who spends his property to
be seen of men and does not believe in God and the last
day; so his parable is as the parable of a smooth rock
with earth upon it, then a heavy rain falls upon it, so it
leaves it bare; they shall not be able to gain anything of
what they have earned; and God does not guide the
unbelieving people. And the parable of those who spend
their property to seek the pleasure of God and for the
certainty of their souls is as the parable of a garden on
an elevated ground, upon which heavy rain falls, so it
brings forth its fruit twofold; but if heavy rains do not
fall upon it, then light rain (is sufficient); and God sees
what you do. Does one of you like to have a garden of
palms and vines with streams flowing in it, having in it
all kinds of fruits, and old age has overtaken him and he
has weak offspring, when (lo!) a whirlwind with fire in it
smites it and it becomes blasted; thus does God make the
communications clear to you that you may reflect.

THE FAMILY OF AMRAN

Section 18.—No Gain to the Enemy

Those who responded to the call of God and the Apostle
after the misfortune had befallen them—those among them
who do good and guard (against evil) shall have a great
reward; those to whom the people said: Men have
gathered against you, therefore fear them; but this increased their faith, and they said: God is sufficient for us
and most excellent is the Protector. So they returned with
favour from God and (His) grace; no evil touched them
and they followed God's pleasure; and God is the Lord
of mighty grace. It is only the devil that causes you to
fear from his friends, but do not fear them, and fear Me
if you are believers. And let not those grieve thee who
fall into unbelief hastily; they cannot injure God in the
least; God intends that He should not give them any

18 portion in the hereafter, and they shall have a grievous chastisement. Those who have bought unbelief at the price of faith shall do no harm at all to God, and they shall have a painful chastisement. And let not those who believe think that Our granting them respite is good for them; We grant them respite only that they may add to (their) sins; and they shall have a disgraceful chastisement. On no account will God leave the believers in the condition which you are in until He separates the evil from the good; nor is God going to make you acquainted with the unseen, but God chooses of His apostles whom He pleases; therefore believe in God and His apostles; and if you believe and guard (against evil), you shall have a great reward. And let not those who are niggardly in giving away that which God has granted them out of His grace think that it is good for them; nay, it is worse for them; they shall have that whereof they were niggardly made to cleave to their necks on the resurrection day; and God's is the heritage of the heavens and the earth; and God is aware of what you do.

Section 20.—*Triumph of the Faithful*

In the creation of the heavens and the earth and the alternation of the night and the day there are signs for men of understanding: those who remember God standing and sitting and lying on their sides and reflect on the creation of the heavens and the earth: Our Lord! Thou hast not created this in vain! glory be to Thee! save us from the chastisement of the fire: Our Lord! whomsoever Thou makest enter the fire, him Thou hast indeed brought to disgrace, and there shall be no helpers for the unjust; Our Lord! we heard a Preacher calling to the faith, saying: Believe in your Lord; so we did believe; our Lord! forgive us our faults, and cover our evil deeds and make us die with the righteous: Our Lord! and grant us what Thou hast promised us by Thy apostles and disgrace us not on the day of resurrection; surely Thou dost not fail to perform the promise. So their Lord accepted their prayer, saying: I will not waste the work of a worker among you, whether male or female, the one of you being from the other; they, therefore, who fled and were turned out of their homes and persecuted in My way and who fought and were slain, I will certainly cover their evil deeds, and I will make them enter gardens in which rivers flow: a reward from God, and with God is yet better reward. Let it not deceive thee that those who disbelieve act in the cities as they please. A brief enjoyment! then their abode is hell; and evil is the resting-place. But as to those who are careful of (their duty to) their Lord, they shall have gardens in which rivers flow, abiding in them; an entertainment from their Lord, and that which is with God is best for the righteous. And of the followers of the Book there are those who believe in God and (in) that which has been revealed to you and (in) that which has been revealed to them, being lowly before God; they do not take a small price for the communications of God; these it is that have their reward with their Lord: surely God is quick in reckoning. O you who believe! be patient and vie in endurance and remain steadfast, and be careful of (your duty to) God that you may be successful.

THE CATTLE

Section 12.—*Triumph of Truth*

God causes the grain and the stone to germinate; He brings forth the living from the dead and He is the bringer forth of the dead from the living; that is God! how are you then turned away? He causes the dawn to break; and He has made the night for rest, and the sun and the moon for reckoning; this is an arrangement of the Mighty, the Knowing. And He it is Who has made the stars for you that you might follow the right way thereby in the darkness of the land and the sea; truly We have made plain the communications for a people who know. And He it is Who has brought you into being from a single soul, then there is (for you) a resting-place and a depository;

20 We have made plain the communications for a people who understand. And He it is Who sends down water from the cloud, then We bring forth with it buds of all (plants), then We bring forth from it green (foliage), from which We produce grain piled up (in the ear); and of the palm-tree, of the sheaths of it, come forth clusters (of dates) within reach; and gardens of grapes and olives and pomegranates, alike and unlike; behold the fruit of it when it yields the fruit and the ripening of it; indeed there are signs in this for a people who believe. And they make the jinn associates with God, while He created them, and they falsely attribute to Him sons and daughters without knowledge; glory be to Him, and highly exalted is He above what they ascribe (to Him).

Section 19.—*Guiding Rules of Life*

Say: Come! I will recite what your Lord has forbidden to you—(remember) that you do not associate anything with Him and show kindness to your parents, and do not slay your children for (fear of) poverty—We provide for you and for them—and do not draw nigh to indecencies, those of them which are apparent and those which are concealed, and do not kill the soul which God has forbidden except for the requirements of justice; this He has enjoined you with that you may understand. And do not approach the property of the orphan except in the best manner until he attains his maturity; and give full measure and weight with justice. We do not impose on any soul a duty except to the extent of its ability; and when you speak, be just, though it be (against) a relative, and fulfil God's covenant; this He has enjoined you with that you may be mindful. And (know) that this is My path, the right one, therefore follow it, and follow not (other) ways, for they will lead you away from His way; this He has enjoined you with that you may guard (against evil). Again, We gave the book to Moses to complete (Our blessings) on him who would do good, and making plain all things and a guidance and a mercy, so that they should believe in the meeting of their Lord.

JONAH

Section 3.—*God's Merciful Dealing*

And when We make people taste of mercy after an affliction touches them, lo! they devise plans against Our communications. Say: God is quicker to plan; Our messengers write down what you plan. He it is Who makes you travel by land and sea; until when you are in the ships, and they sail on with them in a pleasant breeze, and they rejoice at it, a violent wind overtakes them and the billows surge in on them from all sides, and they become certain that they are encompassed about, they pray to God, being sincere to Him in obedience: If Thou deliver us from this, we will be of the grateful ones. But when He delivers them, lo! they are unjustly rebellious in the earth. O men! your rebellion is against your own souls—a provision (only) of this world's life—then to Us shall be your return, so We will inform you of what you did. The likeness of this world's life is only as water which We send down from the cloud, then the herbage of the earth of which men and cattle eat grows luxuriantly thereby; until when the earth puts on its golden raiment and it becomes garnished, and its people think that they have power over it, Our command comes to it, by night or by day; so We render it as reaped seed-produce, as though it had not been in existence yesterday; thus do We make clear the communications for a people who reflect. And God invites to the abode of peace and guides whom He pleases into the right path. For those who do good is good (reward) and more (than this); and blackness shall not cover their faces, nor ignominy; these are the dwellers of the garden; in it they shall abide. And those who have earned evil—the punishment of an evil is the like of it, and abasement shall come upon them—they shall have none to protect them from God—as if their faces had been covered with slices of the dense darkness of

22 night; these are the inmates of the fire, in it they shall abide. And on the day when We will gather them all together, then We will say to those who set up gods (with God): Keep where you are, you and your associates. Then We shall separate them widely one from another and their associates would say: It was not us that you served: and God is sufficient as a witness between us and you that we were quite unaware of your serving (us). There shall every soul become acquainted with what is sent before, and they shall be brought back to God, their true Patron, and what they devised shall escape from them.

THE LIGHT

Section 5.—*Manifestation of Divine Light*

God is the light in the heavens and the earth; a likeness of His light is as a pillar on which is a lamp, the lamp is in a glass, (and) the glass is as it were a brightly shining star, lit from a blessed olive-tree, neither eastern nor western, the oil whereof almost gives light though fire touch it not—light upon light—God guides to His light whom He pleases, and God sets forth parables for men, and God is Cognizant of all things: in houses which God has permitted to be exalted and that His name may be remembered in them; there glorify Him therein in the mornings and the evenings, men whom neither merchandise nor selling diverts from the remembrance of God and the keeping up of prayer and the giving of poor-rate; they fear a day in which the hearts and the eyes shall turn about; that God may give them the best reward of what they have done, and give them more out of His grace; and God gives sustenance to whom He pleases without measure. And those who disbelieve, their deeds are like the mirage in a desert, which the thirsty man deems to be water; until when he comes to it he finds it to be naught, and there he finds God, so He pays back to him his reckoning in full; and God is quick in reckoning; or like darkness in the deep sea: there covers it a wave above which is another wave, above which is a cloud, (layers of) darkness one above another; when h: holds out his hand, he is almost unable to see it; and to whomsoever God does not give light, he has no light.

THE SABA

Section 6.—*Truth shall prosper*

Say: I exhort you only to one thing, that rise up for God's sake in twos and singly, then ponder: there is no madness in your fellow-citizen; he is only a warner to you before a severe chastisement. Say: Whatever reward I ask you, that is only for yourselves. My reward is only with God and He is a witness of all things. Say: My Lord utters the truth, the great Knower of the unseen. Say: The truth has come, and falsehood cannot originate (a thing) nor can it reproduce (it). Say: If I err, I err only against my own soul, and if I follow a right direction, it is because of what my Lord reveals to me; surely He is Hearing, Nigh. And couldst thou see when they shall become terrified, then there shall be no escape and they shall be seized upon from a near place, and they shall say: We believe in it. And whence shall the attaining (of faith) be possible to them from a distant place? And they disbelieved in it before, and they utter conjectures with regard to the unseen from a distant place. And a barrier shall be placed between them and that which they desire, as was done with the likes of them before; surely they are in a disquieting doubt.

THE BELIEVER

Section 7.—*Divine Favours on Man*

God is He Who made for you the night that you may rest therein and the day to see. God is truly Gracious to men, but most men do not give thanks. That is God, your Lord, the Creator of every thing; there is no God but He; whence are you then turned away? Thus were turned away those who denied the communications of God. God is He Who made the earth a resting-place for you and the heaven a structure, and He formed you, then made goodly your forms, and He provided you with goodly things; that is God, your Lord; blessed is God, the Lord of the worlds. He is the Living, there is no god but He; therefore call on Him, being sincere to Him in obedience; (all) praise is due to God, the Lord of the worlds. Say: I am forbidden to serve those whom you call upon besides God when clear arguments have come to me from my Lord, and I am commanded that I should submit to the Lord of the worlds. He it is Who created you from dust, then from a small life-germ, then from a clot, then He brings you forth as a child, then that you may attain your maturity, then that you may be old—and of you there are some who are caused to die before—and that you may reach an appointed term, and that you may understand. He it is Who gives life and brings death; and when He decrees an affair, He only says to it, Be, and it is.

EXTRACTS FROM THE BIBLE

The early history of the Bible is involved in obscurity. The basic factors to observe are that the Bible consists of subjects, secondly that many of its Books are compilations including material taken from older writings, or embodying stories which had for a long time been handed down by word of mouth: and lastly that the form in which we now have the Bible is the result of considerable editing and re-editing.

There seems very little doubt about the divine origin of the Pentateuch, or the Torah which existed as the sacred Laws of the Hebrews from a very ancient period. The only definite date which could be given about the Bible is that it was probably completed about 100 A.D. All the Books of its various authors are believed to be included in it by that date.

Practically all the Books of the Old Testament were written in Hebrew, the New Testament was handed down originally in Greek. Various translations of the Bible were made from Latin into English, the notable ones being that of Tyndale, Miles Coverdale's Version, Matthew's Bible, The Great Bible, the Geneva Bible, Bishop's Bible, the Authorised Version in 1611 and the Revised Version in 1881. The following quotations are from the Revised Version.

I SAMUEL III

And the child Samuel ministered unto the Lord before Eli. And the word of the Lord was precious in those days; there was no open vision.

2. And it came to pass at that time, when Eli was laid down in his place, and his eyes began to wax dim, that he could not see;

3. And ere the lamp of God went out in the temple of the Lord, where the ark of God was, and Samuel was laid down to sleep;

4. That the Lord called Samuel: and he answered, Here am I.

5. And he ran unto Eli, and said, Here am I; for thou

26 calledst me. And he said, I called not; lie down again. And he went and lay down.

6. And the Lord called yet again, Samuel. And Samuel arose and went to Eli, and said, Here am I; for thou didst call me. And he answered, I called not my son; lie down again.

7. Now Samuel did not yet know the Lord, neither was the word of the Lord yet revealed unto him.

8. And the Lord called Samuel again the third time. And he arose and went to Eli, and said, Here am I; for thou didst call me. And Eli perceived that the Lord had called the child.

9. Therefore Eli said unto Samuel, Go, lie down: and it shall be, if he call thee, that thou shalt say, Speak, Lord; for thy servant heareth. So Samuel went and lay down in his place.

10. And the Lord came, and stood, and called as at other times, Samuel, Samuel. Then Samuel answered, Speak; for thy servant heareth.

11. And the Lord said to Samuel, Behold, I will do a thing in Israel, at which both the ears of every one that heareth it shall tingle.

12. In that day I will perform against Eli all things which I have spoken concerning his house: when I begin, I will also make an end.

13. For I have told him that I will judge his house for ever for the iniquity which he knoweth; because his sons made themselves vile, and he restrained them not.

14. And therefore I have sworn unto the house of Eli, that the iniquity of Eli's house shall not be purged with sacrifice nor offering for ever.

15. And Samuel lay until the morning, and opened the doors of the house of the Lord. And Samuel feared to shew Eli the vision.

16. Then Eli called Samuel, and said, Samuel, my son. And he answered, Here am I.

17. And he said, What is the thing that the Lord hath said unto thee? I pray thee hide it not from me: God do so to thee, and more also, if thou hide any thing from me of all the things that he said unto thee.

18. And Samuel told him every whit, and hid nothing from him. And he said, It is the Lord: let him do what seemeth him good.

19. And Samuel grew, and the Lord was with him, and did let none of his words fall to the ground.

20. And all Israel from Dan even to Beer-sheba knew that Samuel was established to be a prophet of the Lord.

21. And the Lord appeared again in Shiloh: for the Lord revealed himself to Samuel in Shiloh by the word of the Lord.

JOB XXVIII

1. Surely there is a vein for the silver, and a place for gold where they fine it.

2. Iron is taken out of the earth, and brass is molten out of the stone.

3. He setteth an end to darkness, and searcheth out all perfection: the stones of darkness, and the shadow of death.

4. The flood breaketh out from the inhabitant; even the waters forgotten of the foot: they are dried up, they are gone away from men.

5. As for the earth, out of it cometh bread: and under it is turned up as it were fire.

6. The stones of it are the place of sapphires: and it hath dust of gold.

7. There is a path which no fowl knoweth, and which the vulture's eye hath not seen:

8. The lion's whelps have not trodden it, nor the fierce lion passed by it.

9. He putteth forth his hand upon the rock; he over-turneth the mountains by the roots.

10. He cutteth out rivers among the rocks; and his eye seeth every precious thing.

11. He bindeth the floods from overflowing; and the thing that is hid bringeth he forth to light.

12. But where shall wisdom be found? and where is the place of understanding?

13. Man knoweth not the price thereof; neither is it found in the land of the living.

28

14. The depth saith, It is not in me: and the sea saith, It is not with me.

15. It cannot be gotten for gold, neither shall silver be weighed for the price thereof.

16. It cannot be valued with the gold of Ophir, with the precious onyx, or the sapphire.

17. The gold and the crystal cannot equal it: and the exchange of it shall not be for jewels of fine gold.

18. No mention shall be made of coral, or of pearls: for the price of wisdom is above rubies.

19. The topaz of Ethiopia shall not equal it, neither shall it be valued with pure gold.

20. Whence then cometh wisdom? and where is the place of understanding?

21. Seeing it is hid from the eyes of all living, and kept close from the fowls of the air.

22. Destruction and death say, We have heard the fame thereof with our ears.

23. God understandeth the way thereof, and he knoweth the place thereof.

24. For he looketh to the ends of the earth, and seeth under the whole heaven;

25. To make the weight for the winds; and he weigheth the waters by measure.

26. When he made a decree for the rain, and a way for the lightning of the thunder:

27. Then did he see it, and declare it; he prepared it, yea, and searched it out.

28. And unto man he said, Behold, the fear of the Lord, that is wisdom; and to depart from evil is understanding.

JOB XXXVIII

1. Then the Lord answered Job out of the whirlwind, and said,

2. Who is this that darkeneth counsel by words without knowledge?

3. Gird up now thy loins like a man; for I will demand of thee, and answer thou me.

4. Where wast thou when I laid the foundations of the earth? declare, if thou hast understanding.

5. Who hath laid the measures thereof, if thou knowest? or who hath stretched the line upon it?

6. Whereupon are the foundations thereof fastened? or who laid the corner stone thereof;

7. When the morning stars sang together, and all the sons of God shouted for joy?

8. Or who shut up the sea with doors, when it brake forth, as if it had issued out of the womb?

9. When I made the cloud the garment thereof, and thick darkness a swaddlingband for it,

10. And brake up for it my decreed place, and set bars and doors,

11. And said, Hitherto shalt thou come, but no further: and here shall thy proud waves be stayed?

12. Hast thou commanded the morning since thy days; and caused the dayspring to know his place;

13. That it might take hold of the ends of the earth, that the wicked might be shaken out of it?

14. It is turned as clay to the seal; and they stand as a garment.

15. And from the wicked their light is withholden, and the high arm shall be broken.

16. Hast thou entered into the springs of the sea? or hast thou walked in the search of the depth?

17. Have the gates of death been opened unto thee? or hast thou seen the doors of the shadow of death?

18. Hast thou perceived the breadth of the earth? declare if thou knowest it all.

19. Where is the way where light dwelleth? and as for darkness, where is the place thereof.

20. That thou shouldest take it to the bound thereof, and that thou shouldest know the paths to the house thereof?

21. Knowest thou it, because thou wast then born? or because the number of thy days is great?

22. Hast thou entered into the treasures of the snow? or hast thou seen the treasures of the hail,

23. Which I have reserved against the time of trouble, against the day of battle and war?

24. By what way is the light parted, which scattereth the east wind upon the earth?

25. Who hath divided a watercourse for the overflowing of waters, or a way for the lightning of thunder;

26. To cause it to rain on the earth, where no man is; on the wilderness wherein there is no man;

27. To satisfy the desolate and waste ground; and to cause the bud of the tender herb to spring forth?

28. Hath the rain a father? or who hath begotten the drops of dew?

29. Out of whose womb came the ice? and the hoary frost of heaven, who hath gendered it?

30. The waters are hid as with a stone, and the face of the deep is frozen.

31. Canst thou bind the sweet influences of Pleiades, or loose the bands of Orion?

32. Canst thou bring forth Mazzaroth in his season? or canst thou guide Arcturus with his sons?

33. Knowest thou the ordinances of heaven? canst thou set the dominion thereof in the earth?

34. Canst thou lift up thy voice to the clouds, that abundance of waters may cover thee?

35. Canst thou send lightnings, that they may go, and say unto thee, Here we are?

36. Who hath put wisdom in the inward parts? or who hath given understanding to the heart?

37. Who can number the clouds in wisdom? or who can stay the bottles of heaven,

38. When the dust groweth into hardness, and the clods cleave fast together?

39. Wilt thou hunt the prey for the lion? or fill the appetite of the young lions.

40. When they couch in their dens, and abide in the covert to lie in wait?

41. Who provideth for the raven his food? when his young ones cry unto God, they wander for lack of meat.

1. Knowest thou the time when the wild goats of the rock bring forth? or canst thou mark when the hinds do calve?

2. Canst thou number the months that they fulfil? or knowest thou the time when they bring forth?

3. They bow themselves, they bring forth their young ones, they cast out their sorrows.

4. Their young ones are in good liking, they grow up with corn; they go forth, and return not unto them.

5. Who hath sent out the wild ass free? or who hath loosed the bands of the wild ass?

6. Whose house I have made the wilderness, and the barren land his dwellings.

7. He scorneth the multitude of the city, neither regardeth he the crying of the driver.

8. The range of the mountains is his pasture, and he searcheth after every green thing.

9. Will the unicorn be willing to serve thee, or abide by thy crib?

10. Canst thou bind the unicorn with his band in the furrow? or will he harrow the valleys after thee?

11. Wilt thou trust him, because his strength is great? or wilt thou leave thy labour to him?

12. Wilt thou believe him, that he will bring home thy seed, and gather it into thy barn?

13. Gavest thou the goodly wings unto the peacocks? or wings and feathers unto the ostrich?

14. Which leaveth her eggs in the earth, and warmeth them in dust,

15. And forgetteth that the foot may crush them, or that the wild beast may break them.

16. She is hardened against her young ones, as though they were not her's: her labour is in vain without fear;

17. Because God hath deprived her of wisdom, neither hath he imparted to her understanding.

18. What time she lifted up herself on high, she scorneth the horse and his rider.

19. Hast thou given the horse strength? hast thou clothed his neck with thunder?

20. Canst thou make him afraid as a grasshopper? the glory of his nostrils is terrible.

21. He paweth in the valley, and rejoiceth in his strength: he goeth on to meet the armed men.

22. He mocketh at fear, and is not affrighted; neither turneth he back from the sword.

23. The quiver rattleth against him, the glittering spear and the shield.

24. He swalloweth the ground with fierceness and rage: neither believeth he that it is the sound of the trumpet.

25. He saith among the trumpets, Ha, ha; and he smelleth the battle afar off, the thunder of the captains, and the shouting.

26. Doth the hawk fly by thy wisdom, and stretch her wings toward the south?

27. Doth the eagle mount up at thy command, and make her nest on high?

28. She dwelleth and abideth on the rock, upon the crag of the rock, and the strong place.

29. From thence she seeketh the prey, and her eyes behold afar off.

30. Her young ones also suck up blood: and where the slain are, there is she.

JOB XL

1. Moreover the Lord answered Job, and said,

2. Shall he that contendeth with the Almighty instruct him? he that reproveth God, let him answer it.

ECCLESIASTES III

1. To every thing there is a season, and a time to every purpose under the heaven:

2. A time to be born, and a time to die; a time to plant, and a time to pluck up that which is planted;

3. A time to kill, and a time to heal; a time to break down, and a time to build up;

4. A time to weep, and a time to laugh; a time to mourn, and a time to dance;

5. A time to cast away stones, and a time to gather stones together; a time to embrace, and a time to refrain from embracing;

6. A time to get, and a time to lose; a time to keep, and a time to cast away;

7. A time to rend, and a time to sew; a time to keep silence, and a time to speak;

8. A time to love, and a time to hate; a time of war, and a time of peace.

9. What profit hath he that worketh in that wherein he laboureth?

10. I have seen the travail, which God hath given to the sons of men to be exercised in it.

11. He hath made every thing beautiful in his time: also he hath set the world in their heart, so that no man can find out the work that God maketh from the beginning to the end.

12. I know that there is no good in them, but for a man to rejoice, and to do good in his life.

13. And also that every man should eat and drink, and enjoy the good of all his labour, it is the gift of God.

14. I know that, whatsoever God doeth, it shall be for ever: nothing can be put to it, nor any thing taken from it: and God doeth it, that men should fear before him.

15. That which hath been is now; and that which is to be hath already been; and God requireth that which is past.

16. And moreover I saw under the sun the place of judgment, that wickedness was there; and the place of righteousness, that iniquity was there.

17. I said in mine heart, God shall judge the righteous and the wicked: for there is a time there for every purpose and for every work.

ECCLESIASTES XI

1. Cast thy bread upon the waters: for thou shalt find it after many days.

2. Give a portion to seven, and also to eight; for thou knowest not what evil shall be upon the earth.

3. If the clouds be full of rain, they empty themselves upon the earth: and if the tree fall toward the south, or toward the north, in the place where the tree falleth, there it shall be.

4. He that observeth the wind shall not sow; and he that regardeth the clouds shall not reap.

5. As thou knowest not what is the way of the spirit, nor how the bones do grow in the womb of her that is with child: even so thou knowest not the works of God who maketh all.

6. In the morning sow thy seed, and in the evening withhold not thine hand: for thou knowest not whether shall prosper, either this or that, or whether they both shall be alike good.

ECCLESIASTES XII

1. Remember now thy Creator in the days of thy youth, while the evil days come not, nor the years draw nigh, when thou shalt say, I have no pleasure in them;

2. While the sun, or the light, or the moon, or the stars, be not darkened, nor the clouds return after the rain:

3. In the day when the keepers of the house shall tremble, and the strong men shall bow themselves, and the grinders cease because they are few, and those that look out of the windows be darkened.

4. And the doors shall be shut in the streets, when the sound of the grinding is low, and he shall rise up at the voice of the bird, and all the daughters of musick shall be brought low;

5. Also when they shall be afraid of that which is high, and fears shall be in the way, and the almond tree shall flourish, and the grasshopper shall be a burden, and desire

shall fail: because man goeth to his long home, and the mourners go about the streets:

6. Or ever the silver cord be loosed, or the golden bowl be broken, or the pitcher be broken at the fountain, or the wheel broken at the cistern.

7. Then shall the dust return to the earth as it was: and the spirit shall return unto God who gave it.

8. Vanity of vanities, saith the preacher; all is vanity.

9. And moreover, because the preacher was wise, he still taught the people knowledge; yea, he gave good heed, and sought out, and set in order many proverbs.

10. The preacher sought to find out acceptable words: and that which was written was upright, even words of truth.

11. The words of the wise are as goads, and as nails fastened by the masters of assemblies, which are given from one shepherd.

12. And further, by these, my son, be admonished: of making many books there is no end; and much study is a weariness of the flesh.

13. Let us hear the conclusion of the whole matter: Fear God, and keep his commandments: for this is the whole duty of man.

14. For God shall bring every work into judgment, with every secret thing, whether it be good, or whether it be evil.

THE SONG OF SOLOMON I

1. The song of songs, which is Solomon's.

2. Let him kiss me with the kisses of his mouth: for thy love is better than wine.

3. Because of the savour of thy good ointments thy name is as ointment poured forth, therefore do the virgins love thee.

4. Draw me, we will run after thee: the king hath brought me into his chambers: we will be glad and rejoice in thee, we will remember thy love more than wine: the upright love thee.

5. I am black, but comely, O ye daughters of Jerusalem, as the tents of Kedar, as the curtains of Solomon.

6. Look not upon me, because I am black, because the sun hath looked upon me: my mother's children were angry with me; they made me the keeper of the vineyards; but mine own vineyard have I not kept.

7. Tell me, O thou whom my soul loveth, where thou feedest, where thou makest thy flock to rest at noon: for why should I be as one that turneth aside by the flocks of thy companions?

THE SONG OF SOLOMON II

3. I sat down under his shadow with great delight, and his fruit was sweet to my taste.

4. He brought me to the banqueting house, and his banner over me was love.

5. Stay me with flagons, comfort me with apples: for I am sick of love.

6. His left hand is under my head, and his right hand doth embrace me.

7. I charge you, O ye daughters of Jerusalem, by the roes, and by the hinds of the field, that ye stir not up, nor awake my love, till he please.

8. The voice of my beloved! behold, he cometh leaping upon the mountains, skipping upon the hills.

9. My beloved is like a roe or a young hart: behold, he standeth behind our wall, he looketh forth at the windows, shewing himself through the lattice.

10. My beloved spake, and said unto me, Rise up, my love, my fair one, and come away.

11. For, lo, the winter is past, the rain is over and gone;

12. The flowers appear on the earth; the time of the singing of birds is come, and the voice of the turtle is heard in our land;

13. The fig tree putteth forth her green figs, and the vines with the tender grape give a good smell. Arise, my love, my fair one, and come away.

14. O my dove, that art in the clefts of the rock, in the

secret places of the stairs, let me see thy countenance, let me hear thy voice; for sweet is thy voice, and thy countenance is comely.

15. Take us the foxes, the little foxes, that spoil the vines: for our vines have tender grapes.

16. My beloved is mine, and I am his: he feedeth among the lilies.

17. Until the day break, and the shadows flee away, turn, my beloved, and be thou like a roe or a young hart upon the mountains of Bether.

ISAIAH XL

1. Comfort ye, comfort ye my people, saith your God.

2. Speak ye comfortably to Jerusalem, and cry unto her, that her warfare is accomplished, that her iniquity is pardoned: for she hath received of the Lord's hand double for all her sins.

3. The voice of him that crieth in the wilderness, Prepare ye the way of the Lord, make straight in the desert a highway for our God.

4. Every valley shall be exalted, and every mountain and hill shall be made low: and the crooked shall be made straight, and the rough places plain:

5. And the glory of the Lord shall be revealed, and all flesh shall see it together: for the mouth of the Lord hath spoken it.

6. The voice said, Cry. And he said, What shall I cry? All flesh is grass, and all the goodliness thereof is as the flower of the field:

7. The grass withereth, the flower fadeth: because the spirit of the Lord bloweth upon it: surely the people is grass.

8. The grass withereth, the flower fadeth: but the word of our God shall stand for ever.

9. O Zion, that bringest good tidings, get thee up into the high mountain; O Jerusalem, that bringest good tidings lift up thy voice with strength; lift it up, be not afraid; say unto the cities of Judah, Behold your God!

10. Behold, the Lord God will come with strong hand, and his arm shall rule for him: behold, his reward is with him, and his work before him.

11. He shall feed his flock like a shepherd: he shall gather the lambs with his arm, and carry them in his bosom, and shall gently lead those that are with young.

12. Who hath measured the waters in the hollow of his hand, and meted out heaven with the span, and comprehended the dust of the earth in a measure, and weighed the mountains in scales, and the hills in a balance?

13. Who hath directed the Spirit of the Lord, or being his counsellor hath taught him?

14. With whom took he counsel, and who instructed him, and taught him in the path of judgment, and taught him knowledge, and shewed to him the way of understanding?

15. Behold, the nations are as a drop of a bucket, and are counted as the small dust of the balance: behold, he taketh up the isles as a very little thing.

16. And Lebanon is not sufficient to burn, nor the beasts thereof sufficient for a burnt offering.

17. All nations before him are as nothing; and they are counted to him less than nothing, and vanity.

18. To whom then will ye liken God? or what likeness will ye compare unto him?

19. The workman melteth a graven image, and the goldsmith spreadeth it over with gold, and casteth silver chains.

20. He that is so impoverished that he hath no oblation chooseth a tree that will not rot; he seeketh unto him a cunning workman to prepare a graven image, that shall not be moved.

21. Have ye not known? have ye not heard? hath it not been told you from the beginning? have ye not understood from the foundations of the earth?

22. It is he that sitteth upon the circle of the earth, and the inhabitants thereof are as grasshoppers; that stretcheth out the heavens as a curtain, and spreadeth them out as a tent to dwell in:

23. That bringeth the princes to nothing; he maketh the judges of the earth as vanity.

24. Yea, they shall not be planted; yea, they shall not be sown: yea, their stock shall not take root in the earth: and he shall also blow upon them, and they shall wither, and the whirlwind shall take them away as stubble.

25. To whom then will ye liken me, or shall I be equal? saith the Holy One.

26. Lift up your eyes on high, and behold who hath created these things, that bringeth out their host by number: he calleth them all by names by the greatness of his might, for that he is strong in power; not one faileth.

27. Why sayest thou, O Jacob, and speakest, O Israel, My way is hid from the Lord, and my judgment is passed over from my God?

28. Hast thou not known? hast thou not heard, that the everlasting God, the Lord, the Creator of the ends of the earth, fainteth not, neither is weary? there is no searching of his understanding.

29. He giveth power to the faint; and to them that have no might he increaseth strength.

30. Even the youths shall faint and be weary, and the young men shall utterly fall:

31. But they that wait upon the Lord shall renew their strength; they shall mount up with wings as eagles; they shall run, and not be weary; and they shall walk, and not faint.

ISAIAH LIII

1. Who hath believed our report? and to whom is the arm of the Lord revealed?

2. For he shall grow up before him as a tender plant, and as a root out of a dry ground: he hath no form nor comeliness; and when we shall see him, there is no beauty that we should desire him.

3. He is despised and rejected of men; a man of sorrows, and acquainted with grief: and we hid as it were our faces from him; he was despised, and we esteemed him not.

4. Surely he hath borne our griefs, and carried our sorrows: yet we did esteem him stricken, smitten of God, and afflicted.

5. But he was wounded for our transgressions, he was bruised for our iniquities: the chastisement of our peace was upon him; and with his stripes we are healed.

6. All we like sheep have gone astray; we have turned every one to his own way; and the Lord hath laid on him the iniquity of us all.

7. He was oppressed, and he was afflicted, yet he opened not his mouth: he is brought as a lamb to the slaughter, and as a sheep before her shearers is dumb, so he openeth not his mouth.

8. He was taken from prison and from judgment: and who shall declare his generation? for he was cut off out of the land of the living: for the transgression of my people was he stricken.

9. And he made his grave with the wicked, and with the rich in his death; because he had done no violence, neither was any deceit in his mouth.

10. Yet it pleased the Lord to bruise him; he hath put him to grief: when thou shalt make his soul an offering for sin, he shall see his seed, he shall prolong his days, and the pleasure of the Lord shall prosper in his hand.

11. He shall see of the travail of his soul, and shall be satisfied: by his knowledge shall my righteous servant justify many; for he shall bear their iniquities.

12. Therefore will I divide him a portion with the great, and he shall divide the spoil with the strong; because he hath poured out his soul unto death: and he was numbered with the transgressors; and he bare the sin of many, and made intercession for the transgressors.

ISAIAH LV

1. Ho, every one that thirsteth, come ye to the waters, and he that hath no money; come ye, buy, and eat; yea, come, buy wine and milk without money and without price.

2. Wherefore do ye spend money for that which is not bread? and your labour for that which satisfieth not?

hearken diligently unto me and eat ye that which is good, and let your soul delight itself in fatness.

3. Incline your ear, and come unto me: hear, and your soul shall live: and I will make an everlasting covenant with you, even the sure mercies of David.

4. Behold, I have given him for a witness to the people, a leader and commander to the people.

5. Behold, thou shalt call a nation that thou knowest not, and nations that knew not thee shall run unto thee because of the Lord thy God, and for the Holy One of Israel; for he hath glorified thee.

6. Seek ye the Lord while he may be found, call ye upon him while he is near:

7. Let the wicked forsake his way, and the unrighteous man his thoughts: and let him return unto the Lord, and he will have mercy upon him; and to our God, for he will abundantly pardon.

8. For my thoughts are not your thoughts, neither are your ways my ways, saith the Lord.

9. For as the heavens are higher than the earth, so are my ways higher than your ways, and my thoughts than your thoughts.

10. For as the rain cometh down, and the snow from heaven, and returneth not thither, but watereth the earth, and maketh it bring forth and bud, that it may give seed to the sower, and bread to the eater:

11. So shall my word be that goeth forth out of my mouth: it shall not return unto me void, but it shall accomplish that which I please, and it shall prosper in the thing whereto I sent it.

12. For ye shall go out with joy, and be led forth with peace: the mountains and the hills shall break forth before you into singing, and all the trees of the field shall clap their hands.

13. Instead of the thorn shall come up the fir tree, and instead of the brier shall come up the myrtle tree: and it shall be to the Lord for a name, for an everlasting sign that shall not be cut off.

1. Take heed that ye do not your alms before men, to be seen of them: otherwise ye have no reward of your Father which is in heaven.

2. Therefore when thou doest thine alms, do not sound a trumpet before thee, as the hypocrites do in the synagogues and in the streets, that they may have glory of men. Verily I say unto you, They have their reward.

3. But when thou doest alms, let not thy left hand know what thy right hand doeth:

4. That thine alms may be in secret: and thy Father which seeth in secret himself shall reward thee openly.

5. And when thou prayest thou shalt not be as the hypocrites are: for they love to pray standing in the synagogues and in the corners of the streets, that they may be seen of men. Verily I say unto you, They have their reward.

6. But thou, when thou prayest, enter into thy closet, and when thou hast shut thy door, pray to thy Father which is in secret; and thy Father which seeth in secret shall reward thee openly.

7. But when ye pray, use not vain repetitions, as the heathen do; for they think that they shall be heard for their much speaking.

8. Be not ye therefore like unto them; for your Father knoweth what things ye have need of, before ye ask him.

9. After this manner therefore pray ye; Our Father which art in heaven, Hallowed be thy name.

10. Thy kingdom come. Thy will be done in earth, as it is in heaven.

11. Give us this day our daily bread.

12. And forgive us our debts, as we forgive our debtors.

13. And lead us not into temptation, but deliver us from evil: For thine is the kingdom, and the power, and the glory, for ever. Amen.

14. For if ye forgive men their trespasses, your heavenly Father will also forgive you:

15. But if ye forgive not men their trespasses, neither will your Father forgive your trespasses.

16. Moreover when ye fast, be not, as the hypocrites, of a sad countenance: for they disfigure their faces, that they may appear unto men to fast. Verily I say unto you, They have their reward.

17. But thou, when thou fastest, anoint thine head, and wash thy face;

18. That thou appear not unto men to fast, but unto thy Father which is in secret: and thy Father, which seeth in secret, shall reward thee openly.

19. Lay not up for yourselves treasures upon earth, where moth and rust doth corrupt, and where thieves break through and steal:

20. But lay up for yourselves treasures in heaven, where neither moth nor rust doth corrupt, and where thieves do not break through nor steal:

21. For where your treasure is, there will your heart be also.

22. The light of the body is the eye: if therefore thine eye be single, thy whole body shall be full of light.

23. But if thine eye be evil, thy whole body shall be full of darkness. If therefore the light that is in thee be darkness, how great is that darkness!

24. No man can serve two masters: for either he will hate the one, and love the other; or else he will hold to the one, and despise the other. Ye cannot serve God and mammon.

25. Therefore I say unto you, Take no thought for your life, what ye shall eat, or what ye shall drink; nor yet for your body, what ye shall put on. Is not the life more than meat, and the body than raiment?

26. Behold the fowls of the air: for they sow not, neither do they reap, nor gather into barns; yet your heavenly Father feedeth them. Are ye not much better than they?

27. Which of you by taking thought can add one cubit unto his stature?

28. And why take ye thought for raiment? Consider

44

the lilies of the field, how they grow; they toil not, neither do they spin:

29. And yet I say unto you, That even Solomon in all his glory was not arrayed like one of these.

30. Wherefore, if God so clothe the grass of the field, which to-day is, and to-morrow is cast into the oven, shall he not much more clothe you, O ye of little faith?

31. Therefore take no thought, saying, What shall we eat? or, What shall we drink? or, Wherewithal shall we be clothed?

32. (For after all these things do the Gentiles seek:) for your heavenly Father knoweth that ye have need of all these things.

33. But seek ye first the kingdom of God, and his righteousness; and all these things shall be added unto you.

34. Take therefore no thought for the morrow: for the morrow shall take thought for the things of itself. Sufficient unto the day is the evil thereof.

ST. MATTHEW VII

1. Judge not, that ye be not judged.

2. For with what judgment ye judge ye shall be judged: and with what measure ye mete, it shall be measured to you again.

3. And why beholdest thou the mote that is in thy brother's eye, but considerest not the beam that is in thine own eye?

4. Or how wilt thou say to thy brother, Let me pull out the mote out of thine eye; and, behold, a beam is in thine own eye?

5. Thou hypocrite, first cast out the beam out of thine own eye; and then shalt thou see clearly to cast out the mote out of thy brother's eye.

6. Give not that which is holy unto the dogs, neither cast ye your pearls before swine, lest they trample them under their feet, and turn again and rend you.

7. Ask, and it shall be given you; seek, and ye shall find; knock, and it shall be opened unto you:

8. For every one that asketh receiveth; and he that seeketh findeth; and to him that knocketh it shall be opened.

9. Or what man is there of you, whom if his son ask bread, will he give him a stone?

10. Or if he ask a fish, will he give him a serpent?

11. If ye then, being evil, know how to give good gifts unto your children, how much more shall your Father which is in heaven give good things to them that ask him?

12. Therefore all things whatsoever ye would that men should do to you, do ye even so to them: for this is the law and the prophets.

13. Enter ye in at the strait gate: for wide is the gate, and broad is the way, that leadeth to destruction, and many there be which go in thereat:

14. Because strait is the gate, and narrow is the way, which leadeth unto life, and few there be that find it.

15. Beware of false prophets, which come to you in sheep's clothing, but inwardly they are ravening wolves.

16. Ye shall know them by their fruits. Do men gather grapes of thorns, or figs of thistles?

17. Even so every good tree bringeth forth good fruit; but a corrupt tree bringeth forth evil fruit.

18. A good tree cannot bring forth evil fruit, neither can a corrupt tree bring forth good fruit.

19. Every tree that bringeth not forth good fruit is hewn down, and cast into the fire.

20. Wherefore by their fruits ye shall know them.

21. Not every one that saith unto me, Lord, Lord, shall enter into the kingdom of heaven; but he that doeth the will of my Father which is in heaven.

22. Many will say to me in that day, Lord, Lord, have we not prophesied in thy name? and in thy name have cast out devils? and in thy name done many wonderful works?

23. And then will I profess unto them, I never knew you: depart from me, ye that work iniquity.

24. Therefore whosoever heareth these sayings of mine,

46 and doeth them, I will liken him unto a wise man, which built his house upon a rock:

25. And the rain descended, and the floods came, and the winds blew, and beat upon that house; and it fell not: for it was founded upon a rock.

26. And every one that heareth these sayings of mine, and doeth them not, shall be likened unto a foolish man, which built his house upon the sand:

27. And the rain descended, and the floods came, and the winds blew, and beat upon that house; and it fell: and great was the fall of it.

28. And it came to pass, when Jesus had ended these sayings, the people were astonished at his doctrine:

29. For he taught them as one having authority, and not as the scribes.

ST. LUKE XV

1. Then drew near unto him all the publicans and sinners for to hear him.

2. And the Pharisees and scribes murmured, saying, This man receiveth sinners, and eateth with them.

3. And he spake this parable unto them, saying.

11. . . . A certain man had two sons:

12. And the younger of them said to his father, Father, give me the portion of goods that falleth to me. And he divided unto them his living.

13. And not many days after the younger son gathered all together, and took his journey into a far country, and there wasted his substance with riotous living.

14. And when he had spent all, there arose a mighty famine in that land; and he began to be in want.

15. And he went and joined himself to a citizen of that country; and he sent him into his fields to feed swine.

16. And he would fain have filled his belly with the husks that the swine did eat: and no man gave unto him.

17. And when he came to himself, he said, How many hired servants of my father's have bread enough and to spare, and I perish with hunger!

18. I will arise and go to my father, and will say unto him, Father, I have sinned against heaven, and before thee,

19. And am no more worthy to be called thy son: make me as one of thy hired servants.

20. And he arose, and came to his father. But when he was yet a great way off, his father saw him, and had compassion, and ran, and fell on his neck, and kissed him.

21. And the son said unto him, Father, I have sinned against heaven, and in thy sight, and am no more worthy to be called thy son.

22. But the father said to his servants, Bring forth the best robe, and put it on him; and put a ring on his hand, and shoes on his feet:

23. And bring hither the fatted calf, and kill it; and let us eat, and be merry:

24. For this my son was dead, and is alive again; he was lost, and is found. And they began to be merry.

25. Now his elder son was in the field: and as he came and drew nigh to the house, he heard musick and dancing.

26. And he called one of the servants, and asked what these things meant.

27. And he said unto him, Thy brother is come; and thy father hath killed the fatted calf, because he hath received him safe and sound.

28. And he was angry, and would not go in: therefore came his father out, and intreated him.

29. And he answering said to his father, Lo, these many years do I serve thee, neither transgressed I at any time thy commandment: and yet thou never gavest me a kid, that I might make merry with my friends:

30. But as soon as this thy son was come, which hath devoured thy living with harlots, thou hast killed for him the fatted calf.

31. And he said unto him, Son, thou art ever with me, and all that I have is thine.

32. It was meet that we should make merry, and be glad: for this thy brother was dead, and is alive again; and was lost, and is found.

1. Though I speak with the tongues of men and of angels, and have not charity, I am become as sounding brass, or a tinkling cymbal.

2. And though I have the gift of prophecy, and understand all mysteries, and all knowledge; and though I have all faith, so that I could remove mountains, and have not charity, I am nothing.

3. And though I bestow all my goods to feed the poor, and though I give my body to be burned, and have not charity, it profiteth me nothing.

4. Charity suffereth long, and is kind; charity envieth not; charity vaunteth not itself, is not puffed up.

5. Doth not behave itself unseemly, seeketh not her own, is not easily provoked, thinketh no evil.

6. Rejoiceth not in iniquity, but rejoiceth in the truth;

7. Beareth all things, believeth all things, hopeth all things, endureth all things.

8. Charity never faileth: but whether there be prophecies they shall fail; whether there be tongues, they shall cease; whether there be knowledge, it shall vanish away.

9. For we know in part, and we prophesy in part.

10. But when that which is perfect is come, then that which is in part shall be done away.

11. When I was a child, I spake as a child, I understood as a child, I thought as a child: but when I became a man, I put away childish things.

12. For now we see through a glass, darkly; but then face to face: now I know in part; but then shall I know even as also I am known.

13. And now abideth faith, hope, charity, these three; but the greatest of these is charity.

HYMN OF CREATION

" Of the four Vedas which constitute the earliest stage of Indian literature, the Rigveda is by far the most ancient and important," says Professor Macdonell, from whose English translation of the " Hymns from the Rigveda " the following is taken. The exact date of this piece of hoary religious literature of the Hindus is not determinable, although it cannot be later than the thirteenth century B.C. The hymns contained in this work were almost exclusively composed by a hereditary priesthood.

Non-being then existed not nor being:
There was no air, nor sky that is beyond it.
What was concealed? Wherein? In whose protection?
And was there deep unfathomable water?

Death then existed not nor life immortal;
Of neither night nor day was any token.
By its inherent force the One breathed windless:
No other thing than that beyond existed.

Darkness there was at first by darkness hidden;
Without distinctive marks, this all was water.
That which, becoming, by the void was covered,
That One by force of heat came into being.

Desire entered the One in the beginning:
It was the earliest seed, of thought the product.
The sages searching in their hearts with wisdom,
Found out the bond of being in non-being.

Their ray extended light across the darkness:
But was the One above or was it under?
Creative force was there, and fertile power:
Below was energy, above was impulse.

Who knows for certain?   Who shall here declare it?
Whence was it born, and whence came this creation?
The gods were born after this world's creation:
Then who can know from whence it has arisen?

None knoweth whence creation has arisen;
And whether he has or has not produced it;
He who surveys it in the highest heaven,
He only knows, or haply he may know not.

SURYA

The gods' refulgent countenance has risen,
The eye of Mitra, Varuna and Agni.
He has pervaded air, and earth, and heaven:
The soul of all that moves and stands is Surya.

The Sun pursues the Dawn, the gleaming goddess,
As a young man a maiden, to the region
Where god-devoted men lay on the harness
Of brilliant offerings for the brilliant godhead.

The brilliant steeds, bay coursers of the sun-god,
Refulgent, dappled, meet for joyful praises,
Wafting our worship, heaven's ridge have mounted,
And in one day round earth and sky they travel.

This is the Sun's divinity, his greatness:
In midst of action he withdraws the daylight.
When from their stand he has withdrawn his coursers,
Then straightway night for him spreads out her garment.

This form the Sun takes in the lap of heaven,
That Varuna and Mitra may regard him.
One glow of his appears unending, splendid;
His bay steeds roll the other up, the black one.

To-day, O gods, do ye at Surya's rising
Release us from distress and from dishonour:
This boon may Varuna and Mitra grant us,
And Aditi and Sindhu, Earth and Heaven.

TEACHINGS FROM THE GITA

Translated by Hari Prasad Shastri

There are three most important metaphysical classics in India which are held as Scriptures by the Hindus: Upnishats, Sastras, and Bhagwad Gita. The philosopher Shankracharya has established the doctrine in his commentary on these classics; as the Gita is believed by the Hindus to have been given by Sri Krishna himself, it is regarded as the best summary of the ethical teachings of ancient India.

THE TRUE SELF

*N*ever was there a time when the self (Atman) of man did not exist, nor shall it cease to exist in the future.

As the embodied soul in the present body experiences childhood, youth and age, so does it in the body it assumes after the death of this body. The souls who have obtained freedom and peace are not deluded by these seeming changes.

Know the Self which pervades all this, to be indestructible. None can destroy the Immutable (self). (Being infinite) It neither kills, nor is killed.

It is above birth and death. It does not come into being out of non-existence. Unborn, eternal, changeless, ever-itself, it does survive the body.

Weapons cannot cut the self, fire cannot burn it, water cannot moisten it, and wind cannot dry it. Immutable, all-pervading, ever-fixed, eternal is the self.

Unmanifested (beyond cause and effect), beyond thought and imagination, unchangeable as it is, you must not mourn for it.

Some consider it a great mystery (wonder), others speak of it as a sublime secret, others hear it as wonder. Many hearing it do not understand it at all.

As true freedom, peace, and joy come only through the

realization of self, the aspirant on the path leading to the realization of self must know that experiences of heat and cold, of pain and joy, are born of the contact of the senses with their objects. They come and go, being impermanent. Bear them with patience and indifference.

The man who is calm and whose equilibrium of mind is not ruffled by pain and pleasure ever self-restrained, he acquires conscious immortality.

The unreal " phenomena " have no existence; the real (self) never suffers extinction. The wise knowing this see the Truth.

As a man casts off worn-out clothes and wears new ones, so does the embodied self leave the worn-out bodies, and enlightens new forms.

To one who knows, there must be no grief, for all things come out of an unmanifested state and staying a while in the state of manifestation go back to the original unmanifested state.

Keeping his inner self calm and undisturbed in the light of this knowledge of truth, the aspirant must lead a life of active struggle against ignorance and duality, ever-engaged in doing good to others.

He must remain the same under pain and pleasure, gain and loss, conquest and defeat, fighting against ignorance.

Then actions will not touch him. Being self-less he will maintain his peace of mind under all circumstances.

One-pointed determination to realize the self is essential to success in the Yoga (Union with God). The undecided have many purposes. They jump from plan to plan, and do not attain complete freedom. Those who are attached to pleasure and power are unfit for self-realization. The seekers after heaven, where desires of the world are fulfilled in an exaggerated form, are deluded by the unwise who themselves are without the bliss of the self-realization. They declare there is no other goal but heaven and its joys. Such go from birth to birth, as they are far from Truth.

The Vedas (all religious scriptures, in fact) teach of the three Gunas, modes of substance. But a true aspirant must rise above the three Gunas, be free from the pairs of opposites, ever established in equilibrium, free from the thoughts of profit and gain. A man who has realized the self does not need the injunctions of the Vedas. He who lives near a river does not need a reservoir.

Under any circumstances we must work for the upliftment of others unselfishly, never attaching ourselves to the fruits of the work, nor courting inaction. Duty for duty's sake is the ideal of the Yoga of action.

Doing your duty, being without attachment, remaining unmindful of success and failure, in evenness of mind is called the path of Yoga.

The real work is that which is performed with the mind unconcerned with the results of it. The work in which desires for results disturb the mind, belongs to an inferior class. Evenness of mind is essential to freedom from vice and virtue. This austerity of work is real Yoga, this leads to freedom from the fetters of birth and death, the transcendental region beyond ignorance and evil.

The illusion of identification of the Self with the body, and general attachment to objects, is a taint. To get rid of it is to go to peace, the supreme goal.

To attain self-realization the intellect, now restless because of conflicting desires and opinions, must become immovable and be firmly established in self.

CHARACTER OF A YOGI

Free from all desires of the mind, satisfied in self alone by the self is the man of perfect wisdom. He does not run after external objects to achieve happiness. Unmoved by adversity, and above fear, anger, and limited (personal) affections is one who has realized the self. Not elated at success, nor cast down by evil, unattached everywhere is the sage.

He withdraws his senses from the objects (being perfectly unattached and not depending on them for his happiness) like the tortoise his limbs. By starving the senses and himself a man can lose attraction for the objects of enjoyment, but by doing so he does not give up the inner relish for them. It is only when he sees the Supreme that his longing ceases.

The senses are turbulent, and they mislead even a clever man engaged in higher knowledge. The wise Yogi steadfastly controls them, and focussing them on God, the supreme reality, sits peaceful. He alone is wise whose senses are under complete control.

If you think of objects of pleasure with a longing (and do not exercise discrimination that they are unreal and passing) you conceive an attachment for them. From attachment comes a yearning to possess them. Impediments in the way to the possession of the desired objects give rise to anger. Anger produces delusion, and delusion loss of discrimination, and the result is ruination. (It is harmful to dwell on the objects of pleasure, giving them objective reality).

To obtain the inner tranquillity, you must be self-controlled, free from attraction and aversion, living among objects. (Running away from the world in aversion is not recommended.)

All griefs and sorrows of life are destroyed when the inner indisturbable peace comes. Only the tranquil-minded has his intellect (and heart) established in firmness.

The man of unsteady mind cannot have self-knowledge, neither can he meditate (on Truth). Inability to meditate is a barrier in the way to spiritual peace. How can there be happiness without peace of the mind?

The mind which follows the wandering senses (runs after pleasures and power) without discrimination, is like a boat without a sailor, left at the mercy of the rising waves.

Verily he is a knower of self (his self-knowledge is steady) whose senses are completely under his control.

The self-controlled man wakes when the world is asleep and that time when all beings wake is night to the self-knowing sage.

(The world wakes in duality and ignorance, but the sage is asleep—unconscious of it.—The sage wakes in Truth—God—while the world is asleep in it.)

The sage is complete and undisturbed like the ocean into which rivers fall day and night, without causing it to overflow. The objects of the senses enter into his mind without creating in him a longing or a delusion of affection. He attains to peace, and not he who is open to desires for pleasures and powers.

Giving up all desires, devoid of thirst for life and pleasures, above the sense of the limited " I," the Yogi obtains eternal peace.

When once this exalted state of consciousness is obtained (God is realized within) all delusion (ignorance or duality) is extinct for ever. Even if at the end of life this Nirvana is attained, it is good for ever.

56

SHARING THE BURDEN

The Talmud

In the first four or six centuries of the Christian era there grew up a great body of sacred writing known as The Talmud, consisting of two parts, the Mishna or the Oral Law and Gemara or the Commentary on the Oral Law. This treasure-house of great wisdom deservedly continues to have profound effect on the lives of the Jewish people.

"When trouble comes upon the congregation, it is not right for a man to say, 'I will eat and drink, and things will be peaceful for me.' Moses, our Teacher, always bore his share in the troubles of the congregation, as it is written, 'They took a stone and put it under him' (Exodus xvii 12). Could they not have given him a chair or a cushion? But then he said, 'Since the Israelites are in trouble, lo, I will bear my part with them, for he who bears his portion of the burden will live to enjoy the hour of consolation.' Woe to one who thinks, 'Ah, well, I will neglect my duty. Who can know whether I bear my part or not?' Even the stones of the house, ay, the limbs of the trees shall testify against him, as it is written, 'For the stones will cry from the wall, and the limbs of the trees will testify.'"

BOOK II

Philosophical, Mystical, and Semi-Religious Literature

POEMS OF SADI

The truism will bear repetition that in no poetry so much grandeur of style and variety of subject is expressed as in the Persian poetry. Both in the realm of mystical illusion and romantic imagery the Persian poets have no compeer, as may be shown by the following quotations from the work of Master Singers of Persia, taken from Costello's *Rose Garden of Persia*.

Contentment (from the " Bostan.")

Smile not, nor think the legend vain,
*   That in old times a worthless stone,*
Such power in holy hands could gain,
*   That straight a silver heap it shone.*
Thy alchemist Contentment be,
Equal is stone or ore to thee.

The infant's pure unruffled breast,
No avarice nor pride molest:
He fills his little hands with earth,
Nor knows that silver has more worth.

The sultan sits in pomp and state,
And sees the dervish at his gate;
But yet of wealth the sage has more
Than the great king, with all his store.

Rich is a beggar, worn and spent,
*   To whom a silver coin is thrown;*
But Feridoun was not content,
*   Though Ajum's kingdom was his own!*

On True Worth

Although a gem be cast away,
And lie obscured in heaps of clay,
* Its precious worth is still the same;*
Although vile dust be whirled to Heaven,
To such no dignity is given,
* Still base as when from earth it came.*

The Vision

I saw the demon in a dream,
* But how unlike he seemed to be,*
To all of horrible we deem,
* And all of fearful that we see.*
His shape was like a cypress bough,
* His eyes like those that Houris wear,*
His face as beautiful as though
* The rays of Paradise were there.*
I near him came, and spoke—" Art thou,"
* I said, " indeed the Evil One?*
No angel has so bright a brow,
* Such yet no eye has looked upon.*
Why should mankind make thee a jest,
* When thou canst show a face like this?*
Fair as the moon in splendour drest,
* An eye of joy, a smile of bliss!*
The painter draws thee vile to sight,
* Our baths thy frightful form display;*
They told me thou wert black as night,
* Behold! thou art as fair as day! "*
The lovely vision's ire awoke,
* His voice was loud, and proud his mien,*
" Believe not, friend," 't was thus he spoke,
* " That thou my likeness yet hast seen:*
The pencil that my portrait made
* Was guided by an envious foe;*
In Paradise I man betrayed,
* And he, from hatred, paints me so."*

POEMS OF ATTAR

The Way to Paradise

Wouldst thou inherit Paradise,
   These maxims keep before thine eyes;
So thy heart's mirror shall appear,
For ever shining bright and clear.
Give thanks when fortune smiles serene,
Be patient when her frown is seen;
If thou hast sinned, for pardon plead,
And help shall follow at thy need.
But shall he hope the prize to hold,
Who with new sins conceals the old?
Be penitent, be watchful still,
And fly the votaries of ill;
Avoid the paths that lead to vice,
And win thy way to Paradise.

The Praise of the Almighty

Unbounded praise to God be given,
Who from His throne, the height of heaven,
Looked on this handful of frail earth—
Unnoticed man—and gave him birth.

On Adam breathed, and bade the wave
Pause, and his servant, Noah, save;
The tempest, with His terrors clad,
And swept from earth the tribe of Ad.

And for His " friend," Oh! blissful name!
To roses changed a bed of flame:
The smallest insect, at His will,
Becomes an instrument of ill.

He spoke, the sea o'erwhelms His foes,
And the hard rock a camel grows!
The iron turns, at His command,
To pliant wax, in David's hand.

To Solomon he gave His sway,
And bade the dives his sign obey;
To one a diadem is given,
Another's head the saw has riven.

Impartial in His goodness still,
Equal to all is good or ill.

One lies on Persian silk reclined,
One naked in a frozen wind;
One scarce can count his heaps of ore,
One faints with hunger at the door.

He bade a virgin's child appear,
And made an infant's witness clear.

The dives before His vengeance fly,
By hosts of stars expelled the sky.
And kings, who hold the world in thrall,
At His great word to ruin fall.

FLOWERS AND BIRDS

By Azz' Eddin Elmocadessi

Learn from birds and flowers, oh man!
Virtues that may gild thy name;
And their faults, if thou would'st scan,
Know thy failings are the same:
The fair narcissus, humble still,
Reflecting on her lowly birth,
And feeling Nature, prone to ill,
Inclines her soft eyes to the earth.

The water-lily, pale with care,
    Mourns as the waters pass her by;
" Alas! " she sighs, " what woes I bear!
    And must submit to misery:
But time can never teach my heart
From love's delusive joy to part! "

The willow is the only tree
    Whose slender boughs for ever wave;
Devotion in their homage see
    To him who leaves and blossoms gave:
And love that gentle willow knows,
Bending its glances towards the rose.
The modest jasmine is content,
She whispers, " Lovers, why lament! "

The bright anemone to view
Is bright and fair in shape and hue;
But in her leaves no perfume dwells,
    And in her heart is wickedness:
With secret scorn her bosom swells;
    Her crimes upon her mem'ry press:
" Behold," she muses, " beauty glows,
    All radiant in each outward part;
But, ah! my soul too sadly knows
    That vice is burning in my heart!

Thou see'st the nightingale in spring—
    He seems as joy were all his own—
From tree to tree, with rapid wing,
    He flits, with love in ev'ry tone;
So volatile, so debonaire,
As though he never knew a care.
But ah! how much art thou deceived!
    His heart is filled with pensive pain,
For earth's frail lot his soul is grieved;
    He sees her glory's fleeting train,
And how each beauty withers fast,
Nor leaves a shadow where it passed.

He knows that ruin soon will seize
The sweetest flowers, the fairest trees;
He knows the garden will decay,
And marks it fading day by day.
Thus, if aright thou read his song,
It tells of grief the whole year long!

Know'st thou why round his neck the dove
  A collar wears?—it is to tell
He is the faithful slave of love,
  And serves all those who serve him well.

The swallow leaves his lowly nest
  And hies him to a foreign shore:
He loves with courtly man to rest,
  From whom he learns a higher lore
Than if he kept amongst his kind,
Nor sought with care to store his mind.
And men the welcome swallow prize,
  For he a kindly guest is known;
No base or selfish ends he tries,
  But friendly converse seeks alone.

The owl has learnt the world's deceit,
  Its vanity and struggles vain;
And deems it flattery unmeet,
  A thought from reason to obtain.
Apart from the perfidious throng,
  In wisdom's contemplative mood.
To Heaven she gives her whole life long,
  And steals to holy solitude.

The peacock, wedded to the world,
  Of all her gorgeous plumage vain,
With glowing banners wide unfurled,
  Sweeps slowly by in proud disdain;
But in her heart a torment lies,
That dims the lustre of those dyes;
She turns away her glance—but no,
Her hideous feet appear below!

And fatal echoes, deep and loud,
Her secret mind's dark caverns stir;
She knows, though beautiful and proud,
That Paradise is not for her.
For, when in Eden's blissful spot
Lost Eblis tempted man, she dared
To join the treach'rous angel's plot,
And thus his crime and sentence shared.
Her frightful claws remind her well,
Of how she sinned and how she fell;
And when they meet her startled eyes,
Her fearful shrieks appal the skies!

The parrot talks and does his best
To make life pass, with cheerful mien,
In hopes that in the regions blest
Man will befriend and take him in.

The bat retires to some lone cell,
Where worldly noise can ne'er intrude;
Where he in shade may calmly dwell,
And spend the day in solitude.
Modest and peaceful, well he knows
How frail is man, how false his ways;
And turns him from day's empty shows,
And from the sun's intemperate blaze.
He is enamoured of the night,
And while no rival comes between,
The stars can yield him ample light,
When he may watch and gaze unseen;
Then he retires to muse once more,
On all her beauty's wondrous store;
And feels fair night has charms for him,
To which day's garish rays are dim.

The bee draws forth from fruit and flower
Sweet dews, that swell his golden dower;
But never injures by his kiss,
Those who have made him rich in bliss.

The moth, though tortured by the flame,
Still hovers round and loves the same:
Nor is his fond attachment less—
 " Alas ! " he whispers, " can it be,
Spite of my ceaseless tenderness,
  That I am doomed to death by thee ? "

THE CUP

By Omar Khyyam

Know'st thou whence the hues are drawn
Which the tulip's leaves adorn?
'Tis that blood has soaked the earth,
Where her beauties had their birth.

Know'st thou why the violet's eyes
Gleam with dewy purple dyes?
'Tis that tears, for love untrue,
Bathed the banks where first she grew.
If no roses bloom for me,
Thorns my only flowers must be:
If no sun shine on my way,
Torches must provide my day,
Let me drink, as drink the wise:
Pardon for our weakness lies
In the cup—for Heaven well knew,
  When I first to being sprung,
I should love the rosy dew,
  And its praise would oft be sung.
'T were impiety to say
We would cast the cup away,
And be votaries no more,
Since it was ordained before.

DISPUTE BETWEEN DAY AND NIGHT

By Essedi of Tus

Day and Night, who each can yield
Joy and solace to the earth,
Thus contended for the field,
Claiming both the highest birth—
Night spoke frowningly:—" 'Twas I
Who from all eternity
Ruled the chaos of the world,
When in dim confusion hurled.
The fervent prayer is heard at night;
Devotion flies day's glaring light.
'Twas night, the Mount when Moses left;
At night was Lot avenged by fire:
At night the moon our prophet cleft,
And saw Heaven's might revealed entire.
The lovely moon for thirty days
Spreads radiant glory from afar:
Her charms for ever night displays,
Crowned, like a queen, with many a star:
Her seal-bearer is Heav'n, a band
Of planets wait on her command.
Day can but paint the skies with blue,
Night's starry hosts amaze the view.
Man measures time but by the moon;
Night shrouds what day reveals too soon.
Day is with toil and care oppressed,
Night comes, and, with her, gentle rest.
Day, busy still, no praise can bring,
All night the saints their anthems sing;
Her shade is cast by Gabriel's wing!

The moon is pure, the sun's broad face
Dark and unsightly spots deface:
The sun shines on with changeless glare,
The moon is ever new and fair."

Day rose, and smiled in high disdain:—
" Cease all this boasting, void and vain;
The Lord of Heaven, and earth, and thee,
　Gave me a place more proud than thine,
And men with joy my rising see,
　And hail the beams that round me shine.
The holy pilgrim takes by day
To many a sacred shrine his way;
By day the pious fast and pray;
And solemn feasts are held by day.

On the last day *the world's career is run,*
As on the first *its being was begun.*

Thou, Night, art friendly, it may be,
For lovers fly for help to thee.
When do the sick thy healing see?
Thieves, by thy aid, may scathless prowl;
Sacred to thee the bat and owl;
And, led by thee, pale spectres grimly howl!

I sprang from Heaven, from dust art thou,
　Light crowns my head with many a gem;
The collier's cap is on thy brow—
　For thee a fitting diadem.
My presence fills the world with joy;
Thou com'st all comfort to annoy.
I am a Moslem—white my vest:
Thou a vile thief, in sable drest.
Out negro-face!—dar'st thou compare
Thy cheeks with mine, so purely fair?

Those ' hosts of stars,' thy boast and pride,
How do they rush their sparks to hide,
How to their native darkness run,
When, in his glory, comes the sun!

True, death was first*; but, tell me, who*
Thinks life least worthy of the two?

'Tis by the moon the Arab counts;
  The lordly Persian tells his year
By the bright sun, that proudly mounts
  The yielding heavens, so wide and clear.
The sun is ruddy, strong, and hale;
The moon is sickly, wan, and pale.
Methinks 't was ne'er in story told
That silver had the worth of gold!
The moon, a slave, is bowed and bent,
She knows her light is only lent;
She hurries on, the way to clear
Till the great Shah himself appear.

What canst thou, idle boaster, say
To prove the night excels the day?
If stubborn still, let Him decide
With whom all truth and law abide;
Let Nasur Ahmed, wise as great,
Pronounce, and give to each his state."

" LAWAIH "

A Treatise on Sufism

Nuruddin Abdur Rahman Jami, from whose treatise the following is taken, was born at Jam in the Khorasan Province of Persia. The date of his birth is uncertain, but after attaining to a ripe old age he died and was buried at Herat in 1492. Not only as a master of romantic verse, but as a great mystic his scholarship is acknowledged. The following extracts are from the translation by Whinfield and Kazvini.

FLASH XXVI

The Shaikh (may God be well pleased with him) says in the *Fass i Shu'aibi*, that the universe consists of accidents all pertaining to a single substance, which is the Reality underlying all existences. This universe is changed and renewed unceasingly at every moment and at every breath. Every instant one universe is annihilated and another resembling it takes its place, though the majority of men do not perceive this, as God most glorious has said: " But they are in doubt regarding the new creation."

Among Rationalists no one has perceived this truth with the exception of the Asharians, who recognize it in certain departments of the universe, to wit, " accidents," as when they say that accidents exist not for two moments together; and also with the exception of the Idealists, called also Sophists, who recognize it in all parts of the universe, whether substances or accidents. But both these sects are in error in one part of their theory. The Asharians are wrong in asserting the existence of numerous substances— other than the One Real Being underlying all existence— on which substances, they say, depend the accidents which continually change and are renewed. They have not grasped the fact that the universe, together with all its parts, is nothing but a number of accidents, ever changing

and being renewed at every breath, and linked together in
a single substance, and at each instant disappearing and
being replaced by a similar set. In consequence of this
rapid succession, the spectator is deceived into the belief
that the universe is a permanent existence. The Asharians
themselves declare this when expounding the succession of
accidents in their substances as involving continuous sub-
stitution of accidents, in such wise that the substances are
never left wholly void of accidents similar to those which
have preceded them. In consequence of this the spectator
is misled into thinking that the universe is something
constant and unique.

> *The ocean does not shrink or vaster grow,*
> *Though the waves ever ebb and ever flow;*
> *The being of the world's a wave, it lasts*
> *One moment, and the next it has to go.*

> *In the world, men of insight may discern*
> *A stream whose currents swirl and surge and churn,*
> *And from the force that works within the stream*
> *The hidden working of the " Truth " may learn.*

As regards the Sophists, though they are right in
asserting the ideality of the whole universe, they are wrong
in failing to recognize the Real Being underlying it, who
clothes Himself with the forms and accidents of the sensible
universe and appears to us under the guise of phenomena
and multiplicity; likewise in denying any manifestation of
Real Being in the grades of visible things under the guise
of these forms and accidents, whereas in truth these
accidents and forms are only manifested to outward view
by the operation of that underlying Real Being.

> *Philosophers devoid of reason find*
> *This world a mere idea of the mind;*
> *'Tis an idea—but they fail to see*
> *The great Idealist who looms behind.*

But the men gifted with spiritual intuition see that the
Majesty of the " Truth," most glorious and most exalted,

reveals Himself at every breath in a fresh revelation, and that He never repeats the same revelation; that is to say, He never reveals Himself during two consecutive moments under the guise of the same phenomena and modes, but every moment presents fresh phenomena and modes.

> *The forms which clothe existence only stay*
> *One moment, in the next they pass away;*
> *This subtle point is proven by the text,*
> *" Its fashion altereth from day to day."*

The root of this mystery lies in the fact that the Majesty of the " Truth " most glorious possesses " names " opposed to one another, some being beautiful and some terrible; and these names are all in continuous operation, and no cessation of such operation is possible for any of them. Thus, when one of the contingent substances, through the concurrence of the requisite conditions, and the absence of opposing conditions, becomes capable of receiving the Very Being, the mercy of the Merciful takes possession of it, and the Very Being is infused into it; and the Very Being thus externalized, through being clothed with the effects and properties of such substances, presents Himself under the form of a particular phenomenon, and reveals Himself under the guise of this phenomenon. Afterwards, by the operation of the terrible Omnipotence which requires the annihilation of all phenomena and all semblance of multiplicity, this same substance is stripped of these phenomena. At the very moment that it is thus stripped this same substance is reclothed with another particular phenomenon, resembling the preceding one, through the operation of the mercy of the Merciful One. The next moment this latter phenomenon is annihilated by operation of the terrible Omnipotence, and another phenomenon is formed by the mercy of the Merciful One; and so on for as long as God wills. Thus, it never happens that the Very Being is revealed for two successive moments under the guise of the same phenomenon. At every moment one universe is annihilated and another similar to it takes its place. But he who is blinded by these veils, to wit, the constant succession of similar phenomena and like conditions, believes that the universe constantly endures in one and the same state, and never varies from time to time.

> *The glorious God, whose bounty, mercy, grace,*
> *And loving-kindness all the world embrace,*
>   *At every moment brings a world to naught,*
> *And fashions such another in its place.*

> *All gifts soever unto God are due,*
> *Yet special gifts from special " names " ensue;*
>   *At every breath one " name " annihilates,*
> *And one creates all outward things anew.*

The proof that the universe is nothing more than a combination of accidents united in a single essence, *i.e.* the " Truth " or Very Being, lies in the fact that when one comes to define the nature of existing things these definitions include nothing beyond " accidents." For example, when one defines man as a " rational animal "; and animal as a " growing and sentient body, possessed of the faculty of voluntary movement "; and body as a " substance possessing three dimensions "; and substance as an " entity which exists *per se* and is not inherent in any other subject "; and entity as " an essence possessed of reality and necessary being "—all the terms used in these definitions come under the category of " accidents," except this vague essence which is discerned behind these terms. For " rational " signifies an essence endued with reason; " that which is growing " signifies an essence endued with the faculty of growth; and so on. This vague essence is, in fact, the " Truth," the Very Being, who is self-existent, and who causes all these accidents to exist. And when the philosophers allege that these terms do not express the difference themselves, but only the invariable marks of these differences whereby we express them, because it is impossible to express the true differences otherwise than by these invariable marks or others more recondite still, this assumption is inadmissible and undeserving of serious attention. And even if we admit it as a hypothesis, we affirm that whatever is essential in relation to special sub-stances is accidental in relation to the Very Truth; for though this alleged essential quality is part of the essence of a particular substance, it is extraneous to the Very Truth upon whom it is dependent. And to say that there is any substantial entity other than the One Essential Being is the height of error, especially when the spiritual intuition of the men of truth, which is borrowed from the lamp of prophecy, attests the contrary, and when their opponents cannot cite any proofs in favour of their own view. " God saith what is true, and directeth man in the right path."

> *Truth is not proved by terms and demonstrations,*
> *Nor seen when hidden by concrete relations;*
> *The " Canon " is no " Cure " for ignorance,*
> *Nor can " Deliv'rance " come from " Indications."*
>
> *If at each " Stage " thy course diverted be*
> *To different " Goals," true goal thou'lt never see;*
> *And till the veil is lifted from thine eyes*
> *The sun of Truth will never " Rise " for thee.*
>
> *Strive to cast off the veil, not to augment*
> *Book-lore: no books will further thy intent.*
> *The germ of love to God grows not in books;*
> *Shut up thy books, turn to God and repent.*

The completest mask and the densest veils of the beauty of the One Real Being are produced by the manifold limitations which are found in the outward aspect of Being and which result from His being clothed with the properties and effects of the archetypes indwelling in the Divine Knowledge, which is the inner side of Being. To those blinded by these veils it seems that the archetypes exist in these outward sensible objects, whereas in point of fact these outward objects never attain a particle of those real archetypes, but are and will always continue in their original not-being. What exists and is manifested is the " Truth," but this is only in regard to His being clothed with the properties and effects of the archetypes, and not in regard to His condition when bare of all these properties; for in this latter case inwardness and concealment are amongst His inherent qualities. Consequently, in reality the Very Being never ceases to abide in His Essential Unity, wherein He was from all eternity and wherein He will endure to all eternity. But to the vulgar, who are blinded by these veils, the Very Being seems to be relative and phenomenal, and wearing the form of the multiplicity of these properties and effects, and He seems manifold to such persons.

> *Being's a sea in constant billows rolled,*
> *'Tis but these billows that we men behold;*
> *Sped from within, they rest upon the sea,*
> *And like a veil its actual form enfold.*

> *Being's the essence of the Lord of all,*
> *All things exist in Him and He in all;*
> *This is the meaning of the Gnostic phrase,*
> *" All things are comprehended in the All."*

When one thing is manifested in another, the thing manifested is different from the thing which is the theatre of the manifestation—*i.e.* the thing manifested is one thing and its theatre another. Moreover, that which is manifested in the theatre is the image or form of the thing manifested, not its reality or essence. But the case of the Very Being, the Absolute, is an exception, all whose manifestations are identical with the theatres wherein they are manifested, and in all such theatres He is manifested in His own essence.

> *They say, How strange! This peerless beauty's face*
> *Within the mirror's heart now holds a place;*
> *The marvel's not the face, the marvel is*
> *That it should be at once mirror and face.*

> *All mirrors in the universe I ween*
> *Display Thy image with its radiant sheen—*
> *Nay, in them all, so vast Thy effluent grace,*
> *'Tis Thyself, not Thine image, that is seen.*

The "Truth," the Very Being, along with all His modes, His attributes, connexions, and relations, which constitute the real existence of all beings, is immanent in the real existence of each being. Hence it has been said, " The All exists in all things." The author of the *Gulshan i Raz* says:

> " *If you cleave the heart of one drop of water*
> *There will issue from it a hundred pure oceans.*"

Every power and every act manifested as proceeding from the theatres of manifestation proceed in reality from the " Truth " manifested in these theatres, and not from the theatres themselves. The Shaikh (may God be well pleased with him) says in the *Hikmat i Aliyya*: " Outward existence (*'ain*) can perform no act of itself; its acts are those of its Lord immanent in it; hence this outward existence is passive, and action cannot be attributed to it." Consequently, power and action are ascribed to the creature (*'abd*) because of the manifestation of the " Truth " under the form of the creature, and not because such action is really effected by the creature himself. Read the text: " God hath created thee, both thee and the works of thy hands," and recognize the fact that thy existence, thy power, and thine actions come from the Majesty of Him who has no equal.

> *Both power and being are denied to us,*
> *The lack of both is what's ordained for us;*
> *But since 'tis He who lives within our forms,*
> *Both power and action are ascribed to us.*

> *Your "self" is non-existent, knowing one!*
> *Deem not your actions by yourself are done;*
> *Make no wry faces at this wholesome truth—*
> *" Build the wall ere the fresco is begun."*

> *Why vaunt thy "self" before those jealous eyes?*
> *Why seek to deal in this false merchandise?*
> *Why feign to be existent of thyself?*
> *Down with these vain conceits and foolish lies!*

Philosophical Literature

APPENDIX

GHAZALI ON FANA, ANNIHILATION OF SELF OR ABSORPTION IN GOD

" Prayers have three veils, whereof the first is prayers uttered only by the tongue; the second is when the mind, by hard endeavour and by firmest resolve, reaches a point at which, being untroubled by evil suggestions, it is able to concentrate itself on divine matters; the third veil is when the mind can with difficulty be diverted from dwelling on divine matters. But the marrow of prayer is seen when He who is invoked by prayer takes possession of the mind of him who prays, and the mind of the latter is absorbed in God whom he addresses, his prayers ceasing and no self-consciousness abiding in him, even to this extent that a mere thought about his prayers appears to him a veil and a hindrance. This state is called ' absorption ' by the doctors of mystical lore, when a man is so utterly absorbed that he perceives nothing of his bodily members, nothing of what is passing without, nothing of what occurs to his mind—yea, when he is, as it were, absent from all these things whatsoever, journeying first *to* his Lord, then *in* his Lord. But if the thought occurs to him that he is totally absorbed, that is a blot; for only that absorption is worthy of the name which is unconscious of absorption.

" I know these words of mine will be called an insipid discourse by narrow theologians, but they are by no means devoid of sense. Why? The condition of which I speak is similar to the condition of the man who loves any other things—*e.g.* wealth, honour, pleasures; and, just as we see some engrossed by love, we see others overpowered by anger so that they do not hear one who speaks, or see one who passes, and are so absorbed by their overwhelming passion that they are not even conscious of being thus absorbed. For so far as you attend to the absorption of your mind, you must necessarily be diverted from Him who is the cause of your absorption. . . .

" And now, being well instructed as to the nature of ' absorption,' and casting aside doubts, do not brand as false what you are unable to comprehend. God most high saith in the Koran: ' They brand as false what they do not comprehend.' The meaning of ' absorption ' having been made clear, you must know that the beginning of the path is the journey *to* God and that the journey *in* God is its goal, for in this latter, absorption in God takes place. At the outset this glides by like a flash of light, barely striking the eye; but thereafter, becoming habitual, it lifts the mind into a higher world, wherein the most pure essential Reality is manifested, and the human mind is imbued with the form of the spiritual world, whilst the majesty of the Deity evolves and discloses itself. Now, what first appears is the substance of angels, spirits, prophets, and saints, for a while under the veil of I know not what beautiful forms, wherefrom certain particular verities are disclosed; but by degrees, as the way is opened out, the Divine Verity begins to uncover His face. Can anyone, I ask, who attains a glimpse of such visions, wherefrom he returns to the lower world disgusted with the vileness of all earthly things, fail to marvel at those who, resting content with the deceits of the world, never strive to ascend to sublimer heights?"

A very similar doctrine is taught by the writer calling himself Dionysius the Areopagite, who has been recently identified with Stephen bar Sudaili, a Syrian monk. He says the soul, following what he calls "the negative way" or method of abstraction, "after completing its ascent into that region of being which, from its very sublimity, is to the impotent human intellect a region of obscurity, becomes completely passive, the voice is stilled, and man becomes united with the Ineffable Being." "Then is he delivered from all seeing and being seen, and passes into the truly mystical darkness of ignorance, where he excludes all intellectual apprehensions and abides in the utterly Impalpable and Invisible; being wholly His who is above all, with no other dependence, either on himself or any other; and is made one, as to his nobler part, with the utterly Unknown, by the cessation of all knowing; and at the same time, in that very knowing nothing, He knows what transcends the mind of man." This is simply a restatement of the doctrine of Plotinus.

ON POVERTY

The following is an extract from Kashful-Mahjub, the Persian Classics of Sufism, by Abul Hasan Ali b. Uthman b. Ali al-Ghaznawi al-Jullabi al Hujwiri of Ghazna (Afghanistan). He was a great traveller and philosopher. His teachings exalted him in the eyes of his followers as a saint. The date of his birth is uncertain, but he died in A.D. 1071 and was buried at Lahore. Kashful Mahjub is not only the ripest fruit of his authorship, but also the oldest Persian treatise on Sufism: the object of the book being to set forth a complete system of Sufism, not to piece together the sayings of other saints.

This extract is from the English translation of Dr. R. A. Nicholson.

*K*now that Poverty has a high rank in the Way of Truth, and that the poor are greatly esteemed, as God said: " (Give alms) *unto the poor, who are kept fighting in God's cause and cannot go to and fro on the earth; whom the ignorant deem rich forasmuch as they refrain* (from begging) " (Kor. ii. 274). And again: " *Their sides are lifted from their beds while they call on their Lord in fear and hope* " (Kor. xxxii. 16). Moreover, the Prophet chose poverty and said: " O God, make me live lowly and die lowly and rise from the dead amongst the lowly! " And he also said: " On the day of Resurrection God will say, ' Bring ye My loved ones nigh unto Me '; then the angels will say, ' Who are Thy loved ones? ' and God will answer them, saying, ' The poor and destitute.' " There are many verses of the Koran and Traditions to the same effect, which on account of their celebrity need not be mentioned here. Among the Refugees in the Prophet's time were poor men who sat in his mosque and devoted themselves to the worship of God, and firmly believed that God would give them their daily bread, and put their trust in Him. The Prophet was enjoined to consort with them and take due care of them; for God said: " *Do not repulse those who call on their Lord in the morning and in* *the evening, desiring His favour*" (Kor. vi. 52). Hence, whenever the Prophet saw one of them, he used to say: "May my father and mother be your sacrifice! since it was for your sakes that God reproached me."

God, therefore, has exalted Poverty and has made it a special distinction of the poor, who have renounced all things external and internal, and have turned entirely to the Causer; whose poverty has become their pride, so that they lamented its going and rejoiced at its coming, and embraced it and deemed all else contemptible.

Now, Poverty has a form and an essence. Its form is destitution and indigence, but its essence is fortune and free choice. He who regards the form rests in the form and, failing to attain his object, flees from the essence; but he who has found the essence averts his gaze from all created things, and in complete annihilation, seeing only the All-One he hastens towards the fullness of eternal life. The poor man has nothing and can suffer no loss. He does not become rich by having anything, nor indigent by having nothing: both these conditions are alike to him in respect of his poverty. It is permitted that he should be more joyful when he has nothing, for the Shaykhs have said: "The more straitened one is in circumstances, the more expansive (cheerful and happy) is one's (spiritual) state," because it is unlucky for a dervish to have property: if he "imprisons" anything for his own use, he himself is "imprisoned" in the same proportion. The friends of God live by means of His secret bounties. Worldly wealth holds them back from the path of quietism.

Story.—A dervish met a king. The king said: "Ask a boon of me." The dervish replied: "I will not ask a boon from one of my slaves." "How is that?" said the king. The dervish said: "I have two slaves who are thy masters: covetousness and expectation."

The Prophet said: "Poverty is glorious to those who are worthy of it." Its glory consists in this, that the poor man's body is divinely preserved from base and sinful acts, and his heart from evil and contaminating thoughts, because his outward parts are absorbed in (contemplation of) the manifest blessings of God, while his inward parts are protected by invisible grace, so that his body is spiritual and his heart divine. Then no relation subsists between him and mankind: this world and the next weigh less than a gnat's wing in the scales of his poverty: he is not contained in the two worlds for a single moment.

The Sufi Shaykhs differ in opinion as to whether poverty or wealth is superior, both being regarded as human attributes; for true wealth belongs to God, who is perfect in all His attributes. Yahyá b. Mu'ádh al-Rázi, Ahmad b. Abi 'l-Hawárí, Hárith al-Muhásibí, Abu 'l-'Abbás b. 'Atá, Ruwaym, Abu 'l-Hasan b. Sim'ún, and among the moderns the Grand Shaykh Abú Sa'íd Fadlallah B. Muhammad al-Mayhaní, all hold the view that wealth is superior to poverty. They argue that wealth is an attribute of God, whereas poverty cannot be ascribed to Him: therefore an attribute common to God and Man is superior to one that is not applicable to God. I answer: " This community of designation is merely nominal, and has no existence in reality: real community involves mutual resemblance, but the Divine attributes are eternal and the human attributes are created; hence your proof is false." I, who am 'Ali b. 'Uthmán al-Jullábí, declare that wealth is a term that may fitly be applied to God, but one to which Man has no right; while poverty is a term that may properly be applied to Man, but not to God. Metaphorically a man is called " rich," but he is not really so. Again, to give a clearer proof, human wealth is an effect due to various causes, whereas the wealth of God, who Himself is the Author of all causes, is not due to any cause. Therefore there is no community in regard to this attribute. It is not allowable to associate anything with God either in essence, attribute, or name. The wealth of God consists in His independence of anyone and in His power to do whatsoever He wills: such He has always been and such He shall be for ever. Man's wealth, on the other hand, is, for example, a means of livelihood, or the presence of joy, or the being saved from sin, or the solace of contemplation;

82

which things are all of phenomenal nature and subject to change.

Furthermore, some of the vulgar prefer the rich man to the poor, on the ground that God has made the former blest in both worlds and has bestowed the benefit of riches on him. Here they mean by "wealth" abundance of worldly goods and enjoyment of pleasures and pursuit of lusts. They argue that God has commanded us to be thankful for wealth and patient in poverty, *i.e.* patient in adversity and thankful in prosperity; and that prosperity is essentially better than adversity. To this I reply that, when God commanded us to be thankful for prosperity He made thankfulness the means of increasing our prosperity; but when He commanded us to be patient in adversity He made patience the means of drawing nigh unto Himself. He said: "*Verily, if ye return thanks, I will give you an increase*" (Kor. xiv. 7), and also, "*God is with the patient*" (Kor. ii. 148).

The Shaykhs who prefer wealth to poverty do not use the term "wealth" in its popular sense. What they intend is not "acquisition of a benefit" but "acquisition of the Benefactor"; to gain union (with God) is a different thing from gaining forgetfulness (of God). Shaykh Abú Saʿíd—God have mercy on him!—says: "Poverty is wealth in God," *i.e.* everlasting revelation of the Truth. I answer to this, that revelation implies the possibility of a veil; therefore, if the person who enjoys revelation is veiled from revelation by the attribute of wealth, he either becomes in need of revelation or he does not; if he does not, the conclusion is absurd, and if he does, need is incompatible with wealth; therefore that term cannot stand. Besides, no one has "wealth in God" unless his attributes are permanent and his object is invariable; wealth cannot coincide with the subsistence of an object or with the affirmation of the attributes of human nature, inasmuch as the essential characteristics of mortality and phenomenal being are need and indigence. One whose attributes still survive is not rich, and one whose attributes are annihilated is not entitled to any name whatever. Therefore "the

rich man is he who is enriched by God," because the
term " rich in God " refers to the agent, whereas the term
" enriched by God " denotes the person acted upon; the
former is self-subsistent, but the latter subsists through the
agent; accordingly self-subsistence is an attribute of human
nature, while subsistence through God involves the annihilation of attributes. I then, who am 'Alí b. 'Uthmán al-
Jullábí, assert that true wealth is incompatible with the
survival of any attribute, since human attributes have
already been shown to be defective and subject to decay;
nor, again, does wealth consist in the annihilation of these
attributes, because a name cannot be given to an attribute
that no longer exists, and he whose attributes are annihilated cannot be called either " poor " or " rich ";
therefore the attribute of wealth is not transferable from
God to Man, and the attribute of poverty is not transferable
from Man to God.

All the Súfí Shaykhs and most of the vulgar prefer
poverty to wealth for the reason that the Koran and the
Sunna expressly declare it to be superior, and herein the
majority of Moslems are agreed. I find, among the anecdotes
which I have read, that on one occasion this question was
discussed by Junayd and Ibn 'Atá. The latter maintained
the superiority of the rich. He argued that at the
Resurrection they would be called to account for their
wealth, and that such an account entails the hearing of the
Divine Word, without any mediation, in the form of
reproach: and reproach is addressed by the Beloved to
the lover. Junayd answered: " If He will call the rich
to account, He will ask the poor for their excuse; and
asking an excuse is better than calling to account." This
is a very subtle point. In true love excuse is " otherness "
and reproach is contrary to unity. Lovers regard both
these things as a blemish, because excuse is made for some
disobedience to the command of the Beloved and reproach
is made on the same score; but both are impossible in
true love, for then neither does the Beloved require an
expiation from the lover nor does the lover neglect to
perform the will of the Beloved.

Every man is "poor," even though he be a prince. Essentially the wealth of Solomon and the poverty of Solomon are one. God said to Job in the extremity of his patience, and likewise to Solomon in the plenitude of his dominion: " *Good servant that thou art!* " (Kor. xxxviii. 29, 44). When God's pleasure was accomplished, it made no difference between the poverty and the wealth of Solomon.

The author says: "I have heard that Abu 'l-Qásim Qushayrí—God have mercy on him!—said: ' People have spoken much concerning poverty and wealth, and have chosen one or the other for themselves, but I choose whichever state God chooses for me and keeps me in; if He keeps me rich I will not be forgetful, and if He wishes me to be poor I will not be covetous and rebellious.' " Therefore, both wealth and poverty are Divine gifts: wealth is corrupted by forgetfulness, poverty by covetousness. Both conceptions are excellent, but they differ in practice. Poverty is the separation of the heart from all but God, and wealth is the preoccupation of the heart with that which does not admit of being qualified. When the heart is cleared (of all except God), poverty is not better than wealth nor is wealth better than poverty. Wealth is abundance of worldly goods and poverty is lack of them: all goods belong to God: when the seeker bids farewell to property, the antithesis disappears and both terms are transcended.

All the Súfí Shaykhs have spoken on the subject of poverty. I will now cite as many of their sayings as it is possible to include in this book.

One of the moderns says: " The poor man is not he whose hand is empty of provisions, but he whose nature is empty of desires." For example, if God gives him money and he desires to keep it, then he is rich; and if he desires to renounce it, he is rich no less, because poverty consists in ceasing to act on one's own initiative. Yahyá b. Mu'ádh al-Rází says: " It is a sign of true poverty that, although one has reached the perfection of saintship and contemplation and self-annihilation, one should always be dreading its decline and departure." And Ruwaym says: "It is characteristic of the poor man that his heart is protected from selfish cares, and that his soul is guarded from contaminations, and that he performs the obligatory duties of religion:" that is to say, his inward meditations do not interfere with his outward acts, nor vice versa; which is a sign that he has cast off the attributes of mortality. Bishr Háfí says: "The best of ' stations ' is a firm resolution to endure poverty continually." Now poverty is the annihilation of all " stations ": therefore the resolution to endure poverty is a sign of regarding works and actions as imperfect, and of aspiring to annihilate human attributes. But in its obvious sense this saying pronounces poverty to be superior to wealth, and expresses a determination never to abandon it. Shibli says: "The poor man does not rest content with anything except God," because he has no other object of desire. The literal meaning is that you will not become rich except by Him, and that when you have gained Him you have become rich. Your being, then, is other than God; and since you cannot gain wealth except by renouncing " other," your " you-ness " is a veil between you and wealth: when that is removed, you are rich. This saying is very subtle and obscure. In the opinion of advanced occult philosophers it means: " Poverty consists in never being independent of poverty." This is what the Pír, *i.e.* Master 'Abdalláh Ansárí—may God be well-pleased with him!—meant when he said that our sorrow is everlasting, that our aspiration never reaches its goal, and that our sum never becomes non-existent in this world or the next, because for the fruition of anything homogeneity is necessary, but God has no congener, and for turning away from Him forgetfulness is necessary, but the dervish is not forgetful. What an endless task, what a difficult road! The dead never become living, so as to be united with Him; the living never become dead, so as to approach His presence. All that His lovers do and suffer is entirely a probation; but in order to console themselves they have invented a fine-sounding phraseology and have produced " stations " and " stages " and a " path."

Their symbolic expressions, however, begin and end in themselves, and their "stations" do not rise beyond their own *genus*, whereas God is exempt from every human attribute and relationship. Abu 'l-Hasan Núrí says: "When he gets nothing he is silent, and when he gets something he regards another person as better entitled to it than himself, and therefore gives it away." The practice enunciated in this saying is of great importance. There are two meanings: (1) His quiescence when he gets nothing is satisfaction, and his liberality when he gets something is love, because "satisfied" means "accepting a robe of honour," and the robe of honour is a token of proximity, whereas the lover rejects the robe of honour inasmuch as it is a token of severance; and (2) his quiescence when he gets nothing is expectation of getting something, and when he has got it, that "something" is other than God: he cannot be satisfied with anything other than God; therefore he rejects it. Both these meanings are implicit in the saying of the Grand Shaykh, Abu 'l-Qásim Junayd: "When his heart is empty of phenomena he is poor." Since the existence of phenomena is "other" (than God), rejection is the only course possible. Shiblí says: "Poverty is a sea of trouble, and all troubles for His sake are glorious." Glory is a portion of "other." The afflicted are plunged in trouble and know nothing of glory, until they forget their trouble and regard the Author thereof. Then their trouble is changed into glory, and their glory into a spiritual state, and their spiritual state into love, and their love into contemplation, so that finally the brain of the aspirant becomes wholly a centre of vision through the predominance of his imagination: he sees without eye, and hears without ear. Again, it is glorious for a man to bear the burden of trouble laid upon him by his Beloved, for in truth misfortune is glory, and prosperity is humiliation. Glory is that which makes one present with God, and humiliation is that which makes one absent from God: the affliction of poverty is a sign of "presence," while the delight of riches is a sign of "absence." Therefore one should cling to trouble of any description that involves contemplation and intimacy. Junayd says: " O ye that are poor, ye are known through God, and are honoured for the sake of God: take heed how ye behave when ye are alone with Him," *i.e.* if people call you " poor " and recognize your claim, see that you perform the obligations of the path of poverty; and if they give you another name, inconsistent with what you profess, do not accept it, but fulfil your professions. The basest of men is he who is thought to be devoted to God, but really is not; and the noblest is he who is not thought to be devoted to God, but really is. The former resembles an ignorant physician, who pretends to cure people, but only makes them worse, and when he falls ill himself needs another physician to prescribe for him; and the latter is like one who is not known to be a physician, and does not concern himself with other folk, but employs his skill in order to maintain his own health. One of the moderns has said: " Poverty is not-being without existence." To interpret this saying is impossible, because what is non-existent does not admit of being explained. On the surface it would seem that, according to this dictum, poverty is nothing, but such is not the case; the explanations and consensus of the Saints of God are not founded on a principle that is essentially non-existent. The meaning here is not " the not-being of the essence," but " the not-being of that which contaminates the essence "; and all human attributes are a source of contamination: when that is removed, the result is annihilation of the attributes, which deprives the sufferer of the instrument whereby he attains, or fails to attain, his object; but his not-going to the essence seems to him annihilation of the essence and casts him into perdition.

I have met with some scholastic philosophers who, failing to understand the drift of this saying, laughed at it and declared it to be nonsense; and also with certain pretenders (to Súfíism) who made nonsense of it and were firmly convinced of its truth, although they had no grasp of the fundamental principle. Both parties are in the wrong: one ignorantly denies the truth, and the other makes ignorance a state (of perfection). Now the expressions " not-being " and " annihilation," as they are used by Súfís, denote the disappearance of a blameworthy instrument and disapproved attribute in the course of seeking a praiseworthy attribute; they do not signify the search for non-reality by means of an instrument which exists.

Dervishhood in all its meanings is a metaphorical poverty, and amidst all its subordinate aspects there is a transcendent principle. The Divine mysteries come and go over the dervish, so that his affairs are acquired by himself, his actions attributed to himself, and his ideas attached to himself. But when his affairs are freed from the bonds of acquisition, his actions are no more attributed to himself. Then he is the Way, not the wayfarer, *i.e.* the dervish is a place over which something is passing, not a wayfarer following his own will. Accordingly, he neither draws anything to himself nor puts anything away from himself: all that leaves any trace upon him belongs to the essence.

I have seen false Súfís, mere tonguesters, whose imperfect apprehension of this matter seemed to deny the existence of the essence of poverty, while their lack of desire for the reality of poverty seemed to deny the attributes of its essence. They called by the name of " poverty " and " purity " their failure to seek Truth and Reality, and it looked as though they affirmed their own fancies but denied all else. Every one of them was in some degree veiled from poverty, because the conceit of Súfísm betokens perfection of saintship, and the claim to be suspected of Súfísm is the ultimate goal, *i.e.* this claim belongs only to the state of perfection. Therefore the seeker has no choice but to journey in their path and to traverse their " stations " and to know their symbolic expressions, in order that he may not be a plebeian among the elect. Those who are ignorant of general principles have no ground to stand on, whereas those who are ignorant only as regards the derivative branches are supported by the principles. I have said all this to encourage you to undertake this spiritual journey and occupy yourself with the due fulfilment of its obligations.

NARGAS

Songs of a Sikh by Bhai Vir Singh
Translated into English by Puran Singh

THE BIRTH OF GANGA

A spark of life, I saw shooting into the heavens.
The half-visible mist, borne on the southern sea-scented
winds, seemed to roll it on,
A ruby glowing in the mist!
It was winging in an aerial cradle, hung on the golden rays of
the sun in midmost sky.
It was the cradle of mists,
And a spark of life was glowing within;
And the angels with their breath were fanning the spark of
life that was soon to have its birth on the earth.
Down below, far below the mist, the white clouds gathered on
the Himalayan summits, like many hoary-headed sages
to receive the spark of life from on high.
A burning ruby, like the morning sun, shot through the air.
And down it fell into the clouds.
The mist rolled on the life-spark to grow and generate on earth!
Those were the clouds of the Himalayas,
With the spark of life glowing within.
The clouds could hardly hold for long the precious gem, so
heavy they were with it.
The clouds dropped down in a storm of snow on the Himalayan
peaks.
And concealed in this storm of snow, the spark of life
descended on the loftiest mountain of the globe!
And the spark of life burned within!

The spark of life, the Ganga of ancient fame, was seated like a
Yogi in the perennial snows;
Her legs were crossed, her backbone straightened as she
brooded in thought;

90

Her eyes were closed, her mind lost in Nirvana *calm!*
Her soul was gathered all within,
There was she seated like a Yogi *in the snows.*
But not the mists, the clouds, not the snows, could hold for
*   long the spark of life;*
No trance of Yogi *nor of* Nirvana *could long hold the moving*
*   life motionless.*
There is a grain of burning fire, a gleam of the seed of eternal
*   life still glowing in the heart of* Ganga.
This little grain of fire melts the glaciers,
And from the opened Gaumukh of the glaciers flows the
*   Ganga down.*
It is a little silver current of crystal joy water,
And the spark of life glows within!

Stealthily tumbling out of the Himalayas' lap,
Down she rolls dancing over rocks and stones,
And sparkles bright, catching the flying rainbows in her
*   hundred waves.*
Undaunted flows the River Ganga, *and nothing bars her way.*
Each little current of water, each little drop of dew, that
*   falls on the Himalayan grass, she beckons to herself,*
*   and every one obeys her call.*
The rivers come, the rivulets come:
And mightier, and larger, and happier flows the River Ganga!
Day and night, unresting, doth the river go,
And the spark of life glows within!
From the Himalayas down she descends on the Sivaliks;
And from the Sivaliks *on to the East,*
On to the East, the river goes,
Still brighter burns the spark of life within!

On to the East the Ganga *flows,*
Scattering the heavenly wealth around!
Plenty and prosperity to each and all!
The gifts of horses, cows and bulls!
The gifts of corn, of fruits and flowers!
Jewels and gems she scatters as she goes.
The mighty cities stand on either side of her banks, waiting,
*   like so many beggars, for her alms.*

Something for all, nothing denied, the Ganga *distributes life
and joy as she rushes down.*
*The thirsty creatures of the forests drink from her cup as she
holds it to their lips.*

Man, bird and beast rejoice!
The Ganga *knows the ways in which heaven does good to all,*
The heat of the heat-oppressed she takes to herself.
She fain would be muddy, if only others may be made clean.
*She gives and forgives; she knows how to serve with her
coolest waves, if only others may be happier thereby.*
Attracted onward by the vision of the ancient teachings,
The Ganga *seeks the sea,*
To be one with the great infinite,
To be lost in the one great stream—the oneness of things,
*At last she goes to the great ocean, blue and broad, one infinite
stretch of things,*
To rest in one unmoving motion.
*All day and night, unresting, through the land she goes, and
never turns back.*

The sea to the approaching Ganga *said, " Who and from
whence art thou?*
Thou art great, full of every gem and scent.
*Thou art fragrant with the fragrance of the earth and of
many a herb!*
*Thou bringest the joys of the land of the people, rich-laden
with gold and pearl thou comest!*
Thou hast been showering joys on all,
Thou hast brought blessing to all!
*Pray, tell me thy tale, where is thy land, thy home, O
beautiful one? "*
Proud of her Father-Himalaya and her high descent from heaven,
The Ganga *raised her head aloft and said:*
" I come from the Himalayas,
From the largest, greatest, highest height,
And the deepest deep,
From him self-lost in Yoga.
All I have now or did ever bring with me is his, O sea!
All I gave to any that met me on my way is his.

The gifts are his, he the giver!
I am but a messenger of the great Himalaya—stern ancient
    lover of men.
His waters are sweet.
His ore and precious stones are so fair and bright.
The gold shines in the sands there.
His air breathes everlasting ecstasies.
His trees are talisman-trees.
His herbs are weighted with charms.
His seasons revolve in endless fascination.
All glorious are his lights.
Those shades of deodar, the moonlit-snows,
The sudden falls of Auroras of the north."

When the sea heard of the greatness of the Himalayas, a snake-
    like wave coiled round his heart, and he angrily replied:
" True," he said, " he is high, but is not a very Hell below,
    in the depths of his valleys?
That greatness is of no avail which has so much low, dark
    littleness by its side.
O beautiful one! those that are high have enough of the low!
Look at me! O fair new-comer from afar!
I am always of one level, neither high nor low,
Nor great nor small; one great vastness I.
I receive a thousand rivers and I increase not,
A thousand rivers go out of me and I decrease not.
Nor have I any high peaks to show,
Nor is there any sudden rise or sudden fall in me.
No deep dark valley is in me, no half-scooped caves,
No cracked fissures or frowning wrinkles are on my face.
One great level, one vastness, one oneness I am! "

The Ganga *collected herself, in supreme wrath,*
And turned her steps back from where she came.
She murmured to herself:
" Back I will go. I will not stay with such a jealous wretch
    as the sea, so proud of his own low level."
And aloud she spoke with the voice of an angry goddess:
" Ah! I had thought that the ocean is ever calm, silent and
    deep.

Thou hast spoken but as a shallow water-pot. Thou hast not weighed what thou hast said.

It is true the Himalaya has deep valleys, deep wrinkles on his face;

But, O sea! his lowest level is higher far than the highest thou canst boast.

The high ones are ever high,

But higher even their lowest pitch than the highest crest of thy waves.

I wonder thou, so low thyself, speakest ill of him who sends thee feeding streams.

Knowest thou not thy Gehenna-depths of hell below this water-garb of honour!

Knowest thou not thy treacherous caves below!

Knowest thou not how mean is this deceptive level of thine!

But thou knowest how to hide thy ugly gulf below this shining water sheet.

And there the high Himalaya, my father, stands bare in his own glory and joy, caring not to conceal even a single blot on his skin.

There stands he, the highest, with all his scars and wrinkles on him.

There rise up his highest peaks, abode of angels and gods, in the transparent blue—

The snowy summits are kissed daily by the rising sun.

Behold the daily showers of gold on the hoary head of my father!

Heaven pouring itself down on him,

How sublime is he! How mean art thou!

How he stands for eternity to feast the world with his flesh and blood!

How thou cringest here eating every crumb that each one throws to thee!

He is the giver.

Thou art but a beggar.

A beggar can brook not the greatness of his benefactor.

Concealing well thy black depths, thou proclaimest thyself without shame and fear, so faultless thou, that art so low.

Go! I curse thee, thou shalt for ever drown in the deeps of
thy own black hate."
Then the Ganga *turned away from the sea.*
And the sea, self-drowned in shame, cried out:
" Go not, Ganga, *go not away! Come back, come back to me,*
I have been waiting so long for thee."
But the Ganga *turned away indignantly from the ocean,*
The spark of life blazing high within!

The sea flatters her;
But on she goes; her eyes turned up to heaven, heaven's eyes
gazing into hers,
Still the sea, catching her by the hands and holding her round
the waist, tries to take her back to his home.
" O God! I will not stay with this monster of winds and
waves,
I will not stay with the slanderer of my great father.
Pray, heaven! send down thy beams and bea. me upwards in
their embraces.
And take me back to the lap of my father!
I will not stay with this monster of the waves."

The Ganga *ascends.*
On the shoulders of the winds, in the cradle woven of the rays
of the sun and moon, she is lifted high to the mid-sky,
To the Himalayas back the Ganga *flies.*
In the cradle of light is her ascent,
Where the spark of life is fanned by angels.

Once again she tries to forget the world,
Once again, in the lap of Himalayas, the Ganga *lies and plays.*
Once again she is lost in Nirvana.
Once again her legs are crossed, her backbone straightened as
she broods in thought.
Her eyes are closed, her mind is lost in calm.
Once again her soul is all gathered within,
Seated like a Yogi *in the snows,*
The eternal unmelting snows,
And buried in them, and aglow is still the spark of life!
The Ganga *sleeps, she sleeps again in trances on the snows.*

But the spark of fire she has in her soul rouses her again.
Again she moves, again she flows; again she goes to bless and love.
Tired and spent, again she returns.
Filled and refreshed, again she flows;
She is alive, and the spark of life in her soul burns for ever.

THE SWING OF LOVE

I

I remember I was on the swing of love, and it was swinging high.
The very height made me pure and selfless.

II

As we swung, the beloved held a bowl to my lips.
I drank of it, my lips were honey-sealed.
It was, I saw, the wine of life, the bestower of love and freedom.
I cast but casual glances downwards: the things on earth looking up with sweet appeal.
I knew not that my very looks and smiles would be my bondage.
My own smiles and looks became the chains by which the things of earth bound me down.
They began to sling their sorrows and shades, and the pains of hell, about my heart.
I blame no one, I only blame my binding looks and smiles.

III

Ah! again the swing of love and the freedom of the air, the sun, and the soul!
These chains would drop, if I could but catch again, as before . . .
As before the hem of the flying garment of him who flies so high!

96   If he would only hale me, and if I could but hold firm his
        helping hand!
Ah! if I could bind him down to myself by his image of love
        within my heart!
If he would only lift me up, and if I could but hold his helping
        hand in mine!

IV

And now I fly again, for thus my chains did drop.
Again I am seated in my swing of love.
It is swinging full and high.
And the bowl is sweet, my love holds to my lips.
I drink of it, and to its lips my lips are honey-sealed:
It is, I see, the wine of life, the bestower of love, and the
        freedom of the air.

RUBAIYAT OF OMAR KHYYAM

Rendered into English Verse by Edward FitzGerald

Omar Khyyam, the astronomer-poet of Persia, was born at Naishapur in the latter half of the eleventh century and died in the first quarter of the century succeeding. He is supposed to have been a tent-maker originally, but was pensioned by an old schoolfellow who had become Vizier, so that he had leisure in which to study, and he became famous as a scientist, and was one of those employed to reform the calendar.

Edward FitzGerald (1809–83) made himself and Omar famous by his free English translation. It was published anonymously in 1859 at 5s., but, proving apparently a failure, the unsold copies soon found their way into the penny box. Few poems in the English language have, however, proved so popular.

In his illuminating *Note on Omar* the late Professor York Powell wrote: " When FitzGerald put Omar into English he did more than he knew. He revealed to us in fixed and memorable form a white, broad tract of thought many moderns and a few ancients had descried, but only in vague and cloudy delineation." And again: " Omar is not often a preacher, seldom a prophet, occasionally a frank counsellor, always a friend. He had learnt to be content to accept men and things as they are. He would have men charitable and sincere. He had no ethical advice beyond this. He recognized that the ultimate explanation is beyond our comprehension, though he did not trouble himself to doubt its existence. He had done with systems and universal theories. He laughed at creeds and mocked at superstitions, but he welcomed facts with a gentle and humorous smile. He had no malice, no grudge against life. He was companionable in his hours, never inhuman. Of the hermit or the ascetic there was no trace in him. He was not the man to shudder at the beauty of women or the splendours of the earth and heavens, because Mutability has set her seal upon them all."

I

Awake! for Morning in the Bowl of Night
Has flung the Stone that puts the Stars to Flight;
And Lo! the Hunter of the East has caught
The Sultan's Turret in a Noose of Light.

II

Dreaming when Dawn's Left Hand was in the Sky
I heard a Voice within the Tavern cry,
  " Awake, my Little ones, and fill the Cup
Before Life's Liquor in its Cup be dry."

III

And, as the Cock crew, those who stood before
The Tavern shouted—" Open then the Door!
  You know how little while we have to stay,
And, once departed, may return no more."

IV

Now the New Year reviving old Desires,
The thoughtful Soul to Solitude retires,
  Where the WHITE HAND OF MOSES *on the Bough*
Puts out, and Jesus from the Ground suspires.

V

Iram indeed is gone with all its Rose,
And Jamshyd's Sev'n-ring'd Cup where no one knows;
  But still the Vine her ancient Ruby yields,
And still a Garden by the Water blows.

VI

And David's Lips are lock't; but in divine
High-piping Pehlevi, with " Wine! Wine! Wine!
  Red Wine!"—the Nightingale cries to the Rose
That yellow Cheek of her's to incarnadine.

VII

Come, fill the Cup, and in the Fire of Spring
The Winter Garment of Repentance fling :
  The Bird of Time has but a little way
To fly—and Lo! the Bird is on the Wing.

VIII

And look—a thousand Blossoms with the Day
Woke—and a thousand scatter'd into Clay:
And this first Summer Month that brings the Rose
Shall take Jamshyd and Kaikobad away.

IX

But come with old Khayyam, and leave the Lot
Of Kaikobad and Kaihosru forgot:
Let Rustum lay about him as he will,
Or Hatim Tai cry Supper—heed them not.

X

With me along some Strip of Herbage strown
That just divides the desert from the sown,
Where name of Slave and Sultan scarce is known,
And pity Sultan Mahmud on his Throne.

XI

Here with a Loaf of Bread beneath the Bough,
A flask of Wine, a Book of Verse—and Thou
Beside me singing in the Wilderness—
And Wilderness is Paradise enow.

XII

" How sweet is mortal Sovranty "—think some:
Others—" How blest the Paradise to come ! "
Ah, take the Cash in hand and waive the Rest;
Oh, the brave Music of a distant Drum !

XIII

Look to the Rose that blows about us—" Lo,
Laughing," she says, " into the World I blow:
At once the silken Tassel of my Purse
Tear, and its Treasure on the Garden throw."

XIV

The Worldly Hope men set their Hearts upon
Turns Ashes—or it prospers; and anon,
   Like Snow upon the Desert's dusty Face
Lighting a little Hour or two—is gone.

XV

And those who husbanded the Golden Grain,
And those who flung it to the Winds like Rain,
   Alike to no such aureate Earth are turn'd
As, buried once, Men want dug up again.

XVI

Think, in this batter'd Caravanserai
Whose Doorways are alternate Night and Day,
   How Sultan after Sultan with his Pomp
Abode his Hour or two, and went his way.

XVII

They say the Lion and the Lizard keep
The Courts where Jamshyd gloried and drank deep:
   And Bahram, that great Hunter—the Wild Ass
Stamps o'er his Head, and he lies fast asleep.

XVIII

I sometimes think that never blows so red
The Rose as where some buried Cæsar bled;
   That every Hyacinth the Garden wears
Dropt in its Lap from some once lovely Head.

XIX

And this delightful Herb whose tender Green
Fledges the River's Lip on which we lean—
   Ah, lean upon it lightly! for who knows
From what once lovely Lip it springs unseen!

XX

Ah, my Beloved, fill the cup that clears
To-DAY *of past Regrets and future Fears—*
    To-MORROW?*—Why, To-morrow I may be*
Myself with Yesterday's Sev'n Thousand Years.

XXI

Lo! some we loved, the loveliest and the best
That Time and Fate of all their Vintage prest,
    Have drunk their Cup a Round or two before,
And one by one crept silently to Rest.

XXII

And we, that now make merry in the Room
They left, and Summer dresses in new Bloom,
    Ourselves must we beneath the Couch of Earth
Descend, ourselves to make a Couch—for whom?

XXIII

Ah, make the most of what we yet may spend,
Before we too into the Dust descend;
    Dust into Dust, and under Dust, to lie,
Sans Wine, sans Song, sans Singer, and—sans End!

XXIV

Alike for those who for TO-DAY *prepare,*
And those that after a TO-MORROW *stare,*
    A Muessin from the Tower of Darkness cries
" Fools! your Reward is neither Here nor There!"

XXV

Why, all the Saints and Sages who discuss'd
Of the Two Worlds so learnedly, are thrust
    Like foolish Prophets forth; their Words to Scorn
Are scatter'd, and their Mouths are stopt with Dust.

XXVI

Oh, come with old Khayyam, and leave the Wise
To talk; one thing is certain, that Life flies;
*   One thing is certain, and the Rest is Lies;*
The Flower that once has blown for ever dies.

XXVII

Myself when young did eagerly frequent
Doctor and Saint, and heard great Argument
*   About it and about: but evermore*
Came out by the same Door as in I went.

XXVIII

With them the Seed of Wisdom did I sow,
And with my own hand labour'd it to grow;
*   And this was all the Harvest that I reap'd—*
" I came like Water, and like Wind I go."

XXIX

Into this Universe, and why not knowing,
Nor whence, like Water willy-nilly flowing:
*   And out of it, as Wind along the Waste,*
I know not whither, willy-nilly blowing.

XXX

What, without asking, hither hurried whence?
And, without asking, whither hurried hence!
*   Another and another Cup to drown*
The Memory of this Impertinence!

XXXI

Up from Earth's Centre through the Seventh Gate
I rose, and on the Throne of Saturn sate,
*   And many Knots unravel'd by the Road;*
But not the Knot of Human Death and Fate.

XXXII

There was a Door to which I found no Key:
There was a Veil past which I could not see:
Some little Talk awhile of ME *and* THEE
There seemed—and then no more of THEE *and* ME.

XXXIII

Then to the rolling Heav'n itself I cried,
Asking, " What Lamp had Destiny to guide
Her little Children stumbling in the Dark? "
And—" A blind Understanding! " Heav'n replied.

XXXIV

Then to this earthen Bowl did I adjourn
My Lip the secret Well of Life to learn:
And Lip to Lip it murmur'd—" While you live
Drink!—for once dead you never shall return."

XXXV

I think the Vessel, that with fugitive
Articulation answer'd, once did live,
And merry make; and the cold Lip I kiss'd
How many Kisses might it take—and give!

XXXVI

For in the Market-place, one Dusk of Day,
I watch'd the Potter thumping his wet Clay:
And with its all obliterated Tongue
It murmur'd—" Gently, Brother, gently, pray! "

XXXVII

Ah, fill the Cup:—what boots it to repeat
How Time is slipping underneath our Feet:
Unborn TO-MORROW *and dead* YESTERDAY,
Why fret about them if TO-DAY *be sweet!*

XXXVIII

One Moment in Annihilation's Waste,
One Moment, of the Well of Life to taste—
The Stars are setting and the Caravan
Starts for the Dawn of Nothing—Oh, make haste!

XXXIX

How long, how long, in infinite Pursuit
Of This and That endeavour and dispute?
Better be merry with the fruitful Grape
Than sadden after none, or bitter, Fruit.

XL

You know, my Friends, how long since in my House
For a new Marriage I did make Carouse:
Divorced old barren Reason from my Bed,
And took the Daughter of the Vine to Spouse.

XLI

For " is " and " is-not " though with Rule and Line,
And " up-and-down " without, I could define,
I yet in all I only cared to know,
Was never deep in anything but—Wine.

XLII

And lately, by the Tavern Door agape,
Came stealing through the Dusk an Angel Shape
Bearing a Vessel on his Shoulder; and
He bid me taste of it; and 'twas—the Grape!

XLIII

The Grape that can with Logic absolute
The Two-and-Seventy jarring Sects confute:
The subtle Alchemist that in a Trice
Life's leaden Metal into Gold transmute.

XLIV

The mighty Mahmud, the victorious Lord,
That all the misbelieving and black Horde
  Of Fears and Sorrows that infest the Soul
Scatters and slays with his enchanted Sword.

XLV

But leave the Wise to wrangle, and with me
The Quarrel of the Universe let be:
  And, in some corner of the Hubbub coucht,
Make Game of that which makes as much of Thee.

XLVI

For in and out, above, about, below,
'Tis nothing but a Magic Shadow-show,
  Play'd in a Box whose Candle is the Sun,
Round which we Phantom Figures come and go.

XLVII

And if the Wine you drink, the Lip you press,
End in the Nothing all Things end in—Yes—
  Then fancy while Thou art, Thou art but what
Thou shall be—Nothing—Thou shalt not be less.

XLVIII

While the Rose blows along the River Brink,
With old Khayyam the Ruby Vintage drink:
  And when the Angel with his darker Draught
Draws up to Thee—take that, and do not shrink.

XLIX

'Tis all a Chequer-board of Nights and Days
Where Destiny with Men for Pieces plays:
  Hither and thither moves, and mates, and slays,
And one by one back in the Closet lays.

L

The Ball no Question makes of Ayes and Noes,
But Right or Left as strikes the Player goes;
*   And He that toss'd Thee down into the Field,*
He knows about it all—HE *knows*—HE *knows!*

LI

The Moving Finger writes; and, having writ,
Moves on: nor all thy Piety nor Wit
*   Shall lure it back to cancel half a Line,*
Nor all thy Tears wash out a word of it.

LII

And that inverted Bowl we call The Sky,
Whereunder crawling coop't we live and die,
*   Lift not thy hands to It for help—for It*
Rolls impotently on as Thou or I.

LIII

With Earth's first Clay They did the Last Man's knead,
And then of the Last Harvest sow'd the Seed:
*   Yea, the first Morning of Creation wrote*
What the Last Dawn of Reckoning shall read.

LIV

I tell Thee this—When, starting from the Goal,
Over the shoulders of the flaming Foal
*   Of Heav'n Parwin and Mushtara they flung,*
In my predestin'd Plot of Dust and Soul.

LV

The Vine had struck a Fibre; which about
If clings my Being—let the Sufi flout;
*   Of my Base Metal may be filed a Key,*
That shall unlock the Door he howls without.

LVI

And this I know: whether the one True Light,
Kindle to Love, or Wrath-consume me quite,
*   One Glimpse of It within the Tavern caught*
Better than in the Temple lost outright.

LVII

Oh Thou, who didst with Pitfall and with Gin
Beset the Road I was to wander in,
*   Thou wilt not with Predestination round*
Enmesh me, and impute my Fall to Sin?

LVIII

Oh, Thou, who Man of baser Earth didst make,
And who with Eden didst devise the Snake;
*   For all the Sin wherewith the Face of Man*
Is blacken'd, Man's Forgiveness give—and take!

.   .   .   .   .

KUZA-NAMA

LIX

Listen again.   One Evening at the Close
Of Ramaẓan, ere the better Moon arose,
*   In that old Potter's Shop I stood alone*
With the clay Population round in Rows.

LX

And, strange to tell, among the Earthen Lot
Some could articulate, while others not:
*   And suddenly one more impatient cried—*
" Who is the Potter, pray, and who the Pot? "

LXI

Then said another—" Surely not in vain
My Substance from the common Earth was ta'en,
*   That He who subtly wrought me into Shape*
Should stamp me back to common Earth again."

LXII

Another said—" Why, ne'er a peevish Boy,
Would break the Bowl from which he drank in Joy;
*   Shall He that* made *the Vessel in pure Love*
And Fancy, in an after Rage destroy!"

LXIII

None answer'd this; but after Silence spake
A Vessel of a more ungainly Make:
*   " They sneer at me for leaning all awry;*
What! did the Hand then of the Potter shake?"

LXIV

Said one—" Folks of a surly Tapster tell,
And daub his Visage with the Smoke of Hell;
*   They talk of some strict Testing of us—Pish!*
He's a Good Fellow, and 'twill all be well."

LXV

Then said another with a long-drawn Sigh,
" My Clay with long oblivion is gone dry:
*   But, fill me with the old familiar Juice,*
Methinks I might recover by and by."

LXVI

So while the Vessels one by one were speaking,
One spied the little Crescent all were seeking:
*   And then they jogg'd each other, " Brother, Brother!*
Hark to the Porter's Shoulder-knot a-creaking!"

.   .   .   .   .   .

LXVII

Ah, with the Grape my fading Life provide,
And wash my Body whence the Life has died,
  And in a Winding-sheet of Vine-leaf wrapt,
So bury me by some sweet Garden-side.

LXVIII

That ev'n my buried Ashes such a Snare
Of Perfume shall fling up into the Air,
  As not a True Believer passing by
But shall be overtaken unaware.

LXIX

Indeed the Idols I have loved so long
Have done my Credit in Men's Eye much wrong:
  Have drown'd my Honour in a shallow Cup,
And sold my Reputation for a Song.

LXX

Indeed, indeed, Repentance oft before
I swore—but was I sober when I swore?
  And then and then came Spring, and Rose-in-hand
My thread-bare Penitence apieces tore.

LXXI

And much as Wine has play'd the Infidel,
And robb'd me of my Robe of Honour—well,
  I often wonder what the Vintners buy
One half so precious as the Goods they sell.

LXXII

Alas, that Spring should vanish with the Rose!
That Youth's sweet-scented Manuscript should close!
  The Nightingale that in the Branches sang,
Ah, whence, and whither flown again, who knows!

LXXIII

Ah Love! could thou and I with Fate conspire
To grasp this sorry Scheme of Things entire,
  Would not we shatter it to bits—and then
Re-mould it nearer to the Heart's Desire!

LXXIV

Ah, Moon of my Delight who know'st no wane,
The Moon of Heav'n is rising once again:
  How oft hereafter rising shall she look
Through this same Garden after me—in vain!

LXXV

And when Thyself with shining Foot shall pass
Among the Guests Star-scatter'd on the Grass,
  And in thy joyous Errand reach the Spot
Where I made one—turn down an empty Glass!

TALES OF MYSTIC MEANING

The following tales are taken from the Persian Mathnawi of Jalaluddin Rumi. Born at Bulkh (Afghanistan) in 1207, he left with his family for a long journey into Iraq, Arabia and Syria, finally settling down at Konia in Asia Minor. Here he started the Order of the Sufis, and wrote a great deal, much of which forms the Text-books of Naqshbundi Philosophy of Sufism. He died at the age of sixty-six in 1273, leaving two sons and a daughter. These English extracts are from Dr. R. A. Nicholson's *Tales of Mystic Meaning*.

THE KING AND THE HANDMAIDEN

*In olden time there was a King to whom belonged the
    power temporal and also the power spiritual.*
*It chanced that one day he rode with his courtiers to the
    chase.*
*On the king's highway the King espied a Handmaiden: the
    soul of the King was enthralled by her.*
*Forasmuch as the bird, his soul, was fluttering in its cage, he
    gave money and bought the Handmaiden.*
*After he had bought her and won to his desire, by Divine
    destiny she sickened.*
*The King gathered the physicians together from left and right
    and said to them, " The life of us both is in your hands.*
*My life is of no account, but she is the life of my life, I am
    in pain and wounded: she is my remedy.*
*Whoever heals her that is my life will bear away with him
    my treasure and pearls, large and small."*
*They all answered him, saying, " We will hazard our lives
    and summon all our skill and put it into the common
    stock.*
*Each one of us the Messiah of a multitude: in our hands is
    a medicine for every pain."*
*In their arrogance they did not say, " If God will "; therefore
    God showed unto them the weakness of Man.*

The more cures and remedies they applied, the more did the illness increase, and their need was not fulfilled.

The sick girl became thin as a hair, while the eyes of the King flowed with tears of blood, like a river.

How it became manifest to the King that the physicians were unable to cure the Handmaiden, and how he turned his face towards God and dreamed of a holy man.

When the King saw the powerlessness of those physicians, he ran bare-footed to the mosque.

He entered the mosque and advanced to the mihrab *to pray: the prayer-carpet was bathed in the King's tears.*

On coming to himself out of the flood of ecstasy he opened his lips in goodly praise and laud,

Saying, " O Thou whose least gift is the empire of the world, what shall I say? for Thou knowest the hidden thing.

O Thou with whom we always take refuge in our need, once again we have lost the way;

But Thou hast said, ' Albeit I know thy secret, nevertheless declare it in thine outward act.' "

When from the depths of his soul he raised a cry of supplication, the sea of Bounty began to surge.

Slumber overtook him in the midst of weeping: he dreamed that an old man appeared

And said, " Good tidings, O King! Thy prayers are granted. If to-morrow a stranger come to thee, he is from me.

He is the skilled physician: deem him veracious, for he is trusty and true.

In his remedy behold absolute magic, in his nature behold the might of God! "

The meeting of the King with the divine Physician whose coming had been announced to him in a dream.

When the promised hour arrived and day broke and the sun, rising from the east, began to burn the stars,

The King was in the belvedere, expecting to see that which had been shown mysteriously.

He saw a person excellent and worshipful, a sun amidst a shadow,

Coming from afar, like the new moon in slenderness and radiance: he was non-existent, though existent in the form of phantasy.

In the stranger's countenance the King discerned the phantom which he had beheld in his dream.

He himself, instead of the chamberlains, went forward to meet his guest from the Invisible.

Both were seamen who had learned to swim, the souls of both were knit together without sewing.

The King said, " Thou wert my Beloved in reality, not she; but in this world one action arises from another.

O thou who art to me as Mustafa, while I am like unto'Umar— I will gird my loins to do thee service."

The King opened his hands and clasped him to his breast and received him, like love, into his heart and soul,

And kissed his hand and brow and inquired concerning his home and journey.

So with many a question he led him to the place of honour. " At last," he said, " I have found a treasure by being patient.

O gift from God and defence against trouble, O thou who art the meaning of ' Patience is the key to joy.'

O thou whose countenance is the answer to every question, by thee hard knots are loosed without discussion.

Thou readest all that is in our hearts, thou givest a helping hand to everyone whose foot is in the mire."

How the King led the Physician to the bedside of the sick girl, that he might see her condition.

When that meeting and bounteous spiritual repast was over, he took his hand and conducted him to the harem.

He rehearsed the tale of the invalid and her sickness and then seated him beside her.

The Physician observed the colour of her face and felt her pulse; he heard both the symptoms and the circumstances of her malady.

He said, " None of the remedies which they have applied
builds health; those false physicians have wrought
destruction.

They were ignorant of the inward state. I seek refuge with
God from that which they devise."

He saw the pain, and the secret became open to him, but he
concealed it and did not tell the King.

Her pain was not caused by black or yellow bile: the smell of
every firewood appears from the smoke.

From her sore grief he perceived that she was heart-sore; well
in body but stricken in heart.

Being in love is made manifest by soreness of heart; there is
no sickness like heart-sickness.

The lover's ailment is separate from all other ailments: Love
is the astrolabe of divine mysteries.

Whether Love be from this side or from that, in the end it
leads us Yonder.

How the Physician demanded of the King to be alone
with the Handmaiden for the purpose of discovering
her malady.

He said, " O King, make the house empty; send away both
kinsfolk and strangers.

Let no one listen in the entrance-halls, that I may ask certain
things of this handmaiden."

The house was left empty, not one inhabitant remained,
nobody save the Physician and the sick girl.

Very gently he asked, " Where is thy native town? for the
treatment suitable to the people of each town is different.

And in that town who is related to thee? With whom hast
thou kinship and affinity? "

She disclosed to the Physician many things touching her
home and former masters and fellow-townsmen,

And he, while listening to her story, continued to observe her
pulse and its beating,

So that, if it throbbed at anyone's name, he might know who
was the object of her desire in the world.

*She told of many a town and many a house, and still no vein
of her quivered nor did her cheek grow pale.*

*Her pulse kept its wonted time, unimpaired, till he asked about
sweet Samarcand.*

*Then it jumped, and her face went red and pale by turns, for she
had been parted from a man of Samarcand, a Goldsmith.*

*When the Physician found out this secret from the sick girl,
he perceived the source of that grief and woe.*

He asked, " In which quarter of the town does he dwell? "

" Sar-i Pul (Bridge-head)," she replied, " and Ghatafar
Street."

*" I know," said he, " what your illness is, and I will at once
display the arts of magic in delivering you.*

*Be glad and care-free and have no fear, for I will do to you
that which rain does to the meadow.*

*I will be anxious for you, be not you anxious: I am kinder to
you than a hundred fathers.*

*Beware! tell not this secret to anyone, not though the King
himself should make much inquiry.*

*Let your heart become the grave of your secret, the sooner will
your desire be gain.*

*When seeds are hidden in the earth, their inward secret becomes
the verdure of the garden."*

How the King sent messengers to Samarcand to fetch the
Goldsmith.

*Then he arose and went to the King and acquainted him with
a part of the matter.*

*" The best plan," said he, " is that we should bring the man
here for the purpose of curing this malady.*

*Summon the Goldsmith from that far country; beguile him
with gold and robes of honour."*

*The King sent thither two messengers, clever men and com-
petent and very just.*

*To Samarcand came the two messengers for the Goldsmith
debonair and wanton,*

*Saying, " O fine master, perfect in knowledge, thy perfection
is famous in all lands.*

Lo, such and such a King hath chosen thee for thy skill in the goldsmith's craft, because thou art eminent.

Look now, receive these robes of honour and gold and silver: when thou comest to the King, thou wilt be his favourite and boon companion."

The man saw the much wealth and the many robes: he was beguiled, he parted from his town and children.

Blithely he set out on the road, unaware that the King had formed a design against his life.

He mounted an Arab horse and sped on joyously: he deemed a robe of honour what really was the price of his blood.

O fool, so willingly with thine own feet to enter on the journey to thy doom!

In his fancy were dreams of riches, power, and lordship. Said Azrael, " Go thy way: yes, thou wilt get them! "

Proudly and delicately they conducted him to the King, that he might burn like a moth on that candle of Taraz.

The King beheld him, showed great regard for him, and entrusted to him the treasure house full of gold.

Then the Physician said, " O mighty Sultan, give thy hand-maiden to this master,

That she may be happy with him and that the water of union may quench the fire of passion."

The King bestowed on him that moon-faced one and wedded the twain who craved each other's company.

During the space of six months they satisfied their desires, till the girl was wholly restored to health.

Afterwards, he prepared a potion for him, so that he began to dwindle away.

When because of sickness his beauty remained not, the soul of the girl remained not in his deadly toils.

Since he appeared ugly and ill-favoured and sallow-cheeked, little by little he became unpleasing to her heart.

Those loves which are for the sake of a colour are not love: in the end they are a disgrace.

Would that he too had lacked all grace, that such an evil doom might not have come to pass upon him!

Blood ran from his eye like a river: his handsome face had become an enemy to his life.

The peacock's plumage is its enemy. How many a king hath been slain by his magnificence!

He said, " I am the muskdeer whose gland caused the hunter to shed its innocent blood,

Or the fox of the field for which they lay in wait to cut off its head for the sake of the fur,

Or the elephant whose blood was shed by the mahout for the sake of the ivory.

He who hath slain me for that which is not myself, does not he know that my blood sleepeth not?

To-day the doom is on me, to-morrow it is on him: how should the blood of one like me rest unavenged?

Although the wall casts a long shadow, yet at last the shadow turns back again towards it.

The world is the mountain, and our action the shout: the echo of the shout comes back to us."

With these words he gave up the ghost. The Handmaiden was purged of love and pain,

Because love of the dead is not enduring, for the dead are never coming back to us;

While love of the living is always fresher than a bud in the spirit and in the sight.

Choose the love of that Living One, who is everlasting and gives thee to drink of the wine that increases life.

Choose the love of Him from whose love all the prophets gained power and glory.

Do not say, " We have no admission to that King." Dealings with the generous are not difficult.

THE FALCON AMONGST THE OWLS

The Falcon is he that comes back to the King. He that has lost the way is the blind falcon.

It lost the way and fell into the wilderness; then in the wilderness it fell amongst owls.

The Falcon is wholly light emanating from the Light of Divine Grace, but Destiny hath blinded it,

Thrown dust in its eyes and led it far from the right way and left it amongst the owls in the wilderness.

To crown all, the owls attack it and tear its lovely wing-feathers and plumes.

A clamour arose amongst the owls—" Ha! the Falcon hath come to seize our dwelling-place."

'Twas as when the street-dogs, wrathful and terrifying, have fallen upon the frock of a strange dervish.

" How am I fit," says the Falcon, " to consort with owls? I give up to the owls a hundred wildernesses like this.

I do not wish to stay here, I am going, I will return to the King of kings.

O ye owls, do not kill yourselves with agitation! I am not settling here, I am going home.

This ruin seems a thriving abode to you, but my pleasure-seat is the King's wrist."

" Beware," said the great Owl to his friends, " the Falcon is plotting to uproot you from house and home.

He will seize our houses by his cunning, he will then turn us out of our nests by his hypocrisy.

He boasts of the King and the King's wrist in order that he may lead us astray, simpletons as we are!

How should a petty bird be familiar with the King? Do not hearken to him, if ye have any understanding.

As for his saying, from deceit and feint and artifice, ' The King with all his retinue is searching after me,'

Here's an absurd mad fancy for you, here's a vain brag and a snare to catch blockheads!

If the smallest owl strike at his brain, where is succour for him from the King? "

The Falcon said, " If a single feather of mine be broken, the King of kings will uproot the whole owlery.

An owl forsooth! Even if a falcon vex my heart and maltreat me,

The King will heap up in every hill and dale hundreds of thousands of stacks of falcons' heads.

His favour keeps watch over me: wherever I go, the King is following behind.

*My image is abiding in the King's heart: sick would the
King be without my image.*

*When the King bids me fl in His Way, I soar up to the
heart's ẓenith, like His beams.*

I fly as a moon and sun, I rend the curtains of the skies.

*O blest is the owl that had the good fortune to apprehend my
mystery!*

*Cling to me, that ye may rejoice and may become royal falcons,
although ye are but owls.*

*I am the owner of the spiritual kingdom, I am not a lickspittle.
The King is beating the falcon-drum for me from Beyond.*

*My falcon-drum is the call, ' Return!' God is my witness in
spite of adversary.*

*I am not a congener of the King of kings—far be it from
Him!—but I have light from His radiance.*

*Since my genus is not the genus of my King, my ego has
passed away for the sake of His ego.*

*My ego has passed away, He remains alone: I roll at the
feet of His horse like the dust.*

*My individual self became dust, and the only trace of it is the
print of His feet upon its dust.*

*Become dust at His feet for the sake of that footprint, in
order that ye may be as the diadem on the head of the
exalted.*

*Let not my puny form deceive you. Partake of my banquet
ere I depart."*

THE FROZEN SNAKE

*A snake-catcher went to the mountains to catch a snake by
his incantations.*

*Whether one be slow or quick, he that is a seeker will be a
finder.*

*Always apply yourself with both hands to seeking, for search
is an excellent guide on the way.*

*Though you be lame and limping and bent in figure and
unmannerly, ever creep towards God and be in quest
of Him.*

Now by speech, now by silence, and now by smelling, catch in every quarter the scent of the King.

Smell all the way from the part to the Whole, O noble one; smell all the way from opposite to opposite, O wise one.

Assuredly wars bring peace; the snake-catcher sought the snake for the purpose of friendship.

Man seeks a snake for his friend and cares for one that is without care for him.

The snake-catcher was searching in the mountains for a big snake in the days of snow.

He espied there a huge dead serpent, at the aspect whereof his heart was filled with fear.

The snake-catcher catches snakes in order to astonish the people—oh, the foolishness of the people!

Man is a mountain: how should he be led into temptation? How should a mountain be astonished by a snake?

Wretched Man does not know himself: he has come from a high estate and fallen into lowlihood.

Man has sold himself cheaply: he was satin, he has patched himself on to a tattered cloak.

Hundreds of thousands of snakes and mountains are amazed at him: how, then, has he become amazed and in love with a snake?

The snake-catcher took up the serpent and came to Baghdad in order to excite astonishment.

For the sake of a paltry fee he carried along with him a serpent like the pillar of a house,

Saying, " I have brought a dead serpent: I have suffered agonies in hunting it."

He thought it was dead, but it was alive, and he had not inspected it very well.

It was frozen by frosts and snow; it was living, though it presented the appearance of the dead.

The World is frozen: its name is jamad *(inanimate); jamid means " frozen," O master.*

Wait till the Sun of the Resurrection shall rise, that thou mayst see the movement of the World's body!

Philosophical Literature

At last the would-be showman arrived at Baghdad, to set up a public show at the cross-roads.

The man set up a show on the bank of the Tigris, and a great hubbub arose in the city——

" A snake-catcher has brought a serpent; he has captured a marvellous rare beast."

Myriads of simpletons assembled, who had become a prey to him as he to his folly.

They were waiting to see the serpent, and he too waited for them to assemble.

The greater the crowd, the better goes the begging and contributing of money.

Myriads of idle babblers gathered round, forming a ring, sole against sole.

Men took no heed of women: all were mingled in the throng, like nobles and common folk at the Resurrection.

When he began to lift the cloth covering the serpent, the people strained their necks,

And saw that the serpent, which had been frozen by intense cold, lay underneath a hundred coarse woollen blankets and coverlets.

He had bound it with thick ropes: the careful keeper had taken great precautions.

During the interval of expectation and coming together, the sun of 'Iraq shone upon the snake.

The sun of the hot country warmed it: the cold humours went out of its limbs.

It was dead, and it revived: the astonished serpent began to uncoil itself.

By the stirring of the dead serpent the people's amazement was increased a hundred thousandfold.

They fled, shrieking, while the cords binding the serpent went crack, crack, one after another.

It burst the bonds and glided out from beneath—a hideous dragon roaring like a lion.

Multitudes were killed in the rout: a hundred heaps were made of the fallen slain.

The snake-catcher stood paralysed with fear, crying, " What have I brought from the mountains and the desert? "

The blind sheep awakened the wolf and unwittingly went to
    meet its Azrael.
The serpent made one mouthful of that dolt: blood-drinking
    is easy for a Hajjaj.
It wound itself on a pillar and crunched the bones of the
    devoured man.

The serpent is thy carnal soul: how is it dead? It is only
    frozen by grief and lack of means.
If it obtain the means of Pharaoh, by whose command the
    Nile would flow,
Then it will begin to act like Pharaoh and waylay a hundred
    such as Moses and Aaron.
That serpent, under stress of poverty, is a little worm; but a
    gnat is made a falcon by power and riches.
Keep the serpent in the snow of separation from its desires.
    Beware, do not carry it into the sun of 'Iraq!

THE PALADIN OF QAZWIN

Now hear a pleasant tale—and mark the scene—
About the way and custom of Qazwin,
Where barbers ply their needles to tattoo
Folk's arms and shoulders with designs in blue.

Once a Qazwini spoke the barber fair:
" Tattoo me, please; make something choice and rare."
" What figure shall I paint, O paladin? "
" A furious lion: punch him boldly in.
Leo is my ascendant: come, tattoo
A lion, and let him have his fill of blue."
" On what place must I prick the deft design? "
" Trace it upon my shoulder, line by line,"
He took the needle and dabbed and dabbed it in.
Feeling his shoulder smart, the paladin
Began to yell—" You have killed me quite, I vow:
What is this pattern you are doing now? "
" Why, sir, a lion, as you ordered me."

" Commencing with what limb ? " demanded he.
" His tail," was the reply. " O best of men,
Leave out the tail, I beg, and start again.
The lion's tail and rump chokes me to death;
It's stuck fast in my windpipe, stops my breath.
O lion-maker, let him have no tail,
Or under these sharp stabs my heart will fail."
Another spot the barber 'gan tattoo,
Without fear, without favour, without rue.
" Oh, oh ! which part of him is this? Oh dear ! "
" This," said the barber " is your lion's ear."
" Pray, doctor, not an ear of any sort!
Leave out his ears and cut the business short."
The artist quickly set to work once more:
Again our hero raised a doleful roar.
" On which third limb now is the needle employed? "
" His belly, my dear sir." " Hold, hold! " he cried.
" Perish the lion's belly, root and branch !
How should the glutted lion want a paunch? "
Long stood the barber there in mute dismay,
His finger 'twixt his teeth; then flung away
The needle, crying, " All the wide world o'er
Has such a thing e'er happened heretofore?
Why, God Himself did never make, I tell ye,
A lion without tail or ears or belly "

Moral

Brother, endure the pain with patience fresh,
To gain deliverance from the miscreant flesh.
Whoso is freed from selfhood's vain conceit,
Sky, sun and moon fall down to worship at his feet.

LUQMAN AND HIS MASTER

Luqman was the favourite of his master, who preferred him to
his own sons,
Because Luqman, though a slave, was master of himself and
free from sensual desire.

A certain King said to a holy man, " Ask a boon that I may bestow it upon thee."

He answered, " O King, are not you ashamed to say such a thing to me?   Mount higher!

I have two slaves, and they are vile, and yet those twain are rulers and lords over you."

Said the King, " Who are those twain?   Surely this is an error."   He replied, " The one is anger and the other is lust."

Luqman was always the first to partake of any viands that were served to his master,

For the master would send them to him, and if Luqman left them untasted his master would throw them away;

Or, if he did eat of them, it would be without heart and without appetite: this is the sign of an affinity without end.

One day he received the gift of a melon.   " Go," said he, " call hither my dear Luqman."

He gave him a slice: Luqman ate it as though it were sugar and honey.

And showed such pleasure that his master went on giving him slice after slice, seventeen in all.

One slice remained.   He said, " I will eat this myself, to see what a sweet melon it is."

No sooner had he tasted it than its sourness blistered his tongue and burnt his throat.

For a while he was almost beside himself; then he cried, " O Luqman, my soul and my world,

How could you have the patience?   What made you endure so long?   Or perhaps life is hateful to you."

Luqman said, " From thy bounteous hand I have eaten so many sweets that I am bent double with shame.

I was ashamed to refuse one bitter thing from thy hand, O wise master.

Since all parts of me have grown from thy bounty and are a prey to thy bait and snare—

If I complain of one bitter thing, may the dust of a hundred roads cover every part of me!

This melon had reposed in thy sugar-bestowing hand: how
   could it retain any bitterness? "
Through Love bitter things become sweet; through Love
   pieces of copper become golden.
Through Love dregs become clear; through Love pains
   become healing.
Through Love the dead is made living; through Love the
   king is made a slave.

THE LION AND THE BEASTS OF CHASE

The Beasts of Chase in a pleasant valley were harassed by
   a Lion,
So they made a plan: they came to the Lion, saying, " We
   will keep thee full-fed by a fixed allowance.
Do not exceed thy allowance, else this pasture will become
   bitter to us."
" Yes," said he, " if I find good faith on your part, for I have
   suffered many a fraud at the hands of Zayd and Bakr.
I am done to death by the cunning of man, I am stung by
   human snake and scorpion.
' The believer is not bitten twice ': I have taken this saying
   of the Prophet to my heart."
The Beasts said, " O sagacious one, let precaution alone: it
   is of no avail against the divine Decree.
Precaution is but trouble and woe: put thy trust in God,
   trust in God is better.
O fierce Lion, do not grapple with Destiny lest Destiny pick
   a quarrel with thee."
" Yes," he said; " but though trust in God is the true guide, yet
   we should use precaution according to the Prophet's rule.
The Prophet spoke plainly, saying, ' Trust in God, and bind
   the knee of thy camel.'
He hath also said, ' God loves the worker.' Let us trust in
   God, but not so as to neglect ways and means."
The Beasts answered him, saying, " There is no work better
   than trust in God: what indeed is dearer to Him than
   resignation?

126

*Man contrives, and his contrivance is a snare to catch him:
that which he thought would save his life sheds his
blood.*

*He locks the door whilst his foe is in the house: the plot of
Pharaoh was a tale of this kind.*

*We are the family of the Lord; like infants, we crave after
milk.*

*God who gives rain from heaven is also able, in His mercy, to
give us bread."*

*" Yes," said the Lion; " but the Lord hath set a ladder
before our feet.*

*Step by step we must climb to the roof: to be a Necessitarian
here is to indulge in foolish hopes.*

*You have feet: why do you pretend to be lame? You have
hands: why do you hide your fingers?*

*When the master puts a spade in his slave's hand, he need
not speak in order to make his object known."*

*The Lion gave many proofs in this style, so that those
Necessitarians became tired of answering him.*

*Fox and deer and hare and jackal abandoned their doctrine
and ceased from disputation.*

*They made a covenant with the Lion, ensuring that he should
incur no loss in the bargain,*

*And that he should receive his daily rations without trouble or
any further demand.*

*Every day the one on whom the lot fell would run to the Lion
as swiftly as a cheetah.*

*When the fatal cup came round to the Hare, " Why," cried
the Hare, " how long shall we endure injustice ? "*

*His companions said, " All this time we have sacrificed our
lives in truth and loyalty.*

*Do not thou give us a bad name, O rebellious one! Quick!
Quick! lest the Lion be aggrieved."*

*" O my friends," said he, " grant me a respite, that by my
cunning ye may escape from this woe*

*And save your lives and leave security as a heritage to your
children."*

*The Beasts replied, " O donkey, listen to us. Keep thyself
within the measure of a hare!*

Eh, what brag is this?   Thy betters never thought of such a thing."

" My friends," said he, " God hath inspired me.   Weak as I am, I am wisely counselled.

God opens the door of knowledge to the bee, so that it builds a house of honey.

God teaches the silkworm a craft beyond the power of the elephant.

When Adam, the earth-born, Gained knowledge of God, his knowledge illumined the Seventh Heaven."

They said, " O nimble Hare, disclose what is in thy mind. The Prophet hath said, ' Take counsel with the trustworthy.' "

" Not every secret may be told," said he; " sometimes an even number turns out odd and an odd one even.

If you breathe the hidden word on a mirror, the mirror immediately becomes dim.

Hold your tongue concerning three things: your departure, your money, and your religion."

The Hare tarried long, rehearsing to himself the trick he was about to play.

At last he took the road and set forth to whisper a few secrets in the Lion's ear.

The Lion, incensed and wrathful and frantic, saw the Hare coming from afar,

Running undismayed and confidently, looking angry and fierce and fell and sour;

For by appearing humble he thought suspicion would be excited, while boldness would remove every cause of doubt.

As soon as he approached, the Lion roared, " Ha, villain!

I who tear oxen limb from limb, I who bruise the ears of the raging elephant—

What! shall a half-witted hare presume to spurn my commands? "

" Mercy! " cried the Hare.   " I have an excuse, please thy Majesty."

" What excuse? " said he.   " O the shortsightedness of fools! Is this the time for them to come into the presence of kings?

The fool's excuse is worse than his crime, 'tis the poison that
kills wisdom."

"Hark!" cried the Hare, "if I am not worthy of thy
clemency, I will lay my head before the dragon of thy
vengeance.

At breakfast-time I set out with another hare which the
Beasts of Chase had appointed, for thy sake, to accom-
pany me.

On the road a lion attacked thy humble slave, attacked both
the companions in travel hastening towards thee.

I said to him, ' We are the slaves of the King of kings, two
lowly fellow-servants of that exalted Court.'

He said, ' The King of kings! Who is he? Be ashamed!
Do not make mention of every base loon in my presence.

Both thee and thy King I will tear to pieces if thou and thy
friend turn back from my portal.'

I said, ' Let me behold the face of my King once more and
acquaint him with the news of thee.'

' Thou must leave thy comrade with me as a pledge,' said he;
' otherwise thy life is forfeit according to my law.'

We entreated him much: 'twas no use. He seized my friend
and left me to go my way alone.

My friend was so big and plump and comely that he would
make three of me.

Henceforth the road is barred by that Lion: the cord of our
covenant is broken.

Abandon hope of thy rations henceforward! I am telling thee
the bitter truth.

If thou want the rations, clear the road! Come on, then, and
drive away that insolent usurper!"

"Come on in God's name," cried the Lion. "Show me
where he is! Lead the way, if you are speaking the
truth,

That I may give him and a hundred like him the punishment
they deserve—or do the same to you if you are lying."

The Hare set off, running ahead in the direction of a deep
well which was to be a snare for the Lion;

But as they drew nigh to it, the Hare shrunk back. "That
lion," said he, "lives here.

*I am consumed with dread of his fury—unless thou wilt take
me beside thee,*

*That with thy support, O Mine of generosity, I may open my
eyes and look in."*

*The Lion took him to his side; they ran together towards the
well and looked in.*

*The Lion saw his own reflection: from the water shone the
image of a lion with a plump hare beside him.*

*No sooner did he espy his adversary than he left the Hare and
sprang into the well.*

*He fell into the well which he had dug: his iniquity recoiled
on his own head.*

*The Lion saw himself in the well: he was so enraged that he
could not distinguish himself from his enemy.*

*O Reader, how many an evil that you see in others is but your
own nature reflected in them!*

*In them appears all that you are—your hypocrisy, iniquity,
and insolence.*

*You do not see clearly the evil in yourself, else you would hate
yourself with all your soul.*

*Like the Lion who sprang at his image in the water, you are
only hurting yourself, O simpleton!*

*When you reach the bottom of the well of your own nature,
then you will know that the wickedness is in you.*

THE MAN WHO PRAYED THAT HE MIGHT RECEIVE
HIS LIVELIHOOD WITHOUT LABOUR

*In the time of the prophet David a certain man, before sage
and simple alike,*

*Used always to utter this prayer: " O God, bestow on me
riches without trouble!*

*For Thou hast created me a lazybones, a receiver of blows,
a slow mover, a sluggard,*

*And one cannot lay upon sore-backed luckless donkeys the load
carried by horses and mules.*

I am lazy and asleep in this world of phenomenal being:
    I sleep in the shade of Thy bounty and munificence.

Surely for them that are lazily sleeping in the shade Thou
    hast ordained a livelihood in another fashion.

I crave the daily bread that comes without effort on my part,
    for I have no work except prayer."

Thus was he praying for a long while, all day until night and
    all night until morning.

The people laughed at his words, at the folly of his hope, and
    at his importunity:

" Marvellous! What is he saying—this idiot? Or has
    somebody given him being, which produces dementia?

The way to get daily bread is work and toil and fatigue; God
    has bestowed on everyone a handicraft and the power to
    seek his livelihood.

At present the King and Ruler and Messenger of God is the
    prophet David, endowed with many accomplishments.

Notwithstanding all his glory and majesty, forasmuch as the
    favours of the Friend have chosen him out,

His livelihood does not come to him without his weaving coats
    of mail and labouring as a craftsman.

Now a God-forsaken abandoned wretch like this, a low scoundrel
    and outcast from Heaven,

A backslider of this sort desires, without trading, at once to
    fill his pockets with gain! "

One would say to him derisively, " Go and get it! Thy
    daily bread has arrived, the messenger has brought the
    good news ";

And another would laugh, saying, " Let us have a share in
    the gift, O headman of the village! "

All this abuse and ridicule could not induce him to desist from
    his petitioning,

So that he became celebrated in the town as one who looks for
    cheese in an empty wallet.

One morning, as he was praying with moans and sighs,
    suddenly a cow ran into his house.

She butted with her horns, broke the bolt, and jumped into the
    house; he sprang up and bound her legs.

*Then he cut her throat without delay, without consideration,
and without mercy,*

*And went to the butcher, in order that he might rip off her hide
forthwith.*

*The owner of the cow espied him and said, " Hey, why did
you kill my cow? Fool! Brigand! Deal fairly
with me."*

*He said, " God answered my ancient prayer. The cow was
my portion of daily bread: I killed her. That is my
reply."*

*The enraged owner seized him by the collar, struck him in the
face with his fist several times,*

*And led him to the prophet David, saying, " Come, you crazy
fool and criminal!*

*What are you saying? What is this prayer of yours?
Don't laugh at my head and beard and your own too,
O rascal!*

*Hey, gather round, O Muslims! For God's sake, how should
his prayer make my property belong to him? "*

*The people said, " He speaks truth, and this prayer-monger
seeks to act unjustly.*

*How should such a prayer be the means of acquiring property?
Give back the cow or go to prison! "*

*Meanwhile the poor man was turning his face to Heaven and
crying, " None knoweth my spiritual experience save
Thee.*

*Thou didst put the prayer into my heart, Thou didst raise a
hundred hopes in my heart.*

*Not idly was I uttering the prayer: like Joseph, I had
dreamed dreams."*

*When the prophet David came forth, he asked, " What is all
this about? What is the matter? "*

*The plaintiff said, " O prophet of God, give me justice. My
cow strayed into his house.*

*He killed my cow. Ask him why he killed my cow and bid
him explain what happened."*

*David said to the poor man, " Speak! Why did you destroy
the property of this honourable person? "*

132 *He replied, " O David, for seven years I was engaged, day and night, in supplication and entreaty,*

Praying to God that He would give me a lawful means of livelihood without trouble on my part.

After all this calling and crying, suddenly I saw a cow in my house.

My eyes became dim, not on account of the food, but for joy that my supplication had been accepted.

I killed her that I might give alms, in thankfulness that He who knoweth things unseen had hearkened to my prayer."

David said, " Wipe out these words and set forth a legal plea in the dispute.

Who gave you the cow? Did you buy or inherit her? Will you take the crop when you are not the farmer?

You must pay this Muslim his money. Go, try to borrow it, and don't seek to do wrong."

" O King," said the poor man, " thou art telling me the same thing as my oppressors."

Then, prostrating himself, he cried, " O Thou who knowest the ardent faith within me, cast that flame into the heart of David;

Put in his heart that which Thou hast secretly let fall into mine, O Benefactor! "

He said this and began to weep and wail so that David was moved exceedingly.

David said to the plaintiff, " Give me a respite to-day. I will go to a solitary place and commune with God."

He shut the door, and then went quickly to the prayer-niche and betook himself to the invocation that God answereth.

God revealed all to him, and he saw who was the man deserving of punishment.

Next day, when the litigants assembled and formed ranks before David, the plaintiff lifted up his voice in reproach.

David said to him, " Be silent! Go, abandon your claim, acquit this true believer of responsibility.

Seeing that God has thrown a veil over you, depart in silence and render due thanks unto God for what He has concealed."

He cried, " Oh, woe is me!   What wisdom is this, what
  justice?   Wilt thou establish a new law in my case?
Such wrong has never been done even to blind dogs; mountains
  and rocks are burst asunder by this iniquity."
Then said David, " O contumacious man, give him on the
  spot all that you possess.
Since 'twas not your fortune to be saved, little by little your
  wickedness has come to light.
Begone!   Your wife and children have now become his slaves.
  Say no more! "
The plaintiff ran up and down in a frenzy, dashing stones
  against his breast with both hands,
While the people too began to blame David, for they were
  ignorant of the hidden circumstances.
The currish mob, which slays the oppressed and worships
  the oppressor, sprang forth from ambush and rushed
  towards David,
Crying, " O chosen prophet, this is unworthy of thee, 'tis
  manifest injustice; thou hast abased an innocent man for
  naught."
He said, " My friend, the time is come for his hidden secret
  to be displayed.
Arise, all of you, let us set out, that we may become acquainted
  with his mystery.
In such and such a plain there is a huge tree, its boughs thick
  and numerous and curved.
Its tent and tent-pegs are very firm; from its roots the smell
  of blood is coming to me.
Murder was done at the foot of that goodly tree: this ill-fated
  man killed his master.
The crime, which God's mercy concealed till now, has at last
  been brought to light through the ingratitude of this
  scoundrel,
Who never once looked upon his master's family, not even at
  Nawruz and other seasons of festival,
And never searched after the destitute children to relieve their
  want, or bethought him of the obligations he had received,
And so proceeded, till for the sake of a cow this accursed
  wretch is now felling his master's son to the earth.

*He himself has lifted the veil from his crime; else God would
have kept it hidden.*

*Wrong is covered up in the depths of the heart: the wrong-
doer exposes it to men,*

*Saying, ' Behold me! I have horns! Behold the cow of
Hell in full view! ' "*

*When they arrived at the tree, David said, " Tie his hands
fast behind him,*

*That I may bring his sin to light and plant the banner of
justice on the field.*

*O dog," said he, " you killed this man's father. You were
a slave; by murder you became a lord.*

*You killed your master and seized his property: God hath
made it manifest.*

*Your wife was his handmaid: she has acted unjustly towards
her master.*

*The children she bore to him, male and female—all of them from
beginning to end are the property of the master's heir.*

*You are a slave: your goods are his property. You have
demanded the Law: take the Law and go: 'tis well.*

*You killed your master miserably, whilst he was crying for
mercy on this very spot,*

*And hastily hid the knife under the soil because of the terrible
apparition which you beheld.*

*On the knife, too, the name of this hound is written who
betrayed and murdered his master.*

*His head together with the knife is beneath! Dig ye back the
soil, thus! "*

*Even so they did, and when they cleft the earth they found
there the knife and the skull.*

*A tumult of lamentation went up from the people: everyone
severed the girdle of unbelief.*

*Then David said to him, " Come, O seeker of justice, and
with that black face of yours receive the justice due
to you! "*

*He ordered him to be killed in retaliation with the same knife:
how should cunning deliver him from the knowledge of
God?*

Kill thy fleshly soul and make the world spiritually alive.
She hath killed her master: make her thy slave.
*The slayer of the cow is thy rational spirit: go, be not offended
with the spirit that kills the flesh.*
*The spirit is a captive, and craves of God daily bread won
without toil, and bounty spread before it on a table.*
*Upon what does its daily bread depend? Upon its killing the
cow, which is the origin of all evil.*

INDIAN EPIGRAMS

The following extracts are from the English translation of Bhartrihari by P. E. More. History is again mute regarding the exact dates of Bhartrihari's life and death, but we are told that in the early centuries of the Christian era he reigned at Ujjan in North India; and that, renouncing the throne, he took to the life of a recluse in the jungle. He was known to have composed the Cataka-trayam or Century-triad, in which he unfolds his experience of life. The first 500 stanzas are devoted to the love of woman, her charm and yet her baleful influence; the second century contains the prudential ethics of worldly wisdom; and the third carries him to a more sublime theme regarding the true wisdom, the finding of peace and the richness of a new life.

VII

The silvery laughter; eyes that sparkle bold,
*   Or droop in virgin rue;*
The prattling words of wonder uncontrolled
When world and life are new;

The startled flight and dallying slow return,
And all their girlish sport;—
Ah me, that they time's ruinous truth must learn,
Their flowering be so short!

X

My love within a forest walked alone,
All in a moonlit dale;
And here awhile she rested, weary grown,
And from her shoulders threw the wimpled veil
To court the little gale.

I peering through the thicket saw it all,
The yellow moonbeams fall,
I saw them mirrored from her bosom fly
Back to the moon on high.

XI

O fair Acoka-tree, with love's own red
Thy boughs are all aflame;
Whither, I pray thee, hath my wanton fled?
This way I know she came.

In vain thy nodding in the wind, thy sigh
Of ignorance assumed;
I know because my flower-love wandered by
For joy thy branches bloomed.

I know thee: ever with thy buds unblown,
Till touched by maiden's foot;
And thou so fair—one fairest maid alone
Hath trod upon thy root.

XX

Harder than faces in a glass designed,
A woman's heart to bind;
Like mountain paths up cragged heights that twist,
Her ways are lightly missed.

Like early dew-drops quivering on a leaf,
Her thoughts are idly brief;
And errors round her grow, as on a vine
The poison-tendrils twine.

XXXI

Oil from the sand a man may strain,
If chance he squeeze with might and main;
The pilgrim at the magic well
Of the mirage his desert thirst may quell.

So travelling far a man by luck
May find a hare horned like a buck;—
But who by art may straighten out
The crooked counsels of a stubborn lout?

XXXIV

I saw an ass who bore a load
Of sandal wood along the road,
And almost with the burden bent,
Yet never guessed the sandal scent;
So pedants bear a ponderous mass
Of books they comprehend not,—like the ass.

XL

This have I done, and that will do,
And this half-done must carry through:—
So busied, bustling, full of care,
Poor fools, Death pounces on us unaware.

To-day is thine, fulfil its work,
Let no loose hour her duty shirk;
Still ere thy task is done, comes Death,
The Finisher,—he ends it with thy breath.

XLV

O'er perilous mountain roads with pain
I've journeyed, yet acquired no gain;
The pride of birth I have forsworn
And toiled in service, yet no profit borne.

In strange homes where I blushed to go
My food I've taken, like the crow,
And eaten shame.—Oh lust of gold!
Oh Greed! that younger grow'st as I wax old!

XLIX

I see a dog—no stone to shy at him;
Yonder a stone—no dog's in view:
There is your dog, here stones to try at him—
The king's dog! what's a man to do?

LIV

The harvest ripens as the seed was sown,
And he that scattered reaps alone;—
So from each deed there falls a germ
That shall in coming lives its source affirm.

UNSEEN *they call it, for it lurks*
The hidden spring of present works;
UNKNOWN BEFORE, *even as the fruit*
Was undiscovered in the vital root.

And he that now impure hath been
Impure shall be, the clean be clean;
We wrestle in our present state
With bonds ourselves we forged,—and call it Fate.

LXV

Seated within this body's car
The silent Self is driven afar;
And the five senses at the pole
Like steeds are tugging restive of control.

And if the driver lose his way,
Or the reins sunder, who can say
In what blind paths, what pits of fear
Will plunge the chargers in their mad career?

Drive well, O Mind, use all thy art,
Thou charioteer!—O feeling Heart,
Be thou a bridle firm and strong!
For the Lord rideth and the way is long.

LXIX

A hundred years we barely keep,
Yet half of this is lost in sleep;
And half our waking time we spend
In the child's folly and the old man's end.

And of the hours remaining, fears
And gaunt disease and parting tears
Are all the prize:—fie on the slave
Who life more values than a bubbling wave!

LXXI

Fallen our father, fallen who bore
For us the pangs—they went before:
And some with our years grew, but they,
They too now tread on memory's dusty way.

And we ourselves from morn to morn
Now shiver like old trees forlorn
Upon a sandy shore, and all
Our care the lapping waves that haste our fall.

Poems from the

DIVAN OF HAFIZ

The following extracts taken from the translation of the Divan of Hafiz by G. L. Bell, portray the greatest glory of the verse of the prince of Persian poets. Born in Shiraz, Mohamed Shamsaddin Hafiz Shirazi was always happy in poverty and never attended any Princes' Court. He was, however, respected for his literary work as well as for his wondrous poems, both mystical and lyrical. The only known date of his life is that of his death in A.D. 1389.

I

Arise, oh Cup-bearer, rise! and bring
*   To lips that are thirsting the bowl they praise,*
For it seemed that love was an easy thing,
But my feet have fallen on difficult ways.
I have prayed the wind o'er my heart to fling
The fragrance of musk in her hair that sleeps—
In the night of her hair—yet no fragrance stays
The tears of my heart's blood my sad heart weeps.

Hear the Tavern-keeper who counsels you:
" With wine, with red wine your prayer carpet dye! "
There was never a traveller like him but knew
The ways of the road and the hostelry.
Where shall I rest, when the still night through,
Beyond thy gateway, oh Heart of my heart,
The bells of the camels lament and cry:
" Bind up thy burden again and depart! "

The waves run high, night is clouded with fears,
And eddying whirlpools clash and roar;
How shall my drowning voice strike their ears
Whose light-freighted vessels have reached the shore?

I sought mine own; the unsparing years
Have brought me mine own, a dishonoured name.
What cloak shall cover my misery o'er
When each jesting mouth has rehearsed my shame!

Oh Hafiz, seeking an end to strife,
Hold fast in thy mind what the wise have writ:
" If at last thou attain the desire of thy life,
Cast the world aside, yea, abandon it!"

II

The bird of gardens sang unto the rose,
New blown in the clear dawn: " Bow down thy head!
As fair as thou within this garden close,
Many have bloomed and died." She laughed and said:
" That I am born to fade grieves not my heart;
But never was it a true lover's part
To vex with bitter words his love's repose."

The tavern step shall be thy hostelry,
For Love's diviner breath comes but to those
That suppliant on the dusty threshold lie.
And thou, if thou would'st drink the wine that flows
From Life's bejewelled goblet, ruby red,
Upon thine eyelashes thine eyes shall thread
A thousand tears for this temerity.

Last night when Irem's magic garden slept,
Stirring the hyacinth's purple tresses curled,
The wind of morning through the alleys stept.
" Where is thy cup, the mirror of the world?
Ah, where is Love, thou Throne of Djem?" I cried.
The breezes knew not; but " Alas," they sighed,
" That happiness should sleep so long!" and wept.

Not on the lips of men Love's secret lies,
Remote and unrevealed his dwelling-place.
Oh Saki, come! the idle laughter dies
When thou the feast with heavenly wine dost grace.

Patience and wisdom, Hafiz, in a sea
Of thine own tears are drowned; thy misery
They could not still nor hide from curious eyes.

VII

From the garden of Heaven a western breeze
Blows through the leaves of my garden of earth;
With a love like a huri I'ld take mine ease,
And wine! bring me wine, the giver of mirth!
To-day the beggar may boast him a king,
His banqueting-hall is the ripening field,
And his tent the shadow that soft clouds fling.

A tale of April the meadows unfold—
Ah, foolish for future credit to slave,
And to leave the cash of the present untold!
Build a fort with wine where thy heart may brave
The assault of the world; when thy fortress falls,
The relentless victor shall knead from thy dust
The bricks that repair its crumbling walls.

Trust not the word of that foe in the fight!
Shall the lamp of the synagogue lend its flame
To set thy monastic torches alight?
Drunken am I, yet place not my name
In the Book of Doom, nor pass judgment on it;
Who knows what the secret finger of Fate
Upon his own white forehead has writ!

And when the spirit of Hafiz has fled,
Follow his bier with a tribute of sighs;
Though the ocean of sin has closed o'er his head,
He may find a place in God's Paradise.

XIV

The nightingale with drops of his heart's blood
Has nourished the red rose, then came a wind,
And catching at the boughs in envious mood,
A hundred thorns about his heart entwined.

Like to the parrot crunching sugar, good
Seemed the world to me who could not stay
The wind of Death that swept my hopes away.

Light of mine eyes and harvest of my heart,
And mine at least in changeless memory!
Ah, when he found it easy to depart,
He left the harder pilgrimage to me!
Oh Camel-driver, though the cordage start,
For God's sake help me lift my fallen load,
And Pity be my comrade of the road!

My face is seamed with dust, mine eyes are wet.
Of dust and tears the turquoise firmament
Kneadeth the bricks for joy's abode; and yet . . .
Alas, and weeping yet I make lament!
Because the moon her jealous glances set
Upon the bow-bent eyebrows of my moon,
He sought a lodging in the grave—too soon!
I had not castled, and the time is gone.
What shall I play? Upon the chequered floor
Of Night and Day, Death won the game—forlorn
And careless now, Hafiz can lose no more.

XVI

What is wrought in the forge of the living and life—
All things are nought! Ho! fill me the bowl,
For nought is the gear of the world and the strife!
One passion has quickened the heart and the soul,
The Beloved's presence alone they have sought—
Love at least exists; yet if Love were not,
Heart and soul would sink to the common lot—
All things are nought!

Like an empty cup is the fate of each,
That each must fill from Life's mighty flood;
Nought thy toil, though to Paradise gate thou reach,
If Another has filled up thy cup with blood;

Neither shade from the sweet-fruited trees could be bought
By thy praying—oh Cypress of Truth, dost not see
That Sidreh and Tuba were nought, and to thee
All then were nought!

The span of thy life is as five little days,
Brief hours and swift in this halting-place;
Rest softly, ah rest! while the Shadow delays,
For Time's self is nought and the dial's face.
On the lip of Oblivion we linger, and short
Is the way from the Lip to the Mouth where we pass—
While the moment is thine, fill, of Saki, the glass
Ere all is nought!

Consider the rose that breaks into flower,
Neither repines though she fade and die—
The powers of the world endure for an hour,
But nought shall remain of their majesty.
Be not too sure of your crown, you who thought
That virtue was easy and recompense yours;
From the monastery to the wine-tavern doors
The way is nought!

What though I, too, have tasted the salt of my tears,
Though I, too, have burnt in the fires of grief,
Shall I cry aloud to unheeding ears?
Mourn and be silent! nought brings relief.
Thou, Hafiz, art praised for the songs thou hast wrought,
But bearing a stained or an honoured name,
The lovers of wine shall make light of thy fame—
All things are nought!

XVIII

Slaves of thy shining eyes are even those
That diadems of might and empire bear;
Drunk with the wine that from thy red lip flows,
Are they that e'en the grape's delight forswear.

K

Drift, like the wind across a violet bed,
Before thy many lovers, weeping low,
And clad like violets in blue robes of woe,
Who feel thy wind-blown hair and bow the head.

Thy messenger the breath of dawn, and mine
A stream of tears, since lover and beloved
Keep not their secret; through my verses shine,
Though other lays my flower's grace have proved
And countless nightingales have sung thy praise.
When veiled beneath thy curls thou passest, see,
To right and leftward those that welcome thee
Have bartered peace and rest on thee to gaze!

But thou that knowest God by heart, away!
Wine-drunk, love-drunk, we inherit Paradise,
His mercy is for sinners; hence and pray
Where wine thy cheek red as red erghwan dyes,
And leave the cell to faces sinister.
Oh Khizr, whose happy feet bathed in life's fount,
Help one who toils afoot—the horsemen mount
And hasten on their way; I scarce can stir.

Ah, loose me not! ah, set not Hafiz free
From out the bondage of thy gleaming hair!
Safe only those, safe, and at liberty,
That fast enchained in thy linked ringlets are.
But from the image of his dusty cheek
Learn this from Hafiz: proudest heads shall bend,
And dwellers on the threshold of a friend
Be crownèd with the dust that crowns the meek.

XX

From out the street of So-and-So,
Oh wind, bring perfumes sweet to me!
For I am sick and pale with woe;
Oh bring me rest from misery!

The dust that lies before her door,
Love's long desired elixir, pour
Upon this wasted heart of mine—
Bring me a promise and a sign!

Between the ambush of mine eyes
And my heart's fort there's enmity—
Her eye-brow's bow, the dart that flies,
Beneath her lashes, bring to me!
Sorrow and absence, glances cold,
Before my time have made me old;
A wine-cup from the hand of Youth
Bring me for pity and for ruth!

Then shall all unbelievers taste
A draught or two of that same wine;
But if they like it not, oh haste!
And let joy's flowing cup be mine.
Cup-bearer, seize to-day, nor wait
Until to-morrow!—or from Fate
Some passport to felicity,
Some written surety bring to me!

My heart threw back the veil of woe,
Consoled by Hafíz' melody:
From out the street of So-and-So,
Oh wind, bring perfumes sweet to me!

XXI

Not all the sum of earthly happiness
Is worth the bowed head of a moment's pain.
And if I sell for wine my dervish dress,
Worth more than what I sell is what I gain!
Land where my Lady dwells, thou holdest me
Enchained; else Fars were but a barren soil,
Not worth the journey over land and sea,
                        Not worth the toil!

Down in the quarter where they sell red wine,
My holy carpet scarce would fetch a cup—
How brave a pledge of piety is mine,
Which is not worth a goblet foaming up!
Mine enemy heaped scorn on me and said:
" Forth from the tavern gate! "   Why am I thrust
From off the threshold? is my fallen head
> *Not worth the dust?*

Wash white that travel-stained sad robe of thine!
Where word and deed alike one colour bear,
The grape's fair purple garment shall outshine
Thy many-coloured rags and tattered gear.
Full easy seemed the sorrow of the sea
Lightened by hope of gain—hope flew too fast!
A hundred pearls were poor indemnity,
> *Not worth the blast.*

The Sultan's crown, with priceless jewels set,
Encircles fear of death and constant dread;
It is a head-dress much desired—and yet
Art sure 'tis worth the danger to the head?
'Twere best for thee to hide thy face from those
That long for thee; the Conqueror's reward
Is never worth the army's long-drawn woes,
> *Worth fire and sword.*

Ah, seek the treasure of a mind at rest
And store it in the treasury of Ease;
Not worth a loyal heart, a tranquil breast,
Were all the riches of thy lands and seas!
Ah, scorn, like Hafiz, the delights of earth,
Ask not one grain of favour from the base,
Two hundred sacks of jewels were not worth
> *Thy soul's disgrace!*

XXXIV

Last night I dreamed that angels stood without
The tavern door, and knocked in vain, and wept;
They took the clay of Adam, and, methought,
Moulded a cup therewith while all men slept.
Oh dwellers in the halls of Chastity!
You brought Love's passionate red wine to me,
Down to the dust I am, your bright feet stept.

For Heaven's self was all too weak to bear
The burden of His love God laid on it,
He turned to seek a messenger elsewhere,
And in the Book of Fate my name was writ.
Between my Lord and me such concord lies
As makes the Huris glad in Paradise,
With songs of praise through the green glades they flit.

A hundred dreams of Fancy's garnered store
Assail me—Father Adam went astray
Tempted by one poor grain of corn!   Wherefore
Absolve and pardon him that turns away
Though the soft breath of Truth reaches his ears,
For two-and-seventy jangling creeds he hears,
And loud-voiced Fable calls him ceaselessly.

That, that is not the flame of Love's true fire
Which makes the torchlight shadows dance in rings,
But where the radiance draws the moth's desire
And sends him forth with scorched and drooping wings.
The heart of one who dwells retired shall break,
Rememb'ring a black mole and a red cheek,
And his life ebb, sapped at its secret springs.

Yet since the earliest time that man has sought
To comb the locks of Speech, his goodly bride,
Not one, like Hafiz, from the Face of Thought
Has torn the veil of Ignorance aside.

XXXV

Forget not when dear friend to friend returned,
Forget not days gone by, forget them not!
My mouth has tasted bitterness, and learned
To drink the envenomed cup of mortal lot;
Forget not when a sweeter draught was mine,
Loud rose the songs of them that drank that wine—
Forget them not!

Forget not loyal lovers long since dead,
Though faith and loyalty should be forgot,
Though the earth cover the enamoured head,
And in the dust wisdom and passion rot.
My friends have thrust me from their memory;
Vainly a thousand thousand times I cry:
Forget me not!

Weary I turn me to my bonds again.
Once there were hands strong to deliver me,
Forget not when they broke a poor slave's chain!
Though from mine eyes tears flow unceasingly,
I think on them whose rose gardens are set
Beside the Zindeh Rud, and I forget
Life's misery.

Sorrow has made her lair in my breast,
And undisturbed she lies—forget them not
That drove her forth like to a hunted beast!
Hafiz, thou and thy tears shall be forgot,
Lock fast the gates of thy sad heart! But those
That held the key to thine unspoken woes—
Forget them not!

XXXVII

Arise! and fill a golden goblet up
Until the wine of pleasure overflow,
Before into thy skull's pale empty cup
A grimmer Cup-bearer the dust shall throw.

Yea, to the Vale of Silence we must come;
Yet shall the flagon laugh and Heaven's dome
Thrill with an answering echo ere we go!

Thou knowest that the riches of this field
Make no abiding, let the goblet's fire
Consume the fleeting harvest Earth may yield!
Oh Cypress-tree! green home of Love's sweet choir,
When I unto the dust I am have passed,
Forget thy former wantonness, and cast
Thy shadow o'er the dust of my desire.

Flow, bitter tears, and wash me clean! for they
Whose feet are set upon the road that lies
'Twixt Earth and Heaven: " Thou shalt be pure," they say,
" Before unto the pure thou lift thine eyes."
Seeing but himself, the Zealot sees but sin;
Grief to the mirror of his soul let in,
Oh Lord, and cloud it with the breath of sighs!

No tainted eye shall gaze upon her face,
No glass but that of an unsullied heart
Shall dare reflect my Lady's perfect grace.
Though like to snakes that from the herbage start,
Thy curling locks have wounded me full sore,
Thy red lips hold the power of the bezoar—
Ah, touch and heal me where I lie apart!

And when from her the wind blows perfume sweet,
Tear, Hafiz, like the rose, thy robe in two,
And cast thy rags beneath her flying feet,
To deck the place thy mistress passes through.

XL

The margin of a stream, the willow's shade,
A mind inclined to song, a mistress sweet,
A Cup-bearer whose cheek outshines the rose,
A friend upon whose heart thy heart is laid:

Oh Happy-starred! let not thine hours fleet
Unvalued; may each minute as it goes
Lay tribute of enjoyment at thy feet,
That thou may'st live and know thy life is sweet.

Let every one upon whose heart desire
For a fair face lies like a burden sore,
That all his hopes may reach their goal unchecked,
Throw branches of wild rue upon his fire.
My soul is like a bride, with a rich store
Of maiden thoughts and jewelled fancies decked,
And in Time's gallery I yet may meet
Some picture meant for me, some image sweet.

Give thanks for nights spent in good company,
And take the gifts a tranquil mind may bring;
No heart is dark when the kind moon doth shine,
And grass-grown river-banks are fair to see.
The Saki's radiant eyes, God favouring,
Are like a wine-cup brimming o'er with wine,
And him my drunken sense goes out to greet,
For e'en the pain he leaves behind is sweet.

Hafiz, thy life has sped untouched by care,
With me towards the tavern turn thy feet!
The fairest robbers thou'lt encounter there,
And they will teach thee what to learn is sweet.

XLIII

Where are the tidings of union? that I may arise—
Forth from the dust I will rise up to welcome thee!
My soul, like a homing bird, yearning for Paradise,
Shall arise and soar, from the snares of the world set free.
When the voice of thy love shall call me to be thy slave,
I shall rise to a greater far than the mastery
Of life and the living, time and the mortal span:

Pour down, oh Lord! from the clouds of thy guiding grace,
The rain of a mercy that quickeneth on my grave,
Before, like dust that the wind bears from place to place,
I arise and flee beyond the knowledge of man.

When to my grave thou turnest thy blessed feet,
Wine and the lute thou shalt bring in thine hand to me,
Thy voice shall ring through the folds of my winding sheet,
And I will arise and dance to thy minstrelsy.
Though I be old, clasp me one night to thy breast,
And I, when the dawn shall come to awaken me,
With the flush of youth on my cheek from thy bosom will rise.
Rise up! let mine eyes delight in thy stately grace!
Thou art the goal to which all men's endeavour has pressed,
And thou the idol of Hafiẓ' worship; thy face
From the world and life shall bid him come forth and arise!

JEWISH TEACHINGS AND PARABLES

ZEDAKAH—CHARITY

By Jacob Ben Asher

The dispensing of charity according to one's means is a positive precept, which demands greater care and diligence in its fulfilment than all the other positive precepts of the Law. For its neglect may possibly lead to the taking of life, inasmuch as the denial of timely aid may compass the death of the poor man who needs our immediate help.

" Whoso closes his eyes to this duty and hardens his heart to his needy brother is called a worthless man, and is regarded as an idolater. But whosoever is careful in the fulfilment of this duty attests himself as belonging to the seed of Abraham, whom the Lord hath blessed: ' For I have known him to the end that he may command his children and his household after him, that they may keep the way of the Lord to do *Zedakah* and justice.'

" Charity is the main foundation of Israel's pre-eminence, and the basis of the Law of Truth. As the prophet says unto Zion: ' By *Zedakah* shalt thou be established ' (Isaiah liv. 14). Its practice will alone bring about Israel's redemption: ' Zion shall be redeemed with justice, and they that return of her with *Zedakah* ' (Isaiah i. 27). Charity is greater than all sacrifices, says Rabbi Eleazar; even as it is written, ' To do *Zedakah* and justice is more acceptable to the Lord than sacrifice ' (Proverbs xxi. 3).

" Whoso pities the poor shall himself receive compassion from the Holy One, blessed be He. Let man further reflect that as there is a wheel of fortune revolving in this world, perchance some day either he himself, or his son, or his son's son, may be brought down to the same lowly state. Nor let it enter his mind to say: ' How can I give to the poor and thus lessen my possessions? ' For man must know that he is not the master of what he has, but only the guardian, to carry out the will of Him who entrusted things to his keeping.

" Whosoever withholds alms from the needy thereby withdraws himself from the lustre of the Shechinah and the light of the Law.

" Let man therefore be exceedingly diligent in the right bestowal of charity."

(Translated by A. Feldman.)

THE TWO NATURES IN MAN

By Moses of Coucy

" It is because man is half angel, half brute, that his inner life witnesses such bitter war between such unlike natures. The brute in him clamours for sensual joy and things in which there is only vanity; but the angel resists and strives to make him know that meat, drink, sleep, are but means whereby the body may be made efficient for the study of the truths, and the doing of the will, of God. Not until the very hour of death can it be certain or known to what measure the victory has been won. He who is but a novice in the fear of God will do well to say audibly each day, as he rises: ' This day I will be a faithful servant of the Almighty. I will be on my guard against wrath, falsehood, hatred, and quarrelsomeness, and will forgive those who wound me.' For whoso forgives is forgiven in his turn; hard-heartedness and a temper that will not make up quarrels are a heavy burden of sin, and unworthy of an Israelite."

THE CITY OF GOD

By Philo-Judaeus

" Do not seek for the City of God on earth, for it is not built of wood or stone; but seek it in the soul of the man who is at peace with himself and is a lover of true wisdom.

" If a man practises ablutions of the body, but defiles

156 his mind—if he offers hecatombs, founds a temple, adorns a shrine, and does nothing for making his soul beautiful— let him not be called religious. He has wandered far from real religion, mistaking ritual for holiness; attempting, as it were, to bribe the Incorruptible and to flatter Him Whom none can flatter. God welcomes the genuine service of a soul, the sacrifice of truth; but from display of wealth He turns away.

"Will any man with impure soul and with no intention to repent, dare to approach the Most High God? The grateful soul of the wise man is the true altar of God."

"WE LIVE IN DEEDS, NOT YEARS"

"A king had a vineyard, and he hired a number of labourers, one of whom worked more diligently and better than the others. What did the king? He took him by the hand and showed him friendship, and walked in the vineyard conversing with him. At eventide, all the labourers came to receive their hire, and the king paid that labourer too for a full day's work.

"Then were the other labourers sorely vexed. They said, 'Behold, we have worked the whole day, whereas this one has only worked a few hours.'

"Then said the king, 'Why do you speak thus? Consider. This one, in a few hours, did more work for me than you who toiled the whole day long.'"

ALEXANDER AT THE GATES OF PARADISE

"Alexander the Great, in his travels in the East, one day wandered to the gate of Paradise. He knocked, and the guardian angel asked, 'Who is there?' 'Alexander,' was the answer. 'Who is Alexander?' 'Alexander, you know—*the* Alexander—Alexander the Great—Conqueror of the world.' 'We know him not—he cannot enter here. *This is the Lord's gate; only the righteous enter here.*'

"Alexander then more humbly begged for something to show he had reached the heavenly gate, and a small fragment of a human skull was thrown to him, with the words, ' Weigh it.' He took it away, and showed it contemptuously to his Wise Men, who brought a pair of scales, and, placing the bone in one, Alexander put some of his silver and gold against it in the other; but the small bone outweighed them all. More and more silver and gold were put into the scale, and at last all his crown jewels and diadems were in, but they all flew upwards like feathers before the weight of the bone, till one of the Wise Men placed a few grains of dust on the bone; up flew the scale! The bone was that which surrounded the eye, and nothing will ever satisfy the eye until covered by the dust of the grave."

VANITY OF HUMAN PLEASURE

" A fox was eyeing longingly some luscious fruit in a very fine garden, but there was no way for him to enter. At last he espied an opening through which, he thought, he might possibly get in, but soon found the hole too small to admit his body. ' True,' he said, ' the hole is small, but if I fast three days my body will become sufficiently reduced to admit me.' He did so, and to his joy he now feasted to his heart's content upon the grapes and all the other good things in the orchard. But, lo! when he desired to escape before the master of the garden came upon him, he saw, to his great consternation, that the opening had again become too small for him. Poor animal! he had a second time to fast three days, and having made good his escape, he cast a farewell glance upon the scene of his late revels, saying: ' O garden, charming art thou and exquisite are thy fruits! But of what avail hast thou been unto me? What have I now for all my labour and cunning? '

" It is even so with man. Naked he comes into the world, naked he must leave it. Of all his toil therein he carries nothing away with him save the fruits of his good deeds."

BOOK III

Romantic Literature

BEYOND THE VERGE OF TIME

By Harindranath Chattopadhyaya

Our dreams and longings cover deeper dreams
And longings in the silence far away.
All things on earth, sweet winds and shining clouds,
Waters and stars and the lone moods of men,
Are cool green echoes of the voice that sings
Beyond the verge of Time. Between two cries of aught,
Of aught on earth, wakes the eternal fire
Wherein the destiny of heaven is wrought,
For what is heaven but the earth grown full,
And God but man unshadowed and afar?

STEPS

By Harindranath Chattopadhyaya

Each moment when we feel alone
In this great world of rush and riot
Is as a jewelled stepping-stone
Which leads into the House of Quiet.
Within it dwell the ancient seers
Beyond unreal griefs and cares,
Beyond unreal smiles and tears,
Beyond the need of chant and prayers.

FIRE

By Harindranath Chattopadhyaya

Kindle your glimmering lamp in the infinite space, O Love!
Let the dark shadows dance in the burning depths of mine eyes.
I am athirst for one glimpse of your beautiful face, O Love!
Veiled in the mystical silence of stars and the purple of skies.

162 *Thrill me with radiant rapture, O Love! of your ravishing*
*   flute,*
Folding my silence in song, and my sorrow in silver eclipse,
Shaping my heart into flower, and the flower of my heart into
*   fruit*
Meet for your orchards of light, and touch of your luminous lips.

Cast in the shadowy deeps of my being, your love, like a
*   spark,*
Fan it to magical flame, till my dead heart burst into fire,
Swing like a censer, my dream of devotion, O Love! through
*   the dark,*
Turn into tumults of incense my richly-pulsating desire!

IMAGERY

By Harindranath Chattopadhyaya

He has fashioned the stars and the moons to the music
Of innermost-flowering joy and desire,
He has tried his own love for himself through the ages
By flooding his limbs with unquenchable fire
Of creation that dances and bubbles and flutters
In peacocks, in seas, and the hearts of the birds.
Behind the rich silence of red-running sunsets
And cool-coloured sundawns he utters his words.

He is finding for ever his infinite fullness
In blossoming buds and the withering flowers.
He shapes through the heart of the world his Ideal
So white in the midst of the many-hued hours.
He weaves a fine trammel of marvellous colours
Around and about him in utter delight,
Till straight through the darkness his laughter comes lambent,
Birdlike from a cage in a freedom of flight.

OPEN THOU THY DOOR OF MERCY

By Hemantabala Dutt

All my guilt of old, sin upon sin, put far, far away. Give, O Lord, give in my heart the melody of a new song.

To stir to life my withered, unfeeling heart, near to death and poor, play thy melody on the *bina*, taking ever a new tune.

As in Nature thy sweetness overflows, so let thy compassion wake in my heart.

In the midst of all things may thy loving face float before my eyes. May no rebel thought against thy wish ever wake in my heart.

Day by day, before I set foot in life's forest, may I crave thy blessing and so advance, my Lord.

Setting thy commands upon my head, may I with unfaltering care accomplish my every task in the remembrance of thy feet.

Giving to thee the fruit of my task fulfilled, at the end of day may my wearied spirit and body find rest.

Hurrying have I come from far away, knowing thee compassionate. A hundred hindrances there were to my coming. How many thorns fill the path to my goal. So, to-day, behold! my heart is wounded, my life is dark. Hurrying have I come from far away, knowing thee compassionate.

Open thou thy door of mercy. My raft of life drifts on the boundless ocean. Fearlessness art thou, and ever powerful. Nought have I, I am weak and poor. My heart is thirsting for thy lotus feet. The day is now far spent. Open thou thy door of mercy. My raft of life drifts on the boundless ocean.

(Translated by Miss Whitehouse.)

THE DANCER

By Nirupama Debi

Lo! the heavy rain has come! With loosened tresses densely dark, lo! the sky is covered. Lightnings rend the thick darkness over the mountains. All around, to my heart's content, I see that beauty has burst forth.

See, frolicsome, she pours forth her loveliness in a thousand streams! Her raiment, hastily flung around her in disarray, mad passion in her eyes, with the voice of the *papiya*, full of sweetness and pity, she sings.

Slowly move her feet. Slipping, slipping, falls her loosely hanging scarf. Her heart throbs with tumultuous feeling. As if a flood of beauty overflows, her green jacket of emerald grass displays the hue of her radiant beauty all around.

The anklets on her feet, keeping time, ring out in swift succession, as if they were sweet cymbals. Round her lovely throat hangs her chain of emerald parrots. The rain has ceased and she garbs herself in silken robes broidered with diamond raindrops.

She gladdens the eye. On the treetops birds play on golden tambourines. Is the dancer dancing in Indra's hall, casting restless glances here and there? Urbasi puts off the chain of jewels from her breast.

How gay her laughter! How fair a dance her tinkling footsteps weave! Her bracelets and bangles circle glittering. She is girdled with melody of murmuring swans. For her earth and sky swoon away, overflowing with love.

Her hands touched the *bina* and by her spell enthralled my infatuated heart. Tears stream from my eyes; infatuation floods my heart. The witch to-day has melted my timid heart. Lo! the heavy rain has come.

(Translated by Miss Whitehouse.)

Romantic Literature

THE VISIBLE

By Priyambada Debi

Dearest, I know that thy body is but transitory; that the kindled life, thy shining eyes, shall be quenched by the touch of death, I know; that this thy body, the meeting-place of all beauty, in seeing which I count my life well-lived, shall become but a heap of bones, I know. Yet I love thy body. Day by day afresh through it have I satisfied a woman's love and desire by serving thy feet and worshipping thee. On days of good omen I have decked thee with a flower-garland; on days of woe I have wiped away with my *sari* end thy tears of grief. O my lord, I know that thy soul is with the Everlasting One, yet waking suddenly some nights I have wept in loneliness, thinking how thou didst drive away my fear, clasping me to thy breast. And so I count thy body as the chief goal of my love, as very heaven.

(Translated by Miss Whitehouse.)

BASANTA PANCHAMI

By Pankajini Basu

To-day, after a year, on the sacred fifth day, Nature has flung away her worn raiment, and with new jewels, see, with fresh buds and new shoots she has begemmed herself and smiles. The birds wing their way, singing with joy; ah, how lovely! The black bee hums as if with sound of " Ulu! ulu! " he wished good fortune to Nature. The south breeze seems to say as it flits from house to house, " To-day Binapani comes here to Bengal." Arrayed in guise that would enrapture even sages, maid Nature has come to worship thy feet, O propitious one! See, O India, at this time all pay no heed to fear of plague, famine, earthquake; all put away pain and grief and gloom; to-day all are drunk with pleasure. For a year Nature was waiting in hope for this day to come. Many folk in many a fashion now summon thee, O white-armed one; I also

166 have a mind to worship. Thy two feet are red lotuses; but, say, with what gift shall we worship thee, O mother Binapani? Ever sorrowful, ever ill-starred are we women of Bengal, all of us. Yet if thou have mercy, this utterly dependent one will worship thee with the gift of a single tear of devotion shed on thy lotus feet. Graciously accept that, and in mercy, O white-armed one, grant this blessing on my head on this propitious, sacred day, that this life may be spent in thy worship, Mother.

(*Translated by Miss Whitehouse.*)

THE LOVERS

By Fredoon Kabraji

From the rose-gardens of Time, fragrant and fresh, in ecstasies of light—Day has come! How many an age of silent love hath breathed and breathed upon his cheeks that tender flush of rose?

The blue in his eyes—from what lakes of enchantment hath he drunk? The radiant colours of his thought—from what infinite wonder hath he made? The glory of his love for whom, for whom hath he brought? For whom, for whom the music of his clouds, his winds, his birds? The secrets of his soul for whom, for whom?

A Lotus-bud has opened; ere she was born the pain of a vast music did fill and fill her soul with a vain constant hope; in the ecstasy of that pain she bloomed into flower.

The Lotus dreams upon the lyric melodies of Day.

In the sunset hush of evening she folds her petals upon the memories of Day, enwoven with her fragrant devotions.

In the secrecy of Night she sings her praise, making the deeps of the dark melodious.

The glory of his love for whom, for whom doth he bring? For whom, for whom the music of his clouds, his winds, his birds?

The secrets of his soul for whom, for whom?

TULIP

By Fredoon Kabraji

Tulip, tell me, what do you hold in your cup?

I hold in my cup the magic that swells the thirst of your soul, O Mother, when you look on the form of your child; the opiate that fills your dream, Mother, with the awe of the Unknown!

But, Tulip, tell me, why do you guard your magic beyond the wing of melody?

Because, ere Thought was, a kiss of Love did capture Death in the Seed of Life. That is why no melody of Life can hold all the magic in my cup, Mother; that is why Love cannot hold your child in Life alone!

IN PRAISE OF HENNA

By Sarojini Naidu

A KOKILA *called from a henna-spray:*
Lira! liree! Lira! liree!
Hasten, maidens, hasten away
To gather the leaves of the henna tree.
Send your pitchers afloat on the tide,
Gather the leaves ere the dawn be old,
Grind them in mortars of amber and gold,
The fresh green leaves of the henna tree.

A kokila called from a henna-spray:
Lira! liree! Lira! liree!
Hasten, maidens, hasten away
To gather the leaves of the henna tree.
The tilka's *red for the brow of a bride,*
And betel-nut's red for lips that are sweet;
But, for lily-like fingers and feet,
The red, the red of the henna tree.

IMPERIAL DELHI

By Sarojini Naidu

Imperial City! dowered with sovereign grace,
To thy renascent glory still there clings
The splendid tragedy of ancient things,
The regal woes of many a vanquished race;
And memory's tears are cold upon thy face
E'en while thy heart's returning gladness rings
Loud on the sleep of thy forgotten Kings,
Who in thine arms sought Life's last resting-place.

Thy changing Kings and Kingdoms pass away,
The gorgeous legends of a bygone day,
But thou dost still immutably remain
Unbroken symbol of proud histories,
Unageing priestess of old mysteries
Before whose shrine the spells of Death are vain.

SPRING

By Sarojini Naidu

Young leaves grow green on the banyan twigs,
And red on the peepul tree,
The honey-birds pipe to the budding figs,
And honey-blooms call to the bee.

Poppies squander their fragile gold
In the silvery aloe-brake;
Coral and ivory lilies unfold
Their delicate lives on the lake.

Kingfishers ruffle the feathery sedge,
And all the vivid air thrills
With butterfly-wings in the wild-rose hedge,
And the luminous blue of the hills.

CRADLE-SONG

By Sarojini Naidu

From groves of spice,
O'er fields of rice,
Athwart the lotus-stream,
I bring for you,
Aglint with dew,
A little lovely dream.

Sweet, shut your eyes,
The wild fire-flies
Dance through the fairy neem;
From the poppy-bole
For you I stole
A little lovely dream.

Dear eyes, good-night,
In golden light
The stars around you gleam;
On you I press
With soft caress
A little lovely dream.

RAJHANS (THE PRINCE OF SWANS)

By Puran Singh

Rajhans! The Golden Swan! Is it thy plumage that shines, or the sunrise on the eternal snows?

The dweller of *Man-Sarowar,* the lake on the roof of the world! Thy golden beak parts milk from water, in the living stream thou art a liberated soul!

A rosary of spotless pearls is in thy beak, and how sublime is the lofty curve of thy neck against the Heaven's vast azure!

Thou livest on pearls, the nectar drops so pure of Hari Nam.

170 Great Soul! lover of the azure transparent Infinite! Thou canst not breathe out of the *Man-Sarowar* air, nor canst thou live out of sight of those loftiest peaks of snow, and away from the diluted perfume of musk blowing from the wild trail of the deer!

Thou art the spirit of Beauty, thou art far beyond the reach of human thought. Thy isolation reflecteth the glory of the starry sky in thy Nectar Lake of Heart in whose waters the sun daily dips himself!

Thou hast the limitless expanse of air, the companionship of fragrant gods,

And yet we know thou leavest those Fair Abodes to come to share the woes of human love;

Thou alightest unawares on the grain-filled barn of the humble farmer, awakening Nature's maiden hearts, thou informest love.

It is thy delight to see woman love man, the small ripplings of a human heart in love flutter thee in thy lofty seat.

Thou art the soul liberated through love; thou knowest the worth of love, flying for its sake even midst the cities' smoke and dust, perchance, to save a human soul through love!

" Sisters of the Spinning-wheel."

OTTOMAN POETS

GHAZEL (80)

The following are extracts from E. J. W. Gibb's *History of Ottoman Poetry*. Ahmed Pasha, whose poems open the series of extracts, was probably wholly a lyrical poet. He is the first singer who demonstrated the powers of the Turkish language as a vehicle of lofty poetic thought. Born in Brusa, he attained many distinctions not only as a writer of verse, but as an administrator, for the poet continued to hold until his death in 902 the Governorship of Brusa Sanjaq during the reign of Bayezid II.

The next poet engaging our attention is Alanddin Sabit, born in Bosnia. He rose from step to step of honour in the service of the Sultan till he received the Mollaship of Dari Bakr a few years before his death in 1124. In style and spirit he is a thorough-going traditionist, and thus his verse is written in the original Turkish of the classical period.

The next, Nadim's work, is a typical example of the transitional period of Ottoman poetry, till you come to the lyrics and even the lullaby sung by a nurse over the cradle of the infant love, to the age of Esrar, in the romanticists of a much later epoch.

For that those thy locks have smit with melancholia the soul,
O thou cordial-lip, with thy sweet healing honey make it whole.

Chide not though my heart be broken by that hard, hard heart o' thine;
For the fragile flask availeth ne'er the stone's assault to thole.

From thy skirt thy tresses shook the perfumed dust by thee betrod,
For that musk while still in China unalloyed remains and sole.

Sovereign of beauty, seek not peace or patience from the heart;
Monarchs gather not from ruined cities aught of tax or toll.

172 When the clay for thee was kneaded, O thou dainty frame,
    meseems
Earth of Paradise was mingled with Life's Water bright
    of roll.

Pure the love of thee is waxen, biding long within the heart;
Clearer groweth wine the longer while it bides in crystal bowl.

Since the dervish Ahmed turned a beggar in the dear one's
    ward
He is grown earth's King with naught of need of throne or
    crown or stole.

GHAZEL (86)

Ah! thy rosebud-face is veiléd mid thy hair!
Midst the clouds the sun is hidden, I would swear!

Whoso sees me kiss the dust before thy gate
Sayeth, " Lo, with golden plate this door is fair! "

Fled the heart from spite, it went to thy dear ward;
Well it knew in Heaven could be nor pain nor care!

Every moment pour mine eyen stained with blood
Where thy feet have trodden, pearls of lustre rare.

Proffering my life, I pray thy lip a hint
Of the mystery of thy mouth, it answers ne'er.

Mid the ruined heart is throned thy fantasy;
Therefore wreck it not with uttermost despair.

Yea, the soul of Jem is sacrifice for thee;
This the saying is " God knoweth best! " for e'er.

ROSE AND ZEPHYR

O radiant pursuivant, O morning breeze,
Thy path is ever over lands and seas.
Thou heal'st the cypress and the narcisse' sight;
Ah, but for thee how sad the narcisse' plight!
When thy blest advent cheers the garden-land,
This opes its eye that on its foot doth stand
Speed there and greet my dearest love from me;
The Seven Seas wet not the skirt of thee!"

QASÎDA (93)

The tide of early spring doth make the earth to smile again,
E'en as the tristful lover's soul who wins his dear to gain.
The party of the flowers is quit the winter-magistrate;
Their heads are bare, their dulcet-savoured cups in hand
    they've ta'en.
" 'T is now the beaker's turn, the season of liesse," they say,
" An thou be wise, beware thou cast it not from thee in vain!"
Each lovesome burgeon which hath donned its cap on rakish
    wise
Meseems a winsome wanton beauty flushed with sweet disdain.
God hath prepared the greeny herbs like Khizrs all around
To rescue those who have been whelmed amid the seas of bane.
To draw the tender herbs from forth the prison dure of earth
The grace of God hath fashioned into cords the falling rain.
Belike this verdant sward is e'en the Resurrection-field,
And so upon one foot there standeth many and many a plane.
Say are they tulips, those that show upon the meadow fair,
Or are they Tartar musk-pods lying there with gory stain;
Or elsewise rolls of musk the which the tulip-land hath wrapped
In crimson say, as offering to the garden-bride full fain?
The tulips put theriaca their ruby pots within
What time they saw the river creeping snake-like o'er the plain.
The streamlet goes to kiss the ground before some cypress dear,
And wandering round and round, it sings the while a sweet
    refrain.

174 *Illumining mine eyes, the lawn hath shown to them the sun*
And all the floret-stars the which the meadow-skies contain.
If that the dewdrop-teeth win not to loose the rosebud-knot,
May pass the winds and may the thorny-nail to loose 't
refrain!
The rose hath stitched her kirtle with the needle of the thorn,
That at the royal feast she be the dancer fair and fain.
How fair a noble banquet, envy of the Bowers Etern!
How fair a gracious feast, wherefrom might Spring monition
gain!
The Irem-garden will no more before our vision rise,
Henceforward none for Paradise itself will sigh or plain.
Is it a cup of purest wine that circles therearound?
Or hath the Sphere let everyone his fondest hope attain?
The sphere hath laid on plate of China-ware sun, moon and
stars,
To serve at this high feast as apple, quince, pomegranate-grain.
The rose is hither come, and hides her face behind her hand,
She blushes red with fire of shame to see her beauty vain.
The narcissi have wrapped their sequins round with paper
white
To scatter at the bridal of the happy-fortuned fain.
The Prince who is the rose unique within the Empire-bower
Hath ta'en to his embrace the Pearl of Fortune in this reign.
Two Saplings grown within the royal garden-land full fair,
And tall and fresh, and jasmine-faced and rosy-cheeked the
twain,
The Age's King hath grafted with the band of Holy Law
For that a sweet and pleasant fruit and lieve may thence
be ta'en.
O Lord, may all fair fortune speed this marriage upon earth;
And may it, like the course of sun and moon, steadfast remain;
And may it dure in sweet delight e'en as the heart would crave,
On such wise even as the Jemshíd-mighty Khusrev's reign!
Sultan Mehemmed, Murád's son, most noble of all Kings!
Darius who doth crowns to all the lords of earth ordain!
The King of starry retinue, the lunar-stirruped Sun!
Prince strong as Fate, and dread as Doom, and bounteous as
main!

He ne'er shall swelter in the heats of tyranny's July
Who refuge 'neath the shadow of the Monarch's grace may gain.
His spear-point and his mace lift high the head and smite
    the ranks,
While bind the foe and pierce the heart his lasso and his flane.
His sword within his ocean-hand is even as that Fish
Who firm doth on his back the ordinance of earth sustain.
None in thy reign hath need to look for refuge to the sphere;
No fortress needeth he who doth in safety's realm remain.
Belike the ocean sought to vie in bounty with thy hand,
And so to place its hand afore its face for shame 'tis fain.
Each day the sun doth kiss the dust before thy glory great,
And thus 'tis honoured that its head doth highest heaven attain.
O King, the genius jewel-radiant of Nejáti's soul
Hath ranged pearls untold upon the page withouten stain,
That he may go upon this festal day and cast them wide
So that they cover all the ground before his Sovereign.

GHAZEL (124)

Ever do the tears of blood the goblet of my eye o'erflow,
Some presentment of thy wine-hued rubies to the folk to show.

Could Ferhád but see my plight for thee, O Shirin-dulcet lip,
Taking in each hand a stone, he'd smite him, like the mill,
    for woe.

Whereso'er I'd flee, the six directions closed on me have these,—
Yonder two locks, yonder two eyes, yonder two eyebrows,
    e'en so.

Winsomeness behoves a beauty that the folk in hand her bear,
Elsewise eke the signet-ring both eye and eyebrow hath, I trow.

Did I fling not art among my verse I should not bide alive;
So that one may gain his living, needful 'tis an art to know.

Should Mesihi from this roll be struck, his like will ne'er
    return;
What is writ o'er an erasure ne'er is writ so fair, ah no.

From the ZAFER-NAME (318)

Arise, reed, thou war-steed of rhetoric's fray,
And o'er speech's field make the battle-dust play.
A stoure do thou raise upon poesy's plain,
And pluck from the meadows of fancy thy strain.
The tale of the rose and the lily forswear,
And bring to us tidings of sabre and spear.
Enow of the musk-scented tresses, enow!
We'd cast up and catch the lasso and the bow.
Enow of the locks falling loop upon loop!
As the links of the mail are mine eyen a-hoop.
Enow of the glance dealing anguish and bane!
That tale let the sword keen of edge cleave atwain.
Enow of the graces and charms of the fair!
Let wave in its beauty that sapling, the spear.
At length let the horsemen of fantasy's plain
Betrample these things in the mire of disdain.
For ancient this building of dolour is grown;
'Tis ruined, there resteth not stone upon stone.
We've heard all these stories a thousand times o'er;
To listen thereto is permitted no more.
Why then to the legend of Qays be heart-bound
Since, thanks be to Allah, our reason is sound?
Repeat not of Leylá and Mejnún the song,
Nor throw words to madmen, let be, pass along.
Or what art and part with a navvy hast thou?
Then run not with Ferhád thy head into woe;
To tell of that rock of distress and dismay
Were reminding the madman of stones, in good fay.
Or wherefore recount thou of Wamiq the tale?
Nor look thou for devils nor lá havla wail.
Beware, nor the praises of Perviz sing thou,
So great a fire-server would burn one I trow.
If the name of Shírin on thy tongue thou dost take,
The taste of thy palate thou'lt ruin, alack.
Then seek, O thou reed-pen, a tract unbeknown,
Disport in a land where no footstep hath gone;
Go, find thee a realm where none other hath been,
Untrodden of Ferhád, of Mejnún unseen.

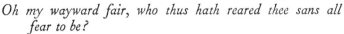

GHAZEL (322)

Oh my wayward fair, who thus hath reared thee sans all
     fear to be?
Who hath tendered thee that thus thou shamest e'en the
     cypress-tree?
Sweeter than all perfume, brighter than all bloom, thy dainty
     frame;
One would deem some rose had nursed thee in her bosom,
     love o' me.
Thou hast donned a rose-enwroughten rich brocade, but sore
     I fear
Lest the shadow of the broidered rose's thorn make thee
     to dree.
Holding in one hand a bowl, in one a rose, thou camest, sweet;
Ah, I knew not which thereof to take, the bowl, the rose, or thee.
Lo, there springs a jetting fountain from the Stream of Life,
     methought,
When thou lettest me that lovely lissom shape o' thine to see.
While the mirror of my bosom clear was as thy frame, alas,
For that even once I clipped thee not, thou darling fair and free.
Whensoe'er I ask it, saying: Who hath bowed thy body so?
Theeward ever points the beaker at the feast of mirth and glee.

GHAZEL (323)

Thy bosom bright hath worked the sun's pavilion dire dismay,
Thy leg diaphanous hath wrought the shaft of dawn's deray.
The vitals of the bud are torn with bitter pangs whene'er
Thy rose-like navel peepeth forth from neath thy shift, my may.
Astound thereat, with mouth agape, e'en like the slipper, bode
The cordwainer what time he saw thy lustrous ankle ray.
Belike thy lips once more have shown how sweetest speech
     should flow;
For all around thee, lo, the grains of sugar strew the way.
Nedim, unless a silvern mirror sparkle therewithin,
What glory hath the bravest wede of gold-enwroughten say?

M

SHARQÍ (331)

Sweet a castanetist maid hath pierced my bosom sore to-day;
   Rosy-cheeked and roseate-vested, prankt with violet watered say;
Silvery-necked and sunny-visaged, fair beseen with moles a tway;
   Rosy-cheeked and roseate-vested, prankt with violet watered say.

Round her head a broidered crenate turban had my lady tied,
And her attar-scented eyebrows black with surma had she dyed.
I should reckon she was only fifteen years of age this tide.
   Rosy-cheeked and roseate-vested, prankt with violet watered say.

Pride of balconies and glory of all clasping arms were she;
Since she parted from her nurse's charge it scarce a year can be.
O my loved one, joyance of my heart, and source of life to me.
   Rosy-cheeked and roseate-vested, prankt with violet watered say.

All, her winsome ways, her airs, her smiles, her voice, beyond compare;
Beautiful her eyes, and mole-besprent her neck exceeding fair:
Silver-necked and slender-waisted, bright with ruffled golden hair;
   Rosy-cheeked and roseate-vested, prankt with violet watered say.

Naught I'll say of yonder fairy-face's anguish-dealing eye,
Neither shall I speak of how Nedim for love of her doth sigh;
I may sing her ways and charms, but tell her name, that, ne'er will I.
   Rosy-cheeked and roseate-vested, prankt with violet watered say.

SHARQÍ (332)

Come forth afield, 'tis now the time o'er mead and plain to
    stray;
  O sapling of the lawn, restore to ancient spring his sway.
Let fall thy tresses, like the sable, round about thy cheek;
  O sapling of the lawn, restore to ancient spring his sway.

Come, Rosebud-mouth, for all thy nightingales are seeking thee;
Come to the bower, and that the rose is o'er forget shall we;
Come forth ere trod 'neath winter's foot the garden-kingdom be;
  O sapling of the lawn, restore to ancient spring his sway.

Around those ruddy cheeks o' thine thy dusky locks unbind,
And let thy sable be this year with crimson camlet lined.
Take thou in hand the bowl, if ne'er a tulip thou canst find.
  O sapling of the lawn, restore to ancient spring his sway.

Again with many fruits and fair is earth like Paradise;
O wilt thou not vouchsafe to us thy union's fruit likewise?
A kiss bestowing secretly on each who lovelorn sighs.
  O sapling of the lawn, restore to ancient spring his sway.

I heard a verse, O wanton bright who mak'st the heart to beam,
I knew not well the meaning that it bore, but yet I deem
'Twas not without reason it was chanted by Nedim:
  O sapling of the lawn, restore to ancient spring his sway

From BEAUTY AND LOVE (402)

Once on a night within this Tribe befell
A passing wondrous thing and strange to tell.
The rolling spheres were each on other swept,
Some smiled among the angels, others wept.
A clamour rang the vault of heaven round,
An earthquake shook the bases of the ground.
A thousand terrors and a thousand joys:
A din of cries, of tabors and hautboys:
Now the thick darkness fold on fold was plied,
Now radiances flashed forth on every side.

Each leaf in adoration bowed the head;
The rivers, for amaƺe dissolving, fled;
Among the stars conjunctions dread arose,
A rain of joyance and a hail of woes.
Amidst the darkness many a dreary cry,
And voices of the illumined lifted high.
The sky pealed, echoing with the wild affray,
And earth through the strange turmoil lost her way,
This fear's contagion to each bosom came,
And peace of heart was but an empty name.
The spheres and all the air were filled with fright:
A thousand destinies were born that night.

GHAZEL (410)

Out on this jugglery! by God! out on this idle snare!
Out on this pomp and circumstance! out on this glore and
  glare!

Since never pasha finds a rag to shroud his lopped off head,
Out on his flag of honour, his badge of horse's hair!

Since ever must the blast of death blow out the lamp of life,
Out on the useless candle that above the tomb doth flare!

How often often have I traced it on the page of earth!
Out on this form of nights and days for aye repeated there!

A mansion whose foundation rests on sighs and bitter tears;
Woe for such show and bravery! out on such beauty fair!

From torment's furnace let them issue forth mid sweat of pain,
Out on them all, these regal pearls, these rubies pure and rare!

To those who, erst of high estate, their rank have forfeited
" Out on thee! " groans the rumbling drum, and " Out! "
  the tabor's blare.

Since that the wedding-revelry must turn to mourning's gloom,
Pugh for the taper of the feast! out on the flambeau-glare!

O Ghálib, be thou dervish-souled, seek poverty's retreat;
Take flute in hand and play, then out on Fortune everywhere!

The while that at Our Master's gate I find my hopes I'll sing:
" Out on the stress and anguish which from earth's duresse
*   I bear! "*

GHAZEL (412)

Hast thou fallen in with Love's clear winsome Fair, O gentle
*   breeze?—*
For thy breath yon Darling's odour sweet doth share, O gentle
*   breeze.*

Thou hast tangled all the curling locks of her who holds the
*   heart,*
Thou hast made her lovers yearning's chain to bear, O gentle
*   breeze.*

Haply 'tis thy zephyr's aim to solve the riddle hard that lies
Hidden in the rosebud's bosom debonair, O gentle breeze.

Sweet a rose-leaf wafted hither from the Heavenly bower above,
Jesus gained from thee his breath of virtue rare, O gentle
*   breeze.*

Hath the way thou camest led thee o'er the dust Our Master
*   trod?—*
Lo, thou hast requickened Esrár with thine air, O gentle
*   breeze.*

From the SÁQÍ-NÁME

MY DESCENT TO THE BANQUET OF HUMANITY (450)

The Hidden Tablet was my royal abode,
Through which high state inebriate I bode.
I looked on nature's feast, and there saw I
The heat, the cold, the humid and the dry.
I won the lofty Empyrean dome,
And downward gazed upon the earth therefrom.
I served the Magian Elder a brief while,

Then sate me on the throne in regal style.
I saw the twelve bowls of the Zodiac,
And drunken, I forgot the pathway back.
I wandered all the Seven Heavens through,
My heart grew wise the hour when drunk I grew.
I hob-a-nobbed with Saturn merrily,
And bode a space with him in mirth and glee.
With Jupiter a while I held debate,
And bade the reeling stars to coruscate.
I made Mars drunken mid the planets roll,
And tutored the Fifth Sphere to quaff the bowl.
The Solar beaker in my hand I seized,
And sighed remembering the Primal Feast.
I bade the lovesome Venus chant her lay
And the Third Heaven dance upon his way.
I learned right goodly lore of Mercury,
And sage and poet turn by turn grew I.
I drained the Crescent bowl, a sun I turned,
Through this hilarity with light I burned.
The Sphere of Fire a tavern-house I deemed,
To me its wayward flashes goblets gleamed.
The Air exhilaration found through me,
I dashed the Waters with the wine of glee.
I reeled into the cloud's carouse elate,
I took the life-bestowing rain to mate.
Drunken, I gazed upon earth's stage astound;
And drunk, dead drunk, made I the blessed ground.
Within the seedling's heart the cup I drained,
And drunken there a twain of days remained.
In the wheat-stalk I strong and goodly grew;
In the grain's heart myself for fair I knew.
I quaffed for nourishment clear wine and bright,
I turned to chyme, and pleasant was my plight.
In hours of grossness wine-dregs I became;
In hours of pureness, spirit pure as flame.
From chyme was one within the liver made,
The other in the father's loins was glad.
At length did I wine seminal become
And lie within the runlet of the womb.

For nine months in the dungeon-womb immured,
What blood I drank! what anguish I endured!—
Then issued to this exile. What should I
But seek the regions where my home doth lie?

DESCRIPTION OF THE CUPBEARER (451)

Polite be the cupbearer and discreet,
Of sunny cheek, moon visaged, angel-sweet.
The fashions of the feast she well should know,
And all the fancies of the rev'llers too;
How some pure undiluted wine require,
While others mingle water with the fire.
A maiden should she be in boyish dress,
Unmatched and peerless in her loveliness.
Gentle and simple should her wit enthral;
Neither untutored nor ill-bred withal.
In minstrelsy and wines she skilled should be,
From all disfigurement and blemish free,
Of sugar-lip, sweet-tongued, and gay of soul,
Of fourteen years, like to the moon at full,
That all the party through her airs be bright
And in her voice the revellers delight.
Her silvern hand the crystal bowl doth bear,—
Radiance on radiance! radiance everywhere!
When to the banquet comes she like the moon,
Her beauty should add splendour to the sun,
That archly stepping like the peacock fine
She deck with lively hues the feast of wine.
As yon fair Torment passeth to and fro
A wild sensation should the banquet know;
And should she drain a cup, her eyen bright
Would smite the royal falcon in his flight.

INDIAN DOHRAS (PEASANT POETRY)

The following selections from the translation of T. D. Broughton give the real meaning to the " spirit of India," inasmuch as these are pieces composed by no literary men, but by illiterate peasants. Most of these Dohras are sung in the village square when the humble husbandmen have sown their crops, or await the burst of monsoon rains to give life to their parched fields: they are thus nature in the nude, and consequently steeped in that simple sweetness which is rustic but not vulgar. Unfortunately, historical data regarding the authors of most of them are lacking. They, in any case, are not modern.

'Tis Sawun; mark—the river flows
With rippling eddies to the sea;
The slender jasmine closer grows,
And clings about its wedded tree.

The lightning wantons with the rain,
And brighter seems to gleam around;
The peacock woos in jocund strain,
While laughing earth returns the sound.

'Tis Sawun, love!—'twixt man and wife
Let no sad parting moment be;
Who journies now? what gain or strife
In Sawun tears my love from me.

A husband preparing to go a journey, is dissuaded from it by his wife; who tells him that it is now the month of Sawun, when all the works of Nature rejoice, and indulge in connubial joys. The Hindoo poets not only feign the various and beautiful creepers that adorn their groves to be wedded to the more robust trees, but with the latitude of Orientalists, assign the sea as a husband to the rivers; and the lightning, which in Sawun, when the rainy season has completely set in, is very frequent, as a consort to the rain. That month falls about the middle of July, and in the reanimation of vegetable life, almost suspended by the preceding heats, presents to the delighted senses all the natural phenomena of the spring of Europe.

> *The lively drum is heard around;*
> *The tambourine and cymbals sound:*
> *I in the flames of absence burn,*
> *And languish for my love's return.*
>
> *The women all around me sing,*
> *And own th' inspiring joys of spring:*
> *While I, from darts of ruthless love,*
> *Never-ending torments prove.*
>
> *The amorous Kokil strains his throat,*
> *And pours his plaintive pleasing note;*
> *My breast responsive heaves with grief,*
> *Hopeless and reckless of relief.*
>
> *When he again shall glad my hours,*
> *Then, girl, I'll take thy blooming flowers;*
> *But now my love is far away,*
> *Where should I place thy Busunt gay?*

The pangs of absence are sung in this little poem by a woman, who observes the general joy diffused around her, upon the approach of the Busunt or Spring.

> *If other voice than his was near,*
> *It seemed a worm within my ear:*
> *He went.—I heard the dreadful sound;*
> *Yet both my ears unhurt I found.*
>
> *Hid by my veil, my eyes have burned;—*
> *Yet weeks past on;—nor he returned.*
> *Then, heart, no more on love rely;*
> *Beat on, and Death himself defy.*

186   A young girl so intoxicated with a first passion as to suppose that she could not survive a separation from her lover, finds, after he had quitted the village for some weeks, that her ears still served her to hear with, though they no longer received the soft sounds of his voice; and her eyes for all the purposes of vision, though no more impressed with the image of her beloved. In the above stanzas she expresses her astonishment at all this, and very wisely determines never again to involve herself in so fleeting and troublesome a passion.

Is it, sweet maid, the breathing flute
That tells to Love some plaintive suit;
While o'er the cup of Indra's bed
Passes a shade of deeper red?

Art thou some Diuta's mistress bright;
Or the fair sister of Delight?
Or Wit's gay parent art thou born,—
Such winning words thy lips adorn?

No;—thou art Music's melting queen;
Or Love's enchanting bride I ween:
And Muttra's shepherd owns thy flame;
And Kokils stay their notes for shame.

O fairest of the Muttra maids!
While thy soft voice my soul pervades,
Seems on thy rosy lips to die
The Beena's heavenly minstrelsy.

    A soft voice has in all ages and by all nations been deemed an irresistible charm, and a proper subject for poetic praise: in the above stanzas of Kesheo Das, Krishna is supposed to celebrate, and certainly not inelegantly, the voice of his beloved Rhada.

TO BURKA

Bright Indra's bow appears; the genial rains
From the full clouds descend, and drench the plains.
Quick lightnings flash along the turbid sky,
Pierce the fresh moisten'd earth, and parch it dry.
O'er the pale moon a showery veil is thrown;
The frequent floods the lily's leaflet drown;
Like curling dust the distant showers appear,
And the swan flies before the watery year.
Dark with her varying clouds, and peacocks gay,
See Burka comes, and steals our hearts away.

Mark,—her slender form bend low,
As the zephyrs lightly blow!
Mark,—her robe, like blossoms rare,
Scatter fragrance on the air!
See, her face as soft moon beaming;
From her smiles ambrosia streaming;
And on brows, more white than snow,
See, the raven tresses glow!
Lotus-like her dewy feet
Treasures yield of nectar'd sweet:
Light as on her footsteps pass,
Blushes all the bending grass;
And rings of jewels, Beauty's powers,
Freshen into living flowers:
While brighter tints, and rosier hues,
All the smiling earth suffuse.

Her forehead some fair moon; her brows a bow;
Love's pointed darts, her piercing eyebeams glow:
Her breath adds fragrance to the morning air;
Her well-turned neck as polished ivory fair:
Her teeth pomegranate seeds,—her smiles soft lightnings are.
Her feet, light leaves of lotus on the lake,
When with the passing breeze they gently shake;

Her movements graceful as the Swan, that laves
His snowy plumage in the rippling waves,
Such, godlike youth, I've seen; a maid so fair;
Than gold more bright, more sweet than flower-fed air!

In the above little poem, an old woman is supposed to describe to Kunya the charms of a nymph who, like all her companions, was a candidate for his notice. The poet has indulged his fancy in particularizing her several attractions. The simile of the lotus is not less just; whose velvet leaf always floats on the surface of the water, seeming scarcely to rest upon it.

To view the waning moon at evening hour,
Fasting, a lovely maid ascends her bower;
Herself a full-orbed moon!—though brighter gleamed
The rays of beauty that around her beamed.
The women, wondering, from their Pooja ceased;
And thus with taunts addressed the wondering Priest:
" To you is heavenly science given!—then say,
Is't the full moon, or only Chout *to-day?"*

On the fourth of the month Katik, the Hindu women fast till the moon rises; when they offer up *Pooja*, or sacrificial rites; praying at the same time that their husbands may now grow prematurely old. The day is called " Kurwa chout "; *chout* signifying fourth, and *kurwa* being the name of certain little earthen vessels, which the women stain with a mixture of rice and turmeric called *aipun*, and filling them with water and grass, place them before figures drawn upon the wall, called *Ahoi*; where they are left till the festival of the Diwalee, which occurs nine days afterwards. The Hindu months commence on the day subsequent to the full moon (Poorun masee); and the foregoing lines describe a beautiful young woman ascending her balcony to await the rising of the planet on the evening of the Kurwa-Chout.

Though hair as black as glossy raven,
On me's bestowed by bounteous Heaven;
The gift I find a source of pain;
Yet who of Heaven may dare complain?
They sneer, and scoff, and taunting swear
I'm proud, because my face is fair:
And how should such a child as I
Restrain their cruel raillery?
My mother, if I stir, will chide;
My sister watches by my side;
And then my brother scolds me so,
My cheeks with constant blushes glow:
Ah then, kind Heaven! restore to me
The happy days of infancy;
And take this boasted youth again,
Productive but of care and pain!

A merry group at evening hour
Kunya spied in shady bower,
Lovely as pearls on lady's breast;
And Rhada shone above the rest.
Sweetly to their chiming bells,
On the glad ear the chorus swells;
And, as so true they strike the ground,
Each heart grows lighter at the sound.
Th' enraptured youth no more concealed,
At once his radiant form revealed:
And how shall I by words convey
Their consternation and dismay!
Their cheeks, till then unknown to shame,
Now redden with the mantling flame;
And their sweet eyes, of lotus hue,
Bend just like lilies filled with dew.

TO KRISHNA

For thy dark form and look divine,
The god of love upon thy shrine
  A million times I'd lay;
And give the riving flame of night
In millions, for those smiles of light,
  Around thy lips that play.

O let a million moons redeem
The glorious sun, whose cheering beam
  Illumes thy awful face!
And let me for thy nature bland
A million suns, with pious hand,
  Upon thy altar place!

The trembling lilies of the lake
In blooming millions let me take,
  Meet offering for thine eyes!
Come then—descend into my soul;—
There dwell and reign without control,
  Bright regent of the skies!

Why should I Baids or Shasturs name,
The venerable leaves, that claim
  Our pious care and love;—
The three vast worlds unawed I'd take,
Nor shrink to offer for thy sake,
  Sweet gardener of the grove!

Pleasure and pain pass away; and wealth and poverty depart from us. O, therefore, learn wisdom.

The land remains not, nor the landholder; the princes of the land remain not: yet be thou fixed, O my soul.

If love or hatred, avarice, passion, or pride, have influenced thee; now, O my heart, receive the rigid lessons of virtue:

They admonish thee night and day to cry, Rhada Krishn! Rhada Krishn! Rhada Krishn!

On an enemy, a prisoner, a trader, a gamester, a thief,
   or a liar,
An adulterer, a diseased man, a debtor, or a whoremaster,
(On the whoremaster especially) place no reliance.
Let them swear an hundred oaths; but believe not one.
The poet Gidhur has said, if an enemy enters your house,
Though he vows eternal friendship, he is still an enemy.

It becometh not a gentleman to desert his patron;
The tiger to skulk from the elephant;
Wisdom to dwell in darkness;
A warrior to shun the combat;
An adviser to speak words of detriment;
A Pundit to forget his learning;
A man of noble birth to associate with the vile;
Nor a wise man to consort with harlots.

Shame to him who solicits without worth,
Shame to him who beholds worth, and is not pleased;
Shame to him who is pleased, yet bestows not,
Shame to him who bestows with reluctance;
Shame to the gift that is without sincerity,
Shame to the sincerity that is without conscience;
Shame to the conscience untempered with mercy,
Shame to mercy when extended to a foe;
Shame to the foe who cannot dive into the heart,
Shame to the heart, where the mind is without honour;
Shame to the honour that is devoid of wisdom,
Shame to wisdom which is without the fear of God.

Your anger cease, and know me still
The humble bearer of his will.
You, who have seen and shared his pleasant ways,
On me your rage and scorn unjustly pour:
Truly I state, what he in pity says;
Nor dare say less, nor add one sentence more.

Lord of three worlds, a present Godhead named,
 What single tongue to speak his praise may dare!
Wanton you've known him still as colt untamed;
 And sportive as the bee in summer air.

With him the days of infancy rolled by;—
 And is he now a traitor deemed by you!
You're doubtless wise;—and poor of wit am I—
 Speak what you will; I'm bound to call it true.

Yet still my heart would heal this mortal hate;
 If I speak false; may wealth, may honour fly!—
Softened, they own 'tis hard the bolts of Fate
 To shun; and sighing, yield to Destiny.

Why on my neck with fondness hang?—
I am not she, who all night long
 Upon thy panting bosom lies;
Who can thy wasted flesh imbue,
With Chumpa's dye, of yellow hue,
 With Goolilala tinge thine eyes.

Go thou perverse; nor foolish, say,
That heart can own another's sway,
 Which once for thee has fondly beat:
With neem-leaves who would heat his lip,
That e'er had known the bliss to sip
 The cooling grapes delicious treat?

In vain I court the noon-tide rays,
In vain I wrap my cloak of baize;—
Fierce winter reigns; nor will give place,
But to a warm and fond embrace.

Yes, genial warmth has fled the earth,
And yields to chilling winter's wrath:
But, banished, finds a place of rest,
Impregnable,—in Woman's breast.

Say, lovely moon,—say, deer-eyed maid
Whose locks like lilies wave in air,
While this green Kewra scorns to fade,
Say, why neglect a form so fair?

O, would the Kewra's leaves were sere!
In ashes would the village lay!
For he, whose false hands placed it here,
From love and me stays far away!

And why should the Kewra's leaves be sere?
Or, tell me, why the village burned?—
For he, whose true hands placed it here,
Behold, in beggar's garb returned.

Was paper then more dear than gold?—
Or ink more scarce than rubies bright?
Were slender reeds for thousands sold;
One line of love you could not write?

I strove;—but only strove, to sigh;—
When memory placed thee in my sight,
My fingers failed, my heart beat high,—
I strove in vain;—I could not write.

A man, soon after his marriage with a beautiful young girl, is obliged to travel into some distant country. Upon taking leave of his bride, he plants a Kewra (supposed to be the spikenard), in the garden, and bids her observe it well; for that, so long as it continued to flourish, all would be right with him; but should she on the contrary behold it wither and die away, she might be assured that some fatal accident had happened to himself. After several years absence, the man returns to his own country; and resolves to appear before his wife in the character of a Jogee, or Hindu mendicant; and thus to ascertain how she had employed herself during his long absence. He finds her listless and sad; her person and dress neglected; and her sole employment, watching and weeping over the still flourishing Kewra plant. The above dialogue then takes place between them.

The terrace now she gains;—and now
  Unwearied seeks again the ground:
Like juggler's ball tossed to and fro,
  And fast in Love's soft fetters bound.

A cord, of eager glances spun,
  They mount; what will not lovers dare!
From roof to roof on eye-beams run,
  And dart like vaulters through the air.

In these stanzas, a girl is described as anxiously expecting the appearance of her lover, upon the terraces of their respective houses: and in a metaphor, allowable perhaps only to an Asiatic poet, their transport upon seeing each other is depicted.

Wife, why thus sadly gaze around,
And why thus heave such sighs profound,
  And whence these strange alarms?
Husband, because thy locks are grey,
And all thy youth hath passed away,
  In wicked syrens' arms.

Disclose that lovely face, sweet maid,
  And glad the eyes of all around.
No;—for the lily's bloom will fade;
  And taunts the vanquished moon confound.

From my Love's hair some loosened tresses hung,
  And angry round her ring of jewels grew:
Just like, at early dawn, a snake's soft young,
  Curling with eager folds to sip the dew.

In this stanza, the poet merely means to say that a lock of his mistress' hair was blown by the wind and entangled in her ear-ring. The constant strife between the natural and artificial ornament is a favourite fiction of the Hindu poets.

How that dark little spot on thy chin
  Enhances thy beauty and power!
'Tis a rose, and a poor bee within,
  Deceived, lies entranced in the flower.

My eyes as sly robbers I use,
  To ensnare silly hearts passing by;
And when bound by a smile for a noose,
  In that dimple I plunge them,—to die.

A fatal dart upon her brow she placed,
  And once upon her lover turned to gaʒe;
Then slow retired, and peeping as she paced,
  Gleamed like the flashing of a sudden blaʒe.

Wear not rings and chains of gold,
And deem the words of friendship true;
Like rust upon a polished mould
Of steel they seem, when worn by you.

These jewels on my neck are tied,
And crimson dyes my feet adorn,
Not to increase my beauty's pride,
But mark a matron's honoured form.

A handsome woman, richly adorned with jewels and
other ornaments, is addressed in the street by a man, who
pays her the compliment contained in the first of the above
stanzas; in the second she replies, and delicately reproves
his presumption. It will be recollected that among the
Hindus married women only are permitted to wear such
ornaments.

Eager my lover tow'rds me ran;
His hand an army, and his plan,
  The careless city to surprise:
But my eyes form a fortress good,
And eye-lashes a fencing wood,
  Where modesty securely lies.

Enter quick, O fly the place!—
Veil, O veil, thy fairer face!—
See, yon planet's fate delayed,
See, the monster's grasp is stayed!—
Thou, whose face no spot defiles,
Dread his force, and dread his wiles;
Soon a meaner prey he'll free,
And quit a moon less pure, for thee.

The popular superstition of the Hindus respecting an eclipse of the moon is that it is caused by a giant, who attacks and devours the planet; in revenge for her having, in conjunction with the sun, discovered him when, in the disguise of a *Deota*, or good spirit, he endeavoured to secure a portion of the *Umvit* or water of life. It is necessary to premise so much, that the English reader may comprehend the foregoing lines, which are supposed to be addressed to a beautiful woman looking at an eclipse of the moon from her terrace.

The spring returns with all its joyous train,
Yet he so fondly lov'd, stays far away:
My fluttering soul will quit its present clay,
In some avenging form to live again ·

A fowler's, to ensnare the murmuring dove,
Or monster's fell, to quench the moon's pale light;
Or his fierce eye, the Lord of wondrous night,
Whose lightning glance consum'd the god of love.

The transmigration of souls is one of the doctrines of the Hindu religion. In the preceding stanzas, a young bride laments the protracted absence of her husband, and wishes that after death she may revive in some form to avenge herself on the objects which now increase her misery, by exciting the tenderest emotions: the ring dove, the full moon, and the God of love himself.

O say, within that coral cell
What mighty magic power can dwell;
That cheats my hopes, my sight misleads,
And makes my pearls seem coral beads!
In those black eyes now fury burns;—
To crabs'-eyes all my coral turns!
But see, she smiles;—my fears were vain;
My worthless beads are pearls again.

The daughter of a certain Raja, young and beautiful, fell suddenly into a deep melancholy. No art was left untried to effect a cure; plays and pantomimes were acted before her; the most ridiculous mimics and buffoons were sent for, and exhibited in her presence: but all in vain; the young Ranee could by no means be induced to smile. At length a facetious Brahman undertook to cure her; and, in the character of a jeweller, offered some fine pearls for sale. The above lines contain the Brahmun's speech, with its effect: the first hyperbole failed; but in the next attempt he was more successful.

A CIRCLE OF THE SEASONS

A Translation of the Ritu-Samhara of Kalidasa made from
various European sources by E. Powys Mathers

SUMMER

*L*o, the season of heat has returned to us, my belovèd, with a sun of fire, and tenderer moons by night; with our long bathing in mirror water broken by plunging bodies, and delicate evening ends in a spent ardour.

Brown nights that are barred with lunar silver, and our palace open to the four breezes; wheels for the spreading and raising of waters, and bright jewel work; lo, these have returned to us, my belovèd, because you desired them.

The glory of our palaces within, a perfume floats there; pure wine that wavers below the breath of the lover; inflaming mystical songs: midnight, and the hour for these things, the hour for lovers.

The fever of Summer thickens in the heart of man, you can assuage and appease it, sorceress whose loins are great in silk, whose breasts are rubbed with sandal and set in pearl, whose hair, coming from the bath, is heavy with winged odour; sorceress having feet reddened by scented lac and arched under gold rings which chime like the song of the rose flamingo, their lines dream upward.

Who would not know enervation because of women whose breasts are wetted with red sandal? Their garments of pearl are mingled with fresh jasmine, who would not feel ardour? Their haunches are held in gold.

Robes are cast off from the tall breasts and quick bodies; there are but tissues afloat over their sweating. Choose out a woman, for they are dressed in youth.

Romantic Literature

Sleep wakes under the kiss of fans, among singing and the calling of guitars and birds. The fans stroke scented breasts. Girls set a man on fire with eye glances on moon evenings.

While lovers, heavy with happiness, lie deep in the palaces, the moon grows white for shame and pales as the night pales.

The hot earth sends up dust to blind the wanderer, and he weeps for his woman. "Will there be water at the edge of the wood?" the deer say anxiously: they have seen a small cloud upon the sky like fard.

The burned snake fails in the ardent dust, she lowers her head and forgets her hatred. She comes to lie under the shade of the prostrate peacock's tail spread high in the sunlight.

The breathless lion is dying, and his mane hangs piteously; the elephant with ivory swords esteems him not. He begs for water along the vanished rivers in the dust and the gold light. Also the wild boars dig into mud hairy with burnt grasses to escape the splendid sun.

The frog leaps from the dry marsh and goes to the snake; he lies under the black shadow of her swollen hood.

The buffaloes are driven, their muzzles are thick with a hot spume; lolling a baked tongue, each wanders wearily seeking for water.

Many birds pant on the spoiled trees. A dying ape draws himself under the thicket. Grasshoppers have fallen on the last cistern.

The lake is a moving slime, filled with dying fishes and dead lilies; the water birds have gone from it; it is poached by the feet of the anxious elephant.

Fear takes us suddenly as we look down upon the dead fields, for there is fire in the forest. In pastures on all that is new and the green latest born. It flares in the brittle windy leaves, and they fly forth.

The fire is a red flower; it eats the trees, the watery lianas and the buds on the branches. The wind is an angry fan, and the world a furnace. The crackings of the cane forest go clap from rock to rock, and the grasses burn; the beasts are cut off by the scarlet flame and go mad.

It climbs to the sky above the cotton trees. It is a gold snake in the crooks of the branches. It leaps at the sun and reddens the high storm of dead leaves.

The beasts come out from the burning forest, the elephants and the wild oxen and the lions come out with sparks upon them. They seek the river bed, but it is filled with islets; then there is peace between them, as with men before death.

Ah, may the season be favourable to you, my belovèd: a procession of mistresses, and nights of terraced pleasure; the palace has beds of lotus over cool water, laughing patalas, rays of distracting moon.

SEASON OF RAINS

The clouds advance like rutting elephants, enormous and full of rain; they come forward as kings among tumultuous armies; their flags are the lightning, the thunder is their drum.

The clouds come forward and mass together, like the dark blue petals of the lotus, like the full breasts of nursing women, like sombre fard upon the face of the sky.

They spread in rain, falling with a new sound and pleasing the soul, in rain the desperate chataka birds have awaited and now drink drop by drop in the high air.

The traveller grows afraid under the thunder, for the clouds have strings of bright lightning and shoot forth arrows of hail. The earth is starred with coloured mushrooms and new shoots, young grasses glittering with lapis. As diamonds upon a woman, so are her fireflies upon the earth, gold shepherds of Indra.

The tails of the peacocks are spread like separate flowers; they wake at the call of love and gather for dancing; the bees, supposing their feathers to be flowers, touch kisses among them.

The rivers are swollen with waves as tainted as harlots; they have burst their banks and snatched the trees away, and ever more swiftly roll to sea.

The woods have taken on a pleasant tiring, shoots on the trees, carpets of young grasses, and lotus fretted by the teeth of gazelles.

We are moved unaware to see the antelopes on guard, with flower eyes, fearful among the clearings.

And women on black nights wrapped with cloud are brave in spite of the thunder; they go to love by paths made bright with lightning. When the rolling of the thunder takes them in the arms of their lovers, they forget their difference; they grip them in terror.

But the neglected woman is weeping, and throws her jewel and her flower and her scent from her. There are tears out of the blue lilies which are her eyes, and her lips drink them; her lips which are the cups of red flowers.

A thick and yellow stream, rolling insects and earth and grasses, comes down like a rearing snake. Its deep throat threatens the frogs, and they watch it with stupefaction.

The black bees forsake the cups of the lotus, being wined with love. They hurl themselves upon the plumes of the peacock, esteeming him to be lotus of a new sort. They make a deep music with their thundering.

The wood elephants run in sounding herds, for the sky is mad, and they would taste its madness. A thunder cloud of bees is about them, lured by the rutting foam on their white tusks, as white as lotus.

The rocks are wet beneath the kisses of the cloud, the streams are hastening: the dance of the mad peacocks, the

202 scented marriage of rain to the young breeze, red nipas and orange kadambas: who is unmoved, my love?

The girls make themselves ready to be desirable, with mastic upon their mouths. They brighten their ears with coloured blossom. They set new pearls about their nipples, and let fall their hair.

Being and nature call in chorus: the rivers move forward and the lovers dream; rain is rustling, the peacock dances; the elephants trumpet and apes hunt for each other and the thickets glisten. And all things live and are moved and seek out their kind.

The sky has her lightnings and the bow of Indra; the women their diamonds and bright belts, but also crimson ketaki for their hair and blue keshara buds, also live jewels of kakubha to be their ear-rings.

The girl runs from her father's house to the bed of her lover; she has rubbed her body with sandal; she has thrown balm blossom among her hair, and sleeked it with black aguru. But the spirit of the deserted bride is rocked in the low clouds slowly, they are heavy with rain and blue with shadows; the lotus is a blue shadow rocking slowly.

Heat dies in the appeasing rain; the woods put out their joy in yellow flowers, in wind-touched branches, and buds breaking their capes like bursts of laughter.

The season has love garments for women, robes of mimosa and jasmine, scarce open blown flowers, and orange ear-rings of the wet kadamba.

Now we see women with strung pearls about red nipples, and with a white garment straining their haunches; a pleasant, an irresistible shade at their dividing, a godlike attraction.

The breeze, sifted with fresh rain, lilts in the flower-bended branches, stealing an odour from the pollens, bearing the souls of parted lovers.

The following quotations, showing the skill of Persian poets in the realm of Romance, are taken from Costello's *Rose Garden of Persia*.

THE FAIREST LAND

By Jelal-ed-din Rûmi

" *Tell me, gentle traveller, thou
    Who hast wandered far and wide,
Seen the sweetest roses blow,
    And the brightest rivers glide;
Say, of all thine eyes have seen,
Which the fairest land has been?* "

" *Lady, shall I tell thee where,
Nature seems most blest and fair,
Far above all climes beside?—
'T is where those we love abide:
And that little spot is best,
Which the loved one's foot hath pressed.*

" *Though it be a fairy space,
Wide and spreading is the place;
Though 't were but a barren mound,
'T would become enchanted ground.*

" *With thee yon sandy waste would seem,
The margin of Al Cawthar's stream;
And thou canst make a dungeon's gloom
A bower where new-born roses bloom.*"

ZULEIKA'S DREAM

By Jami

The ravens of the night were hush'd,
　The bird of dawn began his lay,
The rose-bud, newly-wakened, blush'd
　To feel the touch of springing day;
And bade the roses round unveil,
Roused by the warbling nightingale.
The jasmine stood all bathed in dew;
Wet were the violet's lids of blue.

Zuleika, fairer than the flowers,
　Lay tranced— for 't was not sleep that stole
Her senses, through the night's still hours,
　And raised new visions to her soul.
The heart, unfettered, free to rove,
Turned towards the idol of her love.
No:—'t was not sleep, 't was motionless,
　Unbroken thought, repressed in vain;
The shadow of the day's distress,
　A frenzy of remembered pain.

But, midst those pangs, what rapture still;
　The same dear form is ever there;
Those eyes the rays of Eden fill,
And odours of the blest distil
　From every curl of that bright hair!

His smiles!—such smiles as Houris wear,
　When from their caves of pearl they come,
And bid the true believer share
　The pleasures of their sacred home.
See, on his shoulder shines a star
　That glows and dazzles as he moves;
She feels its influence afar,
　She gazes, worships, hopes—and loves!

Oh! joy too great—oh! hour too blest!
  He comes—they hail him—now, more near,
  His eager courser's feet I hear.
Oh! heart, be hushed within my breast,
Burst not with rapture! Can it be?
  The idol of my life—divine,
All radiant, clothed in mystery,
  And loving me as I adore,
  As none dared ever love before,
Shall be—nay, is—even now, is mine!

I will be patient: but his breath
Seems stealing o'er my senses—death
Were better than suspense like this—
One draught—though 't were the last—of bliss!
One glance, though in that glance I die,
To prove the glorious certainty!

Not he! not he! on whom for years
  My soul has dwelt with sacred truth;
For whom my life has passed in tears,
  And wasted was my bloom of youth:
For whom I breathed, and thought, and moved,
My own, my worshipped, my beloved!
I hailed the night, that I might gaze
Upon his star's unconquered blaze:
The morn but rose that I might pray,
Hope, wish, expect from day to day,
My sole existence was that thought,
And do I wake to know 't is nought?
Vain tears, vain madness, vain endeavour,
Another blasts my sight for ever!

Dawn upon the wide world broke,
And the sun's warm rays awoke;
Scattering o'er the cloudy sky
Hues of rich variety:
Such bright tinting as illumes
With its rays the peacock's plumes,

And the parrot's feathers bright,
Touches with a starry light.
The Asis rides in kingly guise;
Yon curtained litter holds the prize
More precious than all wealth beside—
His own, his young, his peerless bride.

Around, afar, of homage proud,
In countless ranks his warriors crowd,
Well may the lordly Asis boast
The glories of his gorgeous host.

Rich are the veils, profusely spread,
That canopy the fair one's head;
Like some delicious tree that throws
Its shade, inviting to repose:
And, like soft turf, the carpets lie,
Bedecked with gay embroidery.

The temple moves, all glorious, on—
Throned in the midst the happy one.
All heaven resounds with shout and song,
As the bright pageant sweeps along.
The camel-drivers' cries succeed,
Urging their stately beasts to speed,
Whose hoofs, with swift and frequent tread,
The sands with moon-like forms have spread:
The earth is ploughed by coursers' feet,
And still fresh hosts the wounds repeat.
Many a fair and blushing maid
Exulted in the gay parade:
And all, who called the Asis lord,
Hailed the fair idol he adored,

But she—" the beautiful," " the blest "—
What pangs, what tumults shook her breast!
She sat, concealed from every eye,
Alone—in hopeless misery.

" Oh, Fate! " she cried; " Oh, ruthless Fate!
Why am I made thy mark of hate:
Why must my heart thy victim be?
Thus lost, abandoned—crushed by thee!
Thou camest, in troubled dreams, and stole
The peace, the pleasure of my soul,
In visions that the blest might share,
Whose only fruit has been despair.
I see each glittering fabric fall;
But vain reproach, vain trust, vain all!
For help, for rest, where can I fly,
My heart is riven—let me die.
Have I then lingered long in pain,
In sad suspense, in musings vain,
To be—oh, crowning grief!—betrayed,
In foreign lands a victim made.

" Relentless destiny! accurst
Were all the joys thy visions nurst.
Is there no drop of hope left yet?
Must I all promises forget?
Dash not my cup to earth: say, Power benign,
I am be blest—even yet he may be mine! "
Thus raved Zuleika, when without
Arose the sudden deafening shout
That hailed the close of all their toil—
" Lo!—Memphis! and the banks of Nile! "

Then, far and wide, the glittering ranks
Rush to the flowery river's banks.
The Asis' sign his slaves obey,
Gold, silver, flowers, bestrew the way:
And o'er the litter gems are thrown,
Whose countless rays like meteors shone;
As thick they fall as on the rose
Hang the rich dews at evening's close;
The courser's feet on rubies trod,
O'er mounds of gold the camel strode.

On swept the train—one gorgeous mile,
Planting with gems the banks of Nile;
The proud stream rolled its waters deep,
O'er pearls in many a shining heap:
Each shell was filled with pearls; each scale
That clothed the crocodile in mail,
Was changed to silver, as he lay
And basked amidst the fervid ray.

And onward to the palace gate
The train pour'd on, in sumptuous state,
The glowing portals opened wide,—
In flow'd the overwhelming tide,
Ushering the Asis and his bride.

A throne the Peris might have framed,
The sun and moon's pale lustre shamed:
And she, whose radiance all effaced—
Zuleika—on the throne was placed.
Sparkling with jewels, red with gold,
Her heart shrunk, withered, crushed, and cold;
Altho' a feverish sense of pain
Frenzied her mind and seared her brain:
As on a flaming hearth she sat—
Amidst rejoicing—desolate!
Laden with many a priceless gem,
Crown'd with a gorgeous diadem,
Each pearl a poisonous drop appears:
And from her eyes fall scalding tears.

And thus a crown is gained—for this,
We leave all thoughts of present bliss!
We toil, we strive, we live in care,
And in the end possess—despair!
Our sun of youth, of hope, is set,
And all our guerdon is—regret!

Is this a dream!—another dream,
    Like that which stole my senses first,
Which sparkled o'er my life's dull stream,
    By idle, erring fancy nursed?

Was it for this my life I spent
In murmurs deep, and discontent—
Slighted, for this, all homage due,
From gen'rous, faithful love withdrew?
For this, no joy, no pomp have prized;
For this, all honours have despised—
Left all my soul to passion free
To be thus hated—spurn'd—by thee!
Oh, God!—to see thee loathing turn,
While on my cheek swift blushes burn;
Contempt, abhorrence on thy brow,
Where radiant sweetness dwelt—till now!
Thy bitter accents, fierce, severe,
In harsh, unwonted tones to hear:
Thy horror, thy disgust to view,
And know thy accusations true!
All, all but this I could have borne,—
A husband's vengeance and his scorn;
To be reproached, disgraced, reviled,
So Yussuf on his victim smiled.
I would, amidst the desert's gloom,
Have hailed, with thee, a living tomb;
My home, my state, my birth forgot,
And, with thy love, embraced thy lot;
Had taught my heart all pangs to share,
And prove what perfect love can dare.

Let me look back to that dark hour
That bound my spirit to thy power—
Thy grateful words, thy glance recall,
My hopes, my love—and curse them all!
Let me thy tender looks retrace,
The glories of thy heavenly face;
Thy brow where Aden's splendour lies,
And the mild lustre of thine eyes:
Yet, let my heart no weakness prove,
But hate thee as I once could love.

What fearful eloquence was thine,
What awful anger—just—divine!

o

Shuddering, I saw my heart display'd,
And knew all this I should have said!
'T was mine to shrink, withstand, in time,
For, while I sinned, I knew my crime.

Oh! wretched, wavering heart!—as vain
Thy wild resentment as thy pain:
One thought alone expels the rest,
One sole regret distracts my breast,
O'ermastering and subduing all—
More than my crime, more than my fall:
Are not shame, fear, remorse, forgot,
In that one thought—he loves me not!

Though in a dark and narrow cell
The "fair beloved" confined may dwell,
No prison is that dismal place,
'T is filled with dignity and grace:
And the damp vaults and gloom around
Are joyous Spring, with roses crown'd.

Not Paradise to me were fair
If he were not a dweller there;
Without his presence all is night,
My soul awakes but in his sight:
Though this frail tenement of clay
    May here amidst its pomp remain,
My spirit wanders far away,
    And dwells with his in prisoned pain.

Yussuf's Acknowledgment.

Not love thee!—ah! how much I loved
Long absent years of grief have proved.
Severe rebuke, assumed disdain,
Dwelt in my words and looks in vain:
I would not passion's victim be,
And turned from sin—but not from thee.
My love was pure, no plant of earth
From my rapt being sprung to birth:

I loved as angels might adore,
And sought, and wish'd, and hop'd no more.
Virtue was my belov'd: and thou
Hadst virtue's impress on thy brow.
Thy weakness showed how frail is all
That erring mortals goodness call.
I thank'd thee, and reproach'd thee not
For all the sufferings of my lot.
The God we worship was my friend,
And led me to my destined end,
Taught the great lesson to thy heart
That vice and bliss are wide apart;
And join'd us now, that we may prove
With perfect virtue, perfect love.

THE LABOURS OF FERHÂD

By Niẓami

Khosrû Parviz lived A.D. 590: he was a prince of exalted virtues and great magnificence: he fought against the Greek emperors with success, but was at last defeated by Heraclius. He is said to have married a daughter of the Emperor Maurice, named Irene, called by the Persians Shireen, or Sweet.

Ferhâd's history forms a tragical episode in this romance. He was a statuary, celebrated throughout the East for his great genius, but was daring enough to fix his affections on the beloved of a king. The jealousy of Khosrû was excited, and he lamented to his courtiers the existence of a passion which was so violent as not to be concealed, and which gave him great uneasiness. He was recommended to employ Ferhâd in such a manner as to occupy his whole life, and divert him from his dangerous dream: accordingly, as on one occasion the fair Shireen had, somewhat unreasonably, required of her royal lover a *river of milk*, he made her desire a pretext for the labours he imposed on his presumptuous rival.

Ferhâd was summoned to the presence of Khosrû, and

commissioned by the king to execute a work which should render his name immortal, but one which, to accomplish, demanded almost superhuman powers: this was to clear away all impediments which obstructed the passage of the great mountain of Beysitoun, at that time impassable in consequence of its mighty masses of rock and stone. He commanded him, after having done this, to cause the rivers on the opposite side of the mountain to join.

Ferhâd, nothing daunted, replied that he would remove the very heart of the rock from the king's path; but on condition that the lovely Shireen should be the reward of his labours. Khosrû, secretly triumphing in the conviction that what the artist undertook was impossible, consented to his terms, and the indefatigable lover began his work.

> *On lofty Beysitoun the lingering sun*
> *Looks down on ceaseless labours, long begun:*
> *The mountain trembles to the echoing sound*
> *Of falling rocks, that from her sides rebound.*
> *Each day all respite, all repose denied—*
> *No truce, no pause, the thundering strokes are plied;*
> *The mist of night around her summit coils,*
> *But still Ferhâd, the lover-artist, toils,*
> *And still—the flashes of his axe between—*
> *He sighs to ev'ry wind, " Alas! Shireen!*
> *Alas! Shireen!—my task is well-nigh done,*
> *The goal in view for which I strive alone.*
> *Love grants me powers that Nature might deny;*
> *And whatsoe'er my doom, the world shall tell,*
> *Thy lover gave to immortality*
> *Her name he loved—so fatally—so well! "*

The enamoured sculptor prophesied aright; for the wonderful efforts made by this " slave of love " left imperishable monuments of his devotion, in the *carved caverns* which, to this day, excite the amazement and admiration of the traveller who visits the Kesr-e-Shireen, or " Villa of Shireen," and follows the stream called Joui-shur, or

" stream of milk," which flows from the mountain, between Hamadân and Hulwân.

Ferhâd first constructed a recess or chamber in the rock, wherein he carved the figure of Shireen, near the front of the opening: she was represented surrounded by attendants and guards; while in the centre of the cave was an equestrian statue of Khosrû, clothed in armour, the workmanship so exquisite that the nails and buttons of the coat of mail were clearly to be seen, and are said to be so still. An eye-witness says—" Whoso looks on the stone would imagine it to be animated." The chamber and the statues remain still there. As Ferhâd continued to hew away pieces of the rock, which *are like so many columns*, the task was soon performed. The vestiges of the chisel remain, so that the sculptures appear recent. The horse of Khosrû was exquisitely carved: it was called Shebdiz.

THE GREAT WORK

A hundred arms were weak one block to move
Of thousands, moulded by the hand of Love
Into fantastic shapes and forms of grace,
Which crowd each nook of that majestic place.

The piles give way, the rocky peaks divide,
The stream comes gushing on—a foaming tide!
A mighty work, for ages to remain,
The token of his passion and his pain.

As flows the milky flood from Allah's throne,
Rushes the torrent from the yielding stone;
And sculptured there, amazed, stern Khosrû stands,
And sees, with frowns, obeyed his harsh commands:
While she, the fair beloved, with being rife,
Awakes the glowing marble into life.

Ah! hapless youth; ah! toil repaid by woe,—
A king thy rival and the world thy foe!
Will she wealth, splendour, pomp for thee resign?
And only genius, truth, and passion thine!

Around the pair, lo! groups of courtiers wait,
And slaves and pages crowd in solemn state;
From columns imaged wreaths their garlands throw,
And fretted roofs with stars appear to glow;
Fresh leaves and blossoms seem around to spring,
And feathered throngs their loves are murmuring;
The hands of Peris might have wrought those stems,
Where dewdrops hang their fragile diadems;
And strings of pearl and sharp-cut diamonds shine,
New from the wave, or recent from the mine.

" Alas! Shireen! " at every stroke he cries;
At every stroke fresh miracles arise:
" For thee these glories and these wonders all,
For thee I triumph, or for thee I fall;
For thee my life one ceaseless toil has been,
Inspire my soul anew—Alas! Shireen! "

The task of the rival of Khosrû was at length completed, and the king heard with dismay of his success: all the courtiers were terrified at the result of their advice, and saw that some further stratagem was necessary. They therefore engaged an old woman who had been known to Ferhâd, and in whom he had confidence, to report to him tidings which would at once destroy his hopes.

THE MESSENGER

What raven note disturbs his musing mood:
What form comes stealing on his solitude?
Ungentle messenger, whose word of ill,
All the warm feelings of his soul can chill!

" Cease, idle youth, to waste thy days," she said,
" By empty hopes a visionary made;
Why in vain toil thy fleeting life consume
To frame a palace?—rather hew a tomb.
Even like sere leaves that autumn winds have shed,
Perish thy labours, for—Shireen is dead! "

He heard the fatal news—no word, no groan;
He spoke not, moved not,—stood transfixed to stone.
Then with a frenzied start, he raised on high
His arms, and wildly tossed them towards the sky;
Far in the wide expanse, his axe he flung,
And from the precipice at once he sprung.
The rocks, the sculptured caves, the valleys green,
Sent back his dying cry—" Alas! Shireen! "

The legend goes on to relate that the handle of the axe flung away by Ferhâd, being of pomegranate wood, took root on the spot where it fell, and became a flourishing tree: it possessed healing powers, and was much resorted to by believers long afterwards.

Khosrû, on learning this catastrophe, did not conceal his satisfaction, but liberally rewarded the old woman who had caused so fatal a termination to the career of his rival; but the gentle-hearted Shireen heard of his fate with grief, and shed many tears on his tomb.

The charms of Shireen were destined to create mischief, for the king had a son by a former marriage, who became enamoured of his fatally beautiful mother-in-law. His father, Khosrû, was, in the end, murdered by his hand, and Shireen became the object of his importunities. Wearied, at length, with constant struggles, she feigned to give him a favourable answer, and promised, if he would permit her to visit the grave of her husband, *when she returned* she would be his. Shireen accordingly went on her melancholy errand, and true to her affection for her beloved Khosrû, stabbed herself, and died upon his tomb.

From the SHAH NAMAH of Ferdusi :

JAMSHID'S LOVE-MAKING

A weary traveller sat to grieve
  By Gureng's gate, at early eve,
Where fragrant gardens, filled with bloom,
Cast forth their breath of soft perfume,
And wandering o'er his brow and face,
Relieved him for a moment's space.
But sorrow weighed upon his breast,
  And dimmed the lustre of his eye;
He had no home—he sought but rest,
  And laid him down to sleep—or die!

King Gureng's lovely daughter lies
  Beside a fountain gently playing;
She marks not though the waves be bright,
Nor in the roses takes delight:
And though her maids new games devise,
Invent fresh stories to surprise,
  She heeds not what each fair is saying:
Her fav'rite's voice has lost its spell,
The raven charms her ear as well!

But hark! soft whispers, questions gay,
  Amongst the female train prevail;
A young slave, beautiful as day,
  Blushes while she tells her tale.
" Nay, mock me not,—no face so fair
  Was seen on earth till now:
Though on his cheek are hues of care,
  And grief has marked his brow:
Ah! cruel maids, ye smile and doubt,
While the poor stranger faints without! "

The princess heard: " Go hence," she cried,
" And be the stranger's wants supplied:
Let him beneath our shades repose,
And find a refuge for his woes."

The ready damsels straight obey,
And seek the trav'ller where he lay.
" Arise, fair youth, the wine-cup waits,
And roses bloom within our gates,
The tulip bids thee welcome be,
And the young moon has risen for thee."

Meanwhile the princess mused alone,
And thus she sighed, in mournful tone:—
" Alas! they told me 't was my fate;
But ah! I feel 't is all too late:
I cannot now believe—'t was vain—
That dream can never come again!
And yet my nurse—who knows full well
Each herb and ev'ry potent spell,
From the cold wave can conjure fire,
And quell the mighty dragon's ire,
From stones soft dewdrops can distil,
And awe the Dives *with wondrous skill,*
Knows ev'ry star—has said that mine
Glowed with an aspect all divine.
That he, whose image is imprest,
As if by magic on my breast,
Whose portrait cheers my solitude,—
The mighty Jamshid, great and good;
Of whose rare beauty they recount,
When he descended from the mount,
So bright the lustre, those who saw
Proclaimed two suns, and knelt in awe;
For whom the chains of death were riven,
Whom angels clothed in robes of heaven;
That prince whose power was far above
All those who vainly seek my love;
She said he should be mine—vain thought!

Is he not fall'n, to ruin brought;
His kingdom gone, his fortune crost,
And he, perhaps, for ever lost! "

She ceased, when lo! the laughing train
    Came dancing back, with song and jest,
And leading, in a flowery chain,
    The stranger youth their welcome guest.
'T was thus they met—they met and gazed,
    Struck by the self-same power—amazed;
Confused, admiring, pleased, distressed,
    As passion rose in either breast.

The princess spoke—soft as a bird
    In Spring to some dear partner sighing;
And the fair stranger's words were heard,
    Sweet as the bul-bul's *notes replying.*

Her long hair, streaming to the ground
With odours fills the air around;
She moves to music and to song,
As the wild partridge steps along

She leads him to her jasmine bower,
    Midst fountains, birds, and blossoms sweet;
And her attendant maidens shower
    The sparkling wave upon his feet;
Two doves sat near, and softly mourned,
And both their hearts each sigh returned.

With wine, and verse, and wit awhile,
The happy moments they beguile;
But clouds passed o'er the fair one's brow,
    She feared, she doubted,—" Go! " she cried;
" Bring here my long-unbended bow,
    And let my former art be tried.
Two birds are seated on one tree,
Tell me which bird my mark shall be;
And thou shalt know a woman's skill
Can make all captive to her will! "

The stranger smiled with haughty look,
As from her hand the bow he took:
" Thy fame," he said, " to me is known;
Valour, like beauty, is thy own:
But know, though bold in camp and field,
Woman to man is forced to yield.
Princess, a boon! If I have wit
And skill the female bird to hit,
Shall she who makes these groves divine,
She whom I most admire, be mine? "

She blushed assent—the arrow flew;
   The female bird mounts to the skies;
His shaft has struck her pinions through,
   And fluttering on the ground she lies.

The fair one's eyes with triumph shine:
   " The son of Tahúmers I see!
For never yet could hand but mine
   Bend that charmed bow—'t is he—'t is he! "

So spake her heart. " Give me the bow! "
   She said aloud; " if true my aim,
Let him who seeks me take me now,
   No better boon my hopes can claim."

My tale is told. Ye lovers, say,
   Can ye not guess the blissful close?
How Jamshid won a bride that day,
   And found a balm for all his woes.

POEMS

By Sir Rabindranath Tagore

The axe begged humbly, " O thou mighty oak,
  Lend me only a piece of thy branch—
Just enough to fit me with a handle."
The handle was ready, and there was no more wasting of time.
The beggar at once commenced business—and hit hard at the
  root,
And there was the end of the oak.

The favourite damsel said, " Sire, that other wretched queen of
  thine,
Is unfathomably deep in her cunning greed.
Thou didst graciously assign her a corner of thy cowshed,
It is only to give her chances to have milk from thy cow for
  nothing."
The king pondered deeply and said, " I suspect thou hast hit
  the real truth.
But I know not how to put a stop to this thieving."
The favourite said, " 'Tis simple. Let me have the royal cow
And I will take care that none milk her but myself."

Said the beggar's wallet, " Come, my brother purse,
Between us two the difference is so very small,
Let us exchange ! " The purse snapped short and sharp,
" First let that very small difference cease ! "

The highest goes hand in hand with the lowest.
It is only the commonplace who walks at a distance.

The thirsty ass went to the brink of the lake
And came back exclaiming, " O how dark is the water ! "
The lake smiled and said, " Every ass thinks the water black,
But he who knows better is sure that it is white."

Time says, " It is I who create this world."
The clock says, " Then I am thy creator."

The flower cries loudly, " Fruit, my fruit,
Where art thou loitering—Oh how far ! "
" Why is such a clamour ? "   The fruit says in answer,
" I ever live in your heart taking form."

The man says, " I am strong, I do whatever I wish."
" Oh what a shame ! " says the woman with a blush.
" Thou art restrained at every step," says the man.
The poet says, " that is why the woman is so beautiful."

" All my perfume goes out, I cannot keep it shut."
Thus murmurs the flower and beckons back its breath.
The breeze whispers gently, " You must ever remember this—
It is not your perfume at all which is not given out to others."

The water in the pitcher is bright and transparent;
But the ocean is dark and deep.
The little truths have words that are clear;
The great truth is greatly obscure and silent.

A little flower blooms in the chink of a garden wall.
She has no name nor fame.
The garden worthies disdain to give her a glance.
The sun comes up and greets her, " How is my little beauty ? "

Love comes smiling with empty hands.
Flattery asks him, " What wealth didst thou win ? "
Love says, " I cannot show it, it is in my heart."
Flattery says, " I am practical.   What I get I gather in
    both hands."

" Who will take up my work ? " asks the setting sun.
None has an answer in the whole silent world.
The earthen lamp says humbly from a corner,
" I will, my lord, as best as I can."

222

The arrow thinks to himself, " I fly, I am free,
Only the bow is motionless and fixed."
The bow divines his mind and says, " When wilt thou know
the truth,
That thy freedom is ever dependent on me? "

The moon gives light to the whole creation,
But keeps the dark spot only to herself.

" Restless ocean, what endless speech is thine? "
" It is the question eternal," answered the sea.
" What is there in thy stillness, thou ancient line of hills? "
" It is the silence everlasting," came the answer.

In the morn the moon is to lose her sovereignty,
Yet there is smile on her face when she says,
" I wait at the edge of the western sea
To greet the rising sun, bow low, and then depart."

The word says, " When I notice thee, O work,
I am ashamed of my own little emptiness."
The work says, " I feel how utterly poor I am;
I never can attain the fulness which thou hast."

If you at night shed tears for the lost daylight
You get not back the sun but miss all the stars instead.

I ask my destiny—What power is this
That cruelly drives me onward without rest?
My destiny says, " Look round! " I turn back and see
It is I myself that is ever pushing me from behind.

The ashes whisper, " The fire is our brother."
The smoke curls up and says, " We are twins."
" I have no kinship," the firefly says, " with the flame—
But I know I am more than a brother to him."

The night comes stealthily into the forest and loads its branches
With buds and blossoms, then retires with silent steps.
The flowers waken and cry—" To the morning we owe our all."
And the morn asserts with a noise, " Yes, it is doubtlessly true."

The night kissed the departing day and whispered,
" I am death, thy mother, fear me not.
I take thee unto me only to give thee a new birth
And make thee eternally fresh."

Death, if thou wert the void that our fear let us imagine,
In a moment the universe would disappear through the chasm.
But thou art the fulfilment eternal,
And the world ever rocks on thy arms like a child.

Death threatens, " I will take thy dear ones."   The thief says,
*   " Thy money is mine."*
Fate says, " I'll take as my tribute whatever is thine own."
The detractor says, " I'll rob you of your good name."
The poet says, " But who is there to take my joy from me? "

PASSAGES FROM A HYMN DEDICATED TO THE
GODDESS PEACE IN THE ATHARVA VEDA

By Sir Rabindranath Tagore

Peaceful be all motives and peaceful our works done and
yet to be done.

May the past bring us peace and the future, may everything be for our peace.

The Spirit of Speech dwells in and is made active by the
Supreme Being. She is potent in creating fearfulness.
May she offer us peace.

Our five senses and our mind are made active in our soul
by the Supreme Being. They are potent in creating
fearfulness. May they work for our peace.

With the peace that pervades the earth, the sky, the
starry heavens, the water, the plants and trees; with the
peace that dwells with the guardian spirits of the world
and in the divinity within us, let us tranquillize things
fierce and cruel and evil, into the serene and the good.
May everything be for our peace.

By Sir Rabindranath Tagore

We are all the more one because we are many,
For we have made ample room for love in the gap where we
are sundered.
Our unlikeness reveals its breadth of beauty radiant with one
common life,
Like mountain peaks in the morning sun.

AHALYA

(Ahalya, sinning against the purity of married love, incurred
her husband's curse, turning into a stone to be restored
to her humanity by the touch of Ramchandra.)

Struck with the curse in midwave of your tumultuous
passion your life stilled into a stone, clean, cool and
impassive.
You took your sacred bath of dust, plunging deep into the
primitive peace of the earth.
You lay down in the dumb immense where faded days drop,
like dead flowers with seeds, to sprout again into new
dawns.
You felt the thrill of the sun's kiss with the roots of grass
and trees that are like infant's fingers clasping at mother's
breast.
In the night, when the tired children of dust came back to the
dust, their rhythmic breath touched you with the large
and placid motherliness of the earth.
Wild weeds twined round you their bonds of flowering intimacy;
You were lapped by the sea of life whose ripples are the leaves'
flutter, bees' flight, grasshoppers' dance and tremor of
moths' wings.
For ages you kept your ear to the ground, counting the foot-
steps of the unseen comer, at whose touch silence flames
into music.

Woman, the sin has stripped you naked, the curse has washed 225
you pure, you have risen into a perfect life.
The dew of that unfathomed night trembles on your eyelids,
the mosses of ever-green years cling to your hair.
You have the wonder of new birth and the wonder of old time
in your awakening.
You are young as the newborn flowers and old as the hills.

THE MAIDEN'S SMILE

Translated by Sir Rabindranath Tagore

From a Bengali Poem by Devendranath Sen

Methinks, my love, in the dim daybreak of life, before you
came to this shore
You stood by some river-source of run-away dreams filling
your blood with its liquid notes.
Or, perhaps, your path was through the shade of the garden
of gods where the merry multitude of jasmines, lilies and
white oleanders fell in your arms in heaps and entering
your heart became boisterous.
Your laughter is a song whose words are drowned in the tunes,
an odour of flowers unseen.
It is like moonlight rushing through your lips' window when
the midnight moon is high up in your heart's sky.
I ask for no reason, I forget the cause, I only know that your
laughter is the tumult of insurgent life.

MY OFFENCE

Translated by Sir Rabindranath Tagore

From a Bengali Poem by Devendranath Sen

When you smilingly held up to me, my sweet, your child of
six months, and I said, " Keep him in your arms,"
Why did a sudden cloud pass over your face, a cloud of pent-up
rain and hidden lightning?
Was my offence so great?

226 *When the rose-bud, nestling in the branch, smiles back to the laughing morn, is there any cause for anger if I refuse to steal it from its leaves' cradle.*

Or when the Kokil fills the heart of the spring's happy hours with love-dreams, am I to blame if I cannot conspire to imprison it in a cage?

THE UNNAMED CHILD

Translated from the Bengali of Debendra Sen

By Sir Rabindranath Tagore

She is a child of six months, lacking the dignity of a name.
She is like a dewdrop hanging on the tip of a Kamini bud;
like the peep of the first moon through the tresses of the night;
like a pearl in the earring of the tiniest little fairy.
Her elder sister clasps her to her breast, crying, " You are sweet as my new pet doll,"—
and her baby brother likens her to a pink sugar drop.
Thus while the whole household casts about in vain for a simile to fit her, she nods her head opening her eyes wide.

SOME CHINESE CLASSICAL POETRY
Rendered by L. Cranmer-Byng

A FEAST OF LANTERNS

ALONG THE STREAM
By Li Po

The rustling nightfall strews my gown with roses,
   And wine-flushed petals bring forgetfulness
Of shadow after shadow striding past.
I arise with the stars exultantly and follow
The sweep of the moon along the hushing stream,
Where no birds wake; only the far-drawn sigh
Of wary voices whispering farewell.

THE PALACE OF CHAO-YANG
By Li Po

No more the peach-tree droops beneath the snow;
   Spring draws her breath the willow boughs among.
   The mango-bird now maddens into song,
And the swift-building swallows come and go.
'Tis the time of the long daydreams, when laughing maybeams,
   On the mats of slothful revellers play;
'Tis the time of glancing wings, and the dancing
   Of moon-moths whirling the hours away;
When the golden armoured guardians are withdrawn,
And pleasure haunts the rustling woods till dawn.
A warm and perfumed wind
   Strays through the palace blind
And wandering prys into some dim retreat
   Where every whisper stirs the heart to beat.
Now all the gay parterres
   Are rivals for the sun

That drains their jewelled goblets one by one
   From dimpled terrace and green dewy stairs.
And the water-lily renders to the spring
The wonder of her white unbosoming.
   Far away in the tall woods there is an oriole calling;
There are shadows in the blue pavilion of dancers, and music
     rising and falling,
In the month of peach-bloom and plum-bloom, in the silken-
    screened recess
Love is the burden of sweet voices, and the brief night melting,
    and the long caress.

MYSELF

By Po Chü-i

What of myself?
I am like unto the sere chrysanthemum
That is shorn by the frost blade, and, torn from its roots,
Whirled away on the wind.
Once in the valleys of Ch'in and Yung I rambled at will,
Now ring me round the unfriendly plains of the wild folk of Pa.
O galloping dawns with Youth and Ambition riding knee to
    knee!
Ride on, Youth, with the galloping dawns and dappled days!
I am unhorsed, outventured—
I, who crouch by the crumbling embers, old, and grey, and alone.
One great hour of noon with the sky-faring Rukh
I clanged on the golden dome of Heaven.
Now in the long dusk of adversity
I have found my palace of contentment my dream pavilion;
Even the tiny twig of the little humble wren.

ON WAKING FROM SLEEP

By Liu Ch'ang

At noon comes rest from the long routine;
I launch my boat on the lilied pond and float
Till I drift without will into sleep.

Green shadows lattice the waters green;
Courtyard and house the silence keep.
Then a bird breaks over the mountain-side
And falls and calls from the crimson coronals
Of the woods that awake to her cry.
My silken robes in the wind float wide.
O wings of delight, draw nigh! draw nigh!

LINES WRITTEN IN EXILE

By Yang Chi

As pure as autumn water falls the dew;
And cool of night is born when faintly sighs
The wind, that outcast of the twilight, dies,
And the green gloom of random grass anew
Covers the undulating shores.   I see
Far out upon the lake an island gleaming
With a girdle of red nenuphar, and, dreaming,
I fill my sail o' dreams in search of thee.
Cold eyes of strangers follow me, and fears
Start with the trumpet from the ramparts blown.
And on my darkened robes are sown
Two pearls, my tears.

ONE HUNDRED AND SEVENTY CHINESE POEMS

Translated by Arthur Waley

A VISION

By Ts'ao Chih

*I*n the Nine Provinces there is not room enough:
    I want to soar high among the clouds,
And, far beyond the Eight Limits of the compass,
Cast my gaze across the unmeasured void.
I will wear as my gown the red mists of sunrise,
And as my skirt the white fringes of the clouds:
My canopy—the dim lustre of Space:
My chariot—six dragons mounting heavenward:
And before the light of Time has shifted a pace
Suddenly stand upon the World's blue rim.
    The doors of Heaven swing open,
The double gates shine with a red light.
I roam and linger in the palace of Wen-ch'ang,
I climb up to the hall of T'ai-wei.
The Lord God lies at his western lattice:
And the lesser Spirits are together in the eastern gallery.
They wash me in a bath of rainbow-spray
And gird me with a belt of jasper and rubies.
I wander at my ease gathering divine herbs:
I bend down and touch the scented flowers.
Wang-tzu gives me drugs of long-life
And Hsien-men hands me strange potions.
By the partaking of food I evade the rites of Death:
My span is extended to the enjoyment of life everlasting.

By T'ao Ch'ien

In the month of June the grass grows high
And round my cottage thick-leaved branches sway.
There is not a bird but delights in the place where it rests:
And I too—love my thatched cottage.
I have done my ploughing:
I have sown my seed.
Again I have time to sit and read my books.
In the narrow lane there are no deep ruts:
Often my friends' carriages turn back.
In high spirits I pour out my spring wine
And pluck the lettuce growing in my garden.
A gentle rain comes stealing up from the east
And a sweet wind bears it company.
My thoughts float idly over the story of King Chou,
My eyes wander over the pictures of Hills and Seas.
At a single glance I survey the whole Universe.
He will never be happy, whom such pleasures fail to please!

PEOPLE HIDE THEIR LOVE

By Wu-ti

Who says
That it's by my desire,
This separation, this living so far from you?
My dress still smells of the lavender you gave:
My hand still holds the letter that you sent.
Round my waist I wear a double sash:
I dream that it binds us both with a same-heart knot.
Did not you know that people hide their love,
Like a flower that seems too precious to be picked?

ON THE BIRTH OF HIS SON

By Su Tung-p'o

Families, when a child is born
Want it to be intelligent.
I, through intelligence,
Having wrecked my whole life,
Only hope that baby will prove
Ignorant and stupid.
Then he will crown a tranquil life
By becoming a Cabinet Minister.

THE FLOWER MARKET

By Po Chü-i

In the Royal City spring is almost over:
Tinkle, tinkle—the coaches and horsemen pass.
We tell each other " This is the peony season ":
And follow with the crowd that goes to the Flower Market.
" Cheap and dear—no uniform price:
The cost of the plant depends on the number of blossoms.
For the fine flower,—a hundred pieces of damask:
For the cheap flower,—five bits of silk.
Above is spread an awning to protect them:
Around is woven a wattle-fence to screen them.
If you sprinkle water and cover the roots with mud,
When they are transplanted, they will not lose their beauty."
Each household thoughtlessly follows the custom,
Man by man, no one realizing.
There happened to be an old farm labourer who came by
chance that way.
He bowed his head and sighed a deep sigh:
But this sigh nobody understood.
He was thinking, " A cluster of deep-red flowers
Would pay the taxes of ten poor houses."

REALIZING THE FUTILITY OF LIFE

(Written on the wall of a priest's cell)

Ever since the time when I was a lusty boy
Down till now when I am ill and old,
The things I have cared for have been different at different
times,
But my being busy, that *has never changed.*
Then *on the shore,—building sand-pagodas;*
Now, *at Court, covered with tinkling jade.*
This and that,—equally childish games,
Things whose substance passes in a moment of time!
While the hands are busy, the heart cannot understand;
When there are no Scriptures, then Doctrine is sound.
Even should one zealously strive to learn the Way,
That very striving will make one's error more.

BOOK IV

National Literature, Essays, War Songs, and Miscellaneous

LECTURES ON THE RECONSTRUCTION OF RELIGIOUS THOUGHT IN ISLAM

By Sir Mohammad Iqbal

THE CONCEPTION OF GOD AND THE MEANING OF PRAYER

By Sir Mohammad Iqbal

We have seen that the judgment based upon religious experience fully satisfies the intellectual test. The more important regions of experience, examined with an eye on a synthetic view, reveal, as the ultimate ground of all experience, a rationally directed creative will which we have found reasons to describe as an ego. In order to emphasize the individuality of the Ultimate Ego the Quran gives Him the proper name of Allah, and further defines Him as follows:

> " *Say: God is One:*
> *God the mateless!*
> *He begetteth not, and He is not begotten;*
> *And there is none like unto Him.*"

But it is hard to understand what exactly is an individual. As Bergson has taught us in his *Creative Evolution*, individuality is a matter of degrees and is not fully realized even in the case of the apparently closed off unity of the human being. " In particular, it may be said of individuality," says Bergson, " that while the tendency to individuate is everywhere present in the organized world, it is always opposed by the tendency towards reproduction. For the individuality to be perfect, it would be necessary that no detached part of the organism could live separately. But then reproduction would be impossible. For what is reproduction but the building up of a new organism with

238 a detached fragment of the old? Individuality, therefore, harbours its own enemy at home." In the light of this passage it is clear that the perfect individual, closed off as an ego, peerless and unique, cannot be conceived as harbouring its own enemy at home. It must be conceived as superior to the antagonistic tendency of reproduction. This characteristic of the perfect ego is one of the most essential elements in the Quranic conception of God; and the Quran mentions it over and over again, not so much with a view to attack the current Christian conception as to accentuate its own view of a perfect individual. It may, however, be said that the history of religious thought discloses various ways of escape from an individualistic conception of the ultimate Reality which is conceived as some vague, vast and pervasive cosmic element, such as light. This is the view that Farnell has taken in his Gifford lectures on the attributes of God. I agree that the history of religion reveals modes of thought that tend towards pantheism; but I venture to think that in so far as the Quranic identification of God with light is concerned Farnell's view is incorrect. The full text of the verse of which he quotes a portion only is as follows:

" God is the light of the Heavens and of the earth. His light is like a niche in which is a lamp—the lamp encased in a glass,—the glass, as it were, a star." (24: 35).

No doubt, the opening sentence of the verse gives the impression of an escape from an individualistic conception of God. But when we follow the metaphor of light in the rest of the verse, it gives just the opposite impression. The development of the metaphor is meant rather to exclude the suggestion of a formless cosmic element by centralizing the light in a flame which is further individualized by its encasement in a glass likened unto a well-defined star. Personally I think the description of God as light, in the revealed literature of Judaism, Christianity and Islam, must now be interpreted differently. The teaching of modern physics is that the velocity of light cannot be exceeded and is the same for all observers whatever their own system of movement. Thus, in the world of change, light is the nearest approach to the Absolute. The metaphor of light as applied to God, therefore, must, in view of modern knowledge, be taken to suggest the Absoluteness of God and not His Omnipresence which easily lends itself to a pantheistic interpretation.

There is, however, one question which will be raised in this connexion. Does not individuality imply finitude? If God is an ego and as such an individual, how can we conceive Him as infinite? The answer to this question is that God cannot be conceived as infinite in the sense of spatial infinity. In matters of spiritual valuation mere immensity counts for nothing. Moreover, as we have seen before, temporal and spatial infinities are not absolute. Modern science regards Nature not as something static, situate in an infinite void, but a structure of interrelated events out of whose mutual relations arise the concepts of space and time. And this is only another way of saying that space and time are interpretations which thought puts upon the creative activity of the Ultimate Ego. Space and time are possibilities of the Ego, only partially realized in the shape of our mathematical space and time. Beyond Him and apart from His creative activity, there is neither time nor space to close Him off in reference to other egos. The Ultimate Ego is, therefore, neither infinite in the sense of spatial infinity nor finite in the sense of the space-bound human ego whose body closes him off in reference to other egos. The infinity of the Ultimate Ego consists in the infinite inner possibilities of His creative activity of which the universe, as known to us, is only a partial expression. In one word God's infinity is intensive. It involves an infinite series, but is not that series.

The other important elements in the Quranic connexion of God, from a purely intellectual point of view, are Creativeness, Knowledge, Omnipotence and Eternity. I shall deal with them serially.

(a) Finite mind regards Nature as a confronting " other " existing *per se*, which the mind knows but does not make. We are thus apt to regard the act of creation as a specific past event, and the universe appears to us as a manufactured article which has no organic relation to the life of its maker, and of which the maker is nothing more than a mere spectator. All the meaningless theological controversies about the idea of creation arise from this narrow vision of the finite mind. Thus regarded the universe is a mere accident in the life of God and might not have been created. The real question which we are called upon to answer is this: Does the universe confront God as His " other," with space intervening between Him and it? The answer is that, from the Divine point of view, there is no creation in the sense of a specific event having a " before " and an " after." The universe cannot be regarded as an independent reality standing in opposition to Him. This view of the matter will reduce both God and the world to two separate entities confronting each other in the empty receptacle of an infinite space. We have seen before that space, time and matter are interpretations which thought puts on the free creative energy of God. They are not independent realities existing *per se*, but only intellectual modes of apprehending the life of God. The question of creation once arose among the disciples of the well-known saint Ba Yazid of Bistam. One of the disciples very pointedly put the common-sense view, saying: " There was a moment of time when God existed and nothing else existed beside Him." The saint's reply was equally pointed. " It is just the same now," said he, " as it was then." The world of matter, therefore, is not a stuff co-eternal with God, operated upon by Him from a distance as it were. It is, in its real nature, one continuous act which thought breaks up into a plurality of mutually exclusive things. Professor Eddington has thrown further light on this important point, and I take the liberty to quote from his book— *Space, Time and Gravitation*:

" We have a world of point-events with their primary interval-relations. Out of these an unlimited number of more complicated relations and qualities can be built up mathematically, describing various features of the state of the world. These exist in nature in the same sense as an unlimited number of walks exist on an open moor. But the existence is, as it were, latent unless some one gives a significance to the walk by following it; and in the same way the existence of any one of these qualities of the world only acquires significance above its fellows if a mind singles it out for recognition. *Mind filters out matter from the meaningless jumble of qualities, as the prism filters out the colours of the rainbow from the chaotic pulsations of the white light.* Mind exalts the permanent and ignores the transitory; and it appears from the mathematical study of relations, that the only way in which the mind can achieve her object is by picking out one particular quality as the permanent substance of the perceptual world, partitioning a perceptual time and space for it to be permanent in, and, as a necessary consequence of this Hobson's choice, the laws of gravitation and mechanics and geometry have to be obeyed. It is too much to say that the mind's search for permanence has created the world of physics? "

The last sentence in this passage is one of the deepest things in Professor Eddington's book. The physicist has yet to discover by his own methods that the passing show of the apparently permanent world of physics which the mind has created in its search for permanence is rooted in something more permanent, conceivable only as a self which alone combines the opposite attributes of change and permanence, and can thus be regarded as both constant and variable.

There is, however, one question which we must answer before we proceed further. In what manner does the creative activity of God proceed to the work of creation? The most orthodox and still popular school of Muslim theology, I mean the Ash'arite, hold that the creative method of Divine energy is atomic; and they appear to have based their doctrine on the following verse of the Quran:

"And no one thing is here, but with Us are its store-houses; and We send it not down but in fixed quantities." (15 : 21).

Q

242 The rise and growth of atomism in Islam—the first important indication of an intellectual revolt against the Aristotelian idea of a fixed universe—forms one of the most interesting chapters in the history of Muslim thought. The views of the school of Basra were first shaped by Abu Hashim (A.D. 933), and those of the school of Baghdad by that most exact and daring theological thinker, Abu Bakar Bakilani (A.D. 1012). Later in the beginning of the thirteenth century we find a thoroughly systematic description in a book called the *Guide of the Perplexed*, by Moses Mammonides—a Jewish theologian who was educated in the Muslim Universities of Spain. A French translation of this book was made by Munk in 1866, and recently Professor Macdonald of America has given an excellent account of its contents in the Isis from which Dr. Zwemer has reprinted it in the *Muslim World* of January 1928. Professor Macdonald, however, has made no attempt to discover the psychological forces that determined the growth of atomistic "kalam" in Islam. He admits that there is nothing like the Atomism of Islam in Greek thought, but, unwilling as he is to give any credit for original thought to Muslim thinkers, and finding a surface resemblance between the Islamic theory and the views of a certain sect of Buddhism, he jumps to the conclusion that the origin of the theory is due to Buddhistic influences on the thought of Islam. Unfortunately, a full discussion of the sources of this purely speculative theory is not possible in this lecture. I propose only to give you some of its more salient features, indicating at the same time the lines on which the work of reconstruction in the light of modern physics ought, in my opinion, to proceed.

According to the Ash'arite school of thinkers, then, the world is compounded of what they call *jawahir*—infinitely small parts or atoms which cannot be further divided. Since the creative activity of God is ceaseless the number of the atoms cannot be finite. Fresh atoms are coming into being every moment, and the universe is therefore constantly growing. As the Quran says: " God adds to His creation what He wills." The essence of the atom is independent of its existence. This means that existence is a quality imposed on the atom by God. Before receiving this quality the atom lies dormant, as it were, in the creative energy of God, and its existence means nothing more than Divine energy become visible. The atom in its essence, therefore, has no magnitude; it has its position which does not involve space. It is by their aggregation that atoms become extended and generate space. Ibn-i-Hazm, the critic of atomism, acutely remarks that the language of the Quran makes no difference in the act of creation and the thing created. What we call a thing, then, is in its essential nature an aggregation of atomic acts. Of the concept of "atomic act," however, it is difficult to form a mental picture. Modern physics too conceives as action the actual atom of a certain physical quantity. But, as Professor Eddington has pointed out, the precise formulation of the theory of Quanta of action has not been possible so far; though it is vaguely believed that the atomicity of action is the general law and that the appearance of electrons is in some way dependent on it.

Again we have seen that each atom occupies a position which does not involve space. That being so, what is the nature of motion which we cannot conceive except as the atom's passage through space? Since the Ash'arite regarded space as generated by the aggregation of atoms, they could not explain movement as a body's passage through all the points of space intervening between the point of its start and destination. Such an explanation must necessarily assume the existence of void as an independent reality. In order, therefore, to get over the difficulty of empty space, they resorted to the notion of "Tafra" or jump; and imagined the moving body, not as passing through all the discrete positions in space, but as jumping over the void between one position and another. Thus, according to these thinkers, a quick motion and a slow motion possess the same speed; but the latter has more points of rest. I confess I do not quite understand this solution of the difficulty. It may, however, be pointed out that modern atomism has found a similar difficulty and a similar solution has been suggested. In view of the experiments relating to Planck's theory of Quanta, we cannot imagine the moving atom as continuously traversing its path in space. " One of the most hopeful lines of explanation," says Professor Whitehead in his *Science and the Modern World*, " is to assume that an electron does not continuously traverse its path in space. The alternative notion as to its mode of existence is that it appears at a series of discrete positions in space which it occupies for successive durations of time. It is as though an automobile moving at the average rate of thirty miles an hour along a road did not traverse the road continuously, but appeared successively at the successive mile stones remaining for two minutes at each milestone."

Another feature of this theory of creation is the doctrine of accident on the perpetual creation of which depends the continuity of the atom as an existent. If God ceases to create the accidents, the atom ceases to exist as an atom. The atom possesses inseparable positive or negative qualities. These exist in opposed couples, as life and death, motion and rest, and possess practically no duration. Two propositions follow from this:

(i) Nothing has a stable nature.

(ii) There is a single order of atoms, *i.e.* what we call the soul is either a finer kind of matter, or only an accident. I am inclined to think that in view of the idea of continuous creation which the Ash'arite intended to establish there is an element of truth in the first proposition. I have said before that in my opinion the spirit of the Quran is on the whole anti-classical. I regard the Ash'arite thought on this point as a genuine effort to develop on the basis of an Ultimate Will or Energy a theory of creation which, with all its shortcomings, is far more true to the spirit of the Quran than the Aristotelian idea of a fixed universe. The duty of the future theologians of Islam is to reconstruct this purely speculative theory, and to bring it into closer contact with modern science which appears to be moving in the same direction. The second proposition looks like pure materialism. It is my belief that the Ash'arite view that the "Nafs" is an accident is opposed to the real trend of their own theory which makes the continuous existence of the atom dependent on the continuous creation of accidents in it. It is obvious that motion is inconceivable without time. And since time comes from psychic life, the latter is more fundamental than motion. No psychic life, no time: no time, no motion. Thus it is really what the Ash'arite call the accident which is responsible for the continuity of the atom as such. The atom becomes or rather looks spatialized when it receives the quality of existence. Regarded as a phase of Divine energy, it is essentially spiritual. The "Nafs" is the pure act; the body is only the act become visible and hence measurable. In fact the Ash'arite vaguely anticipated the modern notion of point-instant; but they failed rightly to see the nature of the mutual relation between the point and the instant. The instant is the more fundamental of the two; but the point is inseparable from the instant as being a necessary mode of its manifestation. The point is not a thing, it is only a sort of looking at the instant. Rumi is far more true to the spirit of Islam than Ghazali.

Reality is, therefore, essentially spirit. But, of course, there are degrees of spirit. In the history of Muslim thought the idea of degrees of Reality appears in the writings of Shahabuddin Suhrawardi Maqtul. In modern times we find it worked out on a much larger scale in Hegel and, more recently, in the late Lord Haldane's *Reign of Relativity*, which he published shortly before his death. I have conceived the Ultimate Reality as an Ego; and I must add now that from the Ultimate Ego only egos proceed. The creative energy of the Ultimate Ego, in whom deed and thought are identical, functions as ego-unities. The world, in all its details, from the mechanical movement of what we call the atom of matter to the free movement of thought in the human ego, is the self-revelation of the "Great I am." Every atom of Divine energy, however low in the scale of existence, is an ego. But there are degrees in the expression of egohood.

Throughout the entire gamut of being runs the gradually rising note of egohood until it reaches its perfection in man. That is why the Quran declares the Ultimate Ego to be nearer to man than his own neck-vein. Like pearls do we live and move and have our being in the perpetual flow of Divine life.

Thus a criticism, inspired by the best traditions of Muslim thought, tends to turn the Ash'arite scheme of atomism into a spiritual pluralism, the details of which will have to be worked out by the future theologians of Islam. It may, however, be asked whether atomicity has a real seat in the creative energy of God, or presents itself to us as such only because of our finite mode of apprehension. From a purely scientific point of view I cannot say what the final answer to this question will be. From the psychological point of view one thing appears to me to be certain. Only that is, strictly speaking, real which is directly conscious of its own reality. The degree of reality varies with the degree of the feeling of egohood. The nature of the ego is such that, in spite of the capacity to respond to other egos, it is self-centred and possesses a private circuit of individuality excluding all egos other than itself. In this alone consists its reality as an ego. Man, therefore, in whom egohood has reached its relative perfection, occupies a genuine place in the heart of Divine creative energy, and thus possesses a much higher degree of reality than things around him. Of all the creations of God he alone is capable of consciously participating in the creative life of his Maker. Endowed with the power to imagine a better world, and to mould what is into what ought to be, the ego in him aspires, in the interests of an increasingly unique and comprehensive individuality, to exploit all the various environments on which he may be called upon to operate during the course of an endless career. But I would ask you to wait for a fuller treatment of this point till my lecture on the immortality and freedom of the ego. In the meantime, I want to say a few words about the doctrine of atomic time, which I think is the weakest part of the Ash'arite theory of creation. It is necessary to do so for a reasonable view of the Divine attribute of Eternity.

The problem of time has always drawn the attention of Muslim thinkers and mystics. This seems to be due partly to the fact that, according to the Quran, the alternation of day and night is one of the greatest signs of God, and partly to the Prophet's identification of God with " Dahr " (time) in a well known tradition referred to before. Indeed, some of the greatest Muslim Sufis believed in the mystic properties of the word " Dahr." According to Muhyuddin Ibn-ul-Arabi, " Dahr " is one of the beautiful names of God, and Razi tells us in his commentary on the Quran that some of the Muslim saints had taught him to repeat the word " Dahr," " Daihur " or " Daihar." The Ash'arite theory of time is perhaps the first attempt in the history of Muslim thought to understand it philosophically. Time, according to the Ash'arite, is a succession of individual " nows." From this view it obviously follows that between every two individual " nows " or moments of time, there is an unoccupied moment of time, that is to say, a void of time. The absurdity of this conclusion is due to the fact that they looked at the subject of their inquiry from a wholly objective point of view. They took no lesson from the history of Greek thought, which had adopted the same point of view and had reached no results. In our own time Newton described time as " something which in itself and from its own nature flows equally." The metaphor of stream implied in this description suggests serious objections to Newton's equally objective view of time. We cannot understand how a thing is affected on its immersion in this stream, and how it differs from things that do not participate in its flow. Nor can we form any idea of the beginning, the end and the boundaries of time if we try to understand it on the analogy of a stream. Moreover, if flow, movement or " passage " is the last word as to the nature of time, there must be another time to time the movement of the first time, and another which times the second time, and so on to infinity. Thus the notion of time as something wholly objective is beset with

248 difficulties. It must, however, be admitted that the practical Arab mind could not regard time as something unreal like the Greeks. Nor can it be denied that, even though we possess no sense-organ to perceive time, it is a kind of flow and has, as such, a genuine objective, that is to say, atomic aspect. In fact, the verdict of modern science is exactly the same as that of the Ash'arite; for recent discoveries in physics regarding the nature of time assume the discontinuity of matter. The following passage from Professor Rongier's *Philosophy and Physics* is noteworthy in this connexion:—" Contrary to the ancient adage, *Náture non facit saltus*, it becomes apparent that the universe varies by sudden jumps and not by imperceptible degrees. A physical system is capable of only a finite number of distinct states. Since between two different and immediately consecutive states the world remains motionless, time is suspended, so that time itself is discontinuous: there is an atom of time." The point, however, is that the constructive endeavour of the Ash'arite, as of the moderns, was wholly lacking in psychological analysis, and the result of this shortcoming was that they altogether failed to perceive the subjective aspect of time. It is due to this failure that in their theory the systems of material atoms and time-atoms lie apart, with no organic relation between them. It is clear that if we look at time from a purely objective point of view serious difficulties arise; for we cannot apply atomic time to God and conceive Him as a life in the making, as Professor Alexander appears to have done in his Lectures on Space, Time and Deity. Later Muslim theologians fully realized these difficulties. Mulla Jalal-ud-Din Dawani in a passage of his " Zoura," which reminds the modern student of Professor Royce's view of time, tells us that if we take time to be a kind of span which makes possible the appearance of events as a moving procession and conceive this span to be a unity, then we cannot but describe it as an original state of Divine activity, encompassing all the succeeding states of that activity. But the Mulla takes good care to add that a deeper insight into the nature of succession reveals its

relativity, so that it disappears in the case of God to Whom all events are present in a single act of perception. The Sufi poet Iraqi has a similar way of looking at the matter. He conceives infinite varieties of time, relative to the varying grades of being, intervening between materiality and pure spirituality. The time of gross bodies which arises from the revolution of the heavens is divisible into past, present and future; and its nature is such that as long as one day does not pass away the succeeding day does not come. The time of immaterial beings is also serial in character, but its passage is such that a whole year in the time of gross bodies is not more than a day in the time of an immaterial being. Rising higher and higher in the scale of immaterial beings we reach Divine time— time which is absolutely free from the quality of passage, and consequently does not admit of divisibility, sequence and change. It is above eternity; it has neither beginning nor end. The eye of God sees all the visibles, and His ear hears all the audibles in one indivisible act of perception. The priority of God is not due to the priority of time; on the other hand, the priority of time is due to God's priority. Thus Divine time is what the Quran describes as the " Mother of Books " in which the whole of history, freed from the net of causal sequence, is gathered up in a single super-eternal " now." Of all the Muslim theologians, however, it is Fakhr-ud-Din Razi who appears to have given his most serious attention to the problem of time. In his *Eastern Discussions*, which saw the light of publication only a short time ago at Hyderabad, Razi subjects to a searching examination all the contemporary theories of time. He too is, in the main, objective in his method and finds himself unable to reach any definite conclusions. " Until now," he says, " I have not been able to discover anything really true with regard to the nature of time; and the main purpose of my book is to explain what can possibly be said for or against each theory without any spirit of partisanship, which I generally avoid, especially in connexion with the problem of time."

The above discussion makes it perfectly clear that a

purely objective point of view is only partially helpful in our understanding of the nature of time. The right course is a careful psychological analysis of our conscious experience which alone reveals the true nature of time. I suppose you remember the distinction that I drew in the two aspects of the self, appreciative and efficient. The appreciative self lives in pure duration, *i.e.*, change without succession. The life of the self consists in its movement from appreciation to efficiency, from intuition to intellect, and atomic time is born out of this movement. Thus the character of our conscious experience—our point of departure in all knowledge—gives us a clue to the concept which reconciles the opposition of permanence and change, of time regarded as an organic whole or eternity, and time regarded as atomic. If then we accept the guidance of our conscious experience, and conceive the life of the all-inclusive Ego on the analogy of the finite ego, the time of the Ultimate Ego is revealed as change without succession, *i.e.* an organic whole which appears atomic because of the creative movement of the ego. This is what Mir Damad and Mulla Baqir mean when they say that time is born with the act of creation by which the Ultimate Ego realizes and measures, so to speak, the infinite wealth of His own undetermined creative possibilities. On the one hand, therefore, the ego lives in eternity, by which term I mean non-successional change; on the other, it lives in serial time, which I conceive as organically related to eternity in the sense that it is a measure of non-successional change. In this sense alone it is possible to understand the Quranic verse: "To God belongs the alternation of day and night." But on this difficult side of the problem I have said enough in my preceding lecture. It is now time to pass on to the Divine attributes of Knowledge and Omnipotence.

The word knowledge, as applied to the finite ego, always means discursive knowledge—a temporal process which moves round a veritable "other," supposed to exist *per se* and confronting the knowing ego. In this sense knowledge, even if we extend it to the point of omniscience, must always remain relative to its confronting

" other," and cannot, therefore, be predicated of the
Ultimate Ego who, being all-inclusive, cannot be conceived as having a perspective like the finite ego. The
universe, as we have seen before, is not an " other "
existing *per se* in opposition to God. It is only when we
look at the act of creation as a specific event in the life-
history of God that the universe appears as an independent
" other." From the standpoint of the all-inclusive Ego
there is no " other." In Him thought and deed, the act
of knowing and the act of creating, are identical. It may
be argued that the ego, whether finite or infinite, is inconceivable without a confronting non-ego, and if there is
nothing outside the Ultimate Ego, the Ultimate Ego cannot
be conceived as an ego. The answer to this argument is
that logical negations are of no use in forming a positive
concept which must be based on the character of Reality
as revealed in experience. Our criticism of experience
reveals the Ultimate Reality to be a rationally directed life
which, in view of our experience of life, cannot be conceived except as an organic whole, a something closely
knit together and possessing a central point of reference.
This being the character of life, the ultimate life can only
be conceived as an ego. Knowledge, in the sense of discursive knowledge, however infinite, cannot, therefore, be
predicated of an ego who knows, and at the same time
forms the ground of the object known. Unfortunately,
language does not help us here. We possess no word to
express the kind of knowledge which is also creative of
its object. The alternative concept of Divine knowledge
is omniscience in the sense of a single indivisible act of
perception which makes God immediately aware of the
entire sweep of history, regarded as an order of specific
event, in an eternal " now." This is how Jalaluddin
Dawani, Iraqi and Professor Royce in our own times
conceived God's knowledge. There is an element of truth
in this conception. But it suggests a closed universe, a
fixed futurity, a pre-determined, unalterable order of specific
events which, like a superior fate, has once for all determined
the directions of God's creative activity. In fact, Divine

252 knowledge regarded as a kind of passive omniscience is nothing more than the inert void of pre-Einstinian physics, which confers a semblance of unity on things by holding them together, a sort of mirror passively reflecting the details of an already finished structure of things which the finite consciousness reflects in fragments only. Divine knowledge must be conceived as a living creative activity to which the objects that appear to exist in their own right are organically related. By conceiving God's knowledge as a kind of reflecting mirror, we no doubt save His fore-knowledge of future events; but it is obvious that we do so at the expense of His freedom. The future certainly pre-exists in the organic whole of God's creative life, but it pre-exists as an open possibility, not as a fixed order of events with definite outlines. An illustration will perhaps help us in understanding what I mean. Suppose, as sometimes happens in the history of human thought, a fruitful idea with a great inner wealth of applications emerges into the light of your consciousness. You are immediately aware of the idea as a complex whole; but the intellectual working out of its numerous bearings is a matter of time. Intuitively all the possibilities of the idea are present in your mind. If a specific possibility, as such, is not intellectually known to you at a certain moment of time, it is not because your knowledge is defective, but because there is yet no possibility to become known. The idea reveals the possibilities of its application with advancing experience, and sometimes it takes more than one generation of thinkers before these possibilities are exhausted. Nor is it possible, on the view of Divine knowledge as a kind of passive omniscience, to reach the idea of a creator. If history is regarded merely as a gradually revealed photo of a pre-determined order of events, then there is no room in it for novelty and initiation. Consequently, we can attach no meaning to the word creation, which has a meaning for us only in view of our own capacity for original action. The truth is that the whole theological controversy relating to pre-destination is due to pure speculation with no eye on the spontaneity of life, which

is a fact of actual experience. No doubt, the emergence of egos endowed with the power of spontaneous and hence unforeseeable action is, in a sense, a limitation on the freedom of the all-inclusive Ego. But this limitation is not externally imposed. It is born out of His own creative freedom whereby He has chosen finite egos to be participators of His life, power and freedom.

But how, it may be asked, is it possible to reconcile limitation with Omnipotence? The word limitation need not frighten us. The Quran has no liking for abstract universals. It always fixes its gaze on the concrete which the theory of Relativity has only recently taught modern philosophy to see. All activity, creational or otherwise, is a kind of limitation without which it is impossible to conceive God as a concrete operative Ego. Omnipotence, abstractly conceived, is merely a blind, capricious power without limits. The Quran has a clear and definite conception of Nature as a cosmos of mutually related forces. It, therefore, views Divine omnipotence as intimately related to Divine wisdom, and finds the infinite power of God revealed, not in the arbitrary and the capricious, but in the recurrent, the regular and the orderly. At the same time, the Quran conceives God as " holding all goodness in His hands." If, then, the rationally directed Divine will is good, a very serious problem arises. The course of evolution, as revealed by modern science, involves almost universal suffering and wrong-doing. No doubt, wrong-doing is confined to man only. But the fact of pain is almost universal; though it is equally true that men can suffer and have suffered the most excruciating pain for the sake of what they have believed to be good. Thus the two facts of moral and physical evil stand out prominent in the life of Nature. Nor can the relativity of evil and the presence of forces that tend to transmute it be a source of consolation to us; for in spite of all this relativity and transmutation there is something terribly positive about it. How is it, then, possible to reconcile the goodness and omnipotence of God with the immense volume of evil in His creation? This painful problem is really the crux of Theism. No modern writer has put it more accurately than Naumann in his *Briefe Über Religion*. " We possess," he says, " a knowledge of the world which teaches us a God of power and strength, who sends out life and death as simultaneously as shadow and light, and a revelation, a faith as to salvation which declares the same God to be father. The following of the world-God produces the morality of the struggle for existence, and the service of the Father of Jesus Christ produces the morality of compassion. And yet they are not two gods, but one God. Somehow or other, their arms intertwine. Only no mortal can say where and how this occurs." To the optimist Browning all is well with the world; to the pessimist Schopenhauer the world is one perpetual winter wherein a blind will expresses itself in an infinite variety of living things which bemoan their emergence for a moment and then disappear for ever. The issue thus raised between optimism and pessimism cannot be finally decided at the present stage of our knowledge of the universe. Our intellectual constitution is such that we can take only a piecemeal view of things. We cannot understand the full import of the great cosmic forces which work havoc, and at the same time sustain and amplify life. The teaching of the Quran, which believes in the possibility of improvement in the behaviour of man and his control over natural forces, is neither optimism nor pessimism. It is meliorism, which recognizes a growing universe and is animated by the hope of man's eventual victory over evil.

But the clue to a better understanding of our difficulty is given in the legend relating to what is called the fall of man. In this legend the Quran partly retains the ancient symbols, but the legend is materially transformed with a view to put an entirely fresh meaning into it. The Quranic method of complete or partial transformation of legends in order to besoul them with new ideas, and thus to adapt them to the advancing spirit of time is an important point, which has nearly always been overlooked both by Muslim and non-Muslim students of Islam. The object of the Quran in dealing with these legends is seldom historical;

it nearly always aims at giving them a universal moral or philosophical import. And it achieves this object by omitting the names of persons and localities which tend to limit the meaning of a legend by giving it the colour of a specific historical event, and also by deleting details which appear to belong to a different order of feeling. This is not an uncommon method of dealing with legends. It is common in non-religious literature. An instance in point is the legend of Faust, to which the touch of Goethe's genius has given a wholly new meaning.

Turning to the legend of the Fall we find it in a variety of forms in the literatures of the ancient world. It is, indeed, impossible to demarcate the stages of its growth, and to set out clearly the various human motives which must have worked in its slow transformation. But confining ourselves to the Semitic form of the myth, it is highly probable that it arose out of the primitive man's desire to explain to himself the infinite misery of his plight in an uncongenial environment, which abounded in disease and death and obstructed him on all sides in his endeavour to maintain himself. Having no control over the forces of Nature, a pessimistic view of life was perfectly natural to him. Thus, in an old Babylonian inscription, we find the serpent (phallic symbol), the tree and the woman offering an apple (symbol of virginity) to the man. The meaning of the myth is clear—the fall of man from a supposed state of bliss was due to the original sexual act of the human pair. The way in which the Quran handles this legend becomes clear when we compare it with the narration of the Book of Genesis. The remarkable points of difference between the Quranic and the Biblical narrations suggest unmistakably the purpose of the Quranic narration.

1. The Quran omits the serpent and the rib-story altogether. The former omission is obviously meant to free the story from its phallic setting and its original suggestion of a pessimistic view of life. The latter omission is meant to suggest that the purpose of the Quranic narration is not historical, as in the case of the Old Testament, which gives us an account of the origin of the first

human pair by way of a prelude to the history of Israel. Indeed, in the verses which deal with the origin of man as a living being, the Quran uses the words " Bashar," or " Insan," not " Adam," which it reserves for man in his capacity of God's vicegerent on earth. The purpose of the Quran is further secured by the omission of proper names mentioned in the Biblical narration—Adam and Eve. The word Adam is retained and used more as a concept than as the name of a concrete human individual. This use of the word is not without authority in the Quran itself. The following verse is clear on the point:

" We created you; then fashioned you; then said We to the angels, ' prostrate yourself unto Adam.' " (7: 10).

2. The Quran splits up the legend into two distinct episodes—the one relating to what it describes simply as " the tree " and the other relating to the " tree of eternity " and the " kingdom that faileth not." The first episode is mentioned in the 7th and the second in the 20th Sura of the Quran. According to the Quran Adam and his wife, led astray by Satan whose function is to create doubts in the minds of men, tasted the fruit of both the trees, whereas according to the Old Testament man was driven out of the garden of Eden immediately after his first act of disobedience, and God placed, at the eastern side of the garden, angels and a flaming sword, turning on all sides, to keep the way to the tree of life.

3. The Old Testament curses the earth for Adam's act of disobedience; the Quran declares the earth to be the " dwelling place " of man and a " source of profit " to him for the possession of which he ought to be grateful to God. " And We have established you on the earth and given you therein the supports of life. How little do ye give thanks! " (7: 9). Nor is there any reason to suppose that the word " Jannat " (garden) as used here means the supersensual paradise from which man is supposed to have fallen on this earth. According to the Quran man is not a stranger on this earth. " And we have

caused you to grow from the earth," says the Quran. 257 The " Jannat," mentioned in the legend, cannot mean the eternal abode of the righteous. In the sense of the eternal abode of the righteous, " Jannat " is described by the Quran to be the place " wherein the righteous will pass to one another the cup which shall engender no light discourse, no motive to sin." It is further described to be the place " wherein no weariness shall reach the righteous, nor forth from it shall they be cast." In the " Jannat " mentioned in the legend, however, the very first event that took place was man's sin of disobedience followed by his expulsion. In fact, the Quran itself explains the meaning of the word as used in its own narration. In the second episode of the legend the garden is described as a place " where there is neither hunger, nor thirst, neither heat nor nakedness." I am, therefore, inclined to think that the " Jannat " in the Quranic narration is the conception of a primitive state in which man is practically unrelated to his environment, and consequently does not feel the sting of human wants, the birth of which alone marks the beginning of human culture.

Thus we see that the Quranic legend of the Fall has nothing to do with the first appearance of man on this planet.. Its purpose is rather to indicate man's rise from a primitive state of instinctive appetite to the conscious possession of a free self, capable of doubt and disobedience. The fall does not mean any moral depravity; it is man's transition from simple consciousness to the first flash of self-consciousness, a kind of waking from the dream of nature with a throb of personal causality in one's own being. Nor does the Quran regard the earth as a torture-hall where an elementally wicked humanity is imprisoned for an original act of sin. Man's first act of disobedience was also his first act of free choice; and that is why, according to the Quranic narration, Adam's first transgression was forgiven. Now goodness is not a matter of compulsion; it is the self's free surrender to the moral ideal and arises out of a willing co-operation of free egos. A being whose movements are wholly determined like a

258 machine cannot produce goodness. Freedom is thus a condition of goodness. But to permit the emergence of a finite ego who has the power to choose, after considering the relative values of several courses of action open to him, is really to take a great risk; for the freedom to choose good involves also the freedom to choose what is the opposite of good. That God has taken this risk shows His immense faith in man; it is for man now to justify this faith. Perhaps such a risk alone makes it possible to test and develop the potentialities of a being who was created of the " goodliest fabric " and " brought down to be the lowest of the low." As the Quran says: " And for trial will We test you with evil and with good." (21 : 36). Good and evil, therefore, though opposites, must fall within the same whole. There is no such thing as an isolated fact; for facts are systematic wholes, the elements of which must be understood by mutual reference. Logical judgment separates the elements of a fact only to reveal their interdependence.

Further, it is the nature of the self to maintain itself as a self. For this purpose it seeks knowledge, self-multiplication and power, or, in the words of the Quran, " the kingdom that never faileth." The first episode in the Quranic legend relates to man's desire for knowledge, the second to his desire for self-multiplication and power. In connexion with the first episode it is necessary to point out two things. Firstly, the episode is mentioned immediately after the verses describing Adam's superiority over the angels in remembering and reproducing the names of things. The purpose of these verses, as I have shown before, is to bring out the conceptual character of human knowledge. Secondly, Madame Blavatski, who possessed a remarkable knowledge of ancient symbolism, tells us in her book, called *Secret Doctrine*, that with the ancients the tree was a cryptic symbol for occult knowledge. Adam was forbidden to taste the fruit of this tree obviously because his finitude as a self, his sense-equipment, and his intellectual faculties were, on the whole, attuned to a different type of knowledge, *i.e.* the type of knowledge which necessitates the toil of patient observation and admits only of slow accumulation. Satan, however, persuaded him to eat the forbidden fruit of occult knowledge and Adam yielded, not because he was elementally wicked, but because being "hasty" (ajul) by nature he sought a short cut to knowledge. The only way to correct this tendency was to place him in an environment which, however painful, was better suited to the unfolding of his intellectual faculties. Thus Adam's insertion into a painful physical environment was not meant as a punishment; it was meant rather to defeat the object of Satan who, as an enemy of man, diplomatically tried to keep him ignorant of the joy of perpetual growth and expansion. But the life of a finite ego in an obstructing environment depends on the perpetual expansion of knowledge based on actual experience. And the experience of a finite ego to whom several possibilities are open expands only by method of trial and error. Therefore, error which may be described as a kind of intellectual evil is an indispensable factor in the building up of experience.

The second episode of the Quranic legend is as follows:—

" But Satan whispered him (Adam): said he, O Adam! shall I show thee the tree of Eternity and the Kingdom that faileth not? And they both ate thereof, and their nakedness appeared to them, and they began to sew of the leaves of the garden to cover them, and Adam disobeyed his Lord, and went astray. Afterwards his Lord chose him for Himself, and was turned towards him, and guided him." (20: 114).

The central idea here is to suggest life's irresistible desire for a lasting dominion, an infinite career as a concrete individual. As a temporal being, fearing the termination of its career by death, the only course open to it is to achieve a kind of collective immortality by self-multiplication. The eating of the forbidden fruit of the tree of eternity is life's resort to sex-differentiation by which it multiplies itself with a view to circumvent total extinction. It is as if life says to death—" if you sweep away one generation of living things, I will produce another." The Quran rejects the phallic symbolism of ancient art, but suggests the original sexual act by the birth of the sense of shame disclosed in Adam's anxiety to cover the nakedness of his body. Now to live is to possess a definite outline, a concrete individuality. It is in the concrete individuality, manifested in the countless varieties of living forms that the Ultimate Ego reveals the infinite wealth of His Being. Yet the emergence and multiplication of individualities, each fixing its gaze on the revelation of its own possibilities and seeking its own dominion, inevitably brings in its wake the awful struggle of ages. " Descend ye as enemies of one another," says the Quran. This mutual conflict of opposing individualities is the world-pain which both illuminates and darkens the temporal career of life. In the case of man in whom individuality deepens into personality, opening up possibilities of wrong-doing, the sense of the tragedy of life becomes much more acute. But the acceptance of selfhood as a form of life involves the acceptance of all the imperfections that flow from the finitude of selfhood. The Quran represents man as having accepted at his peril the trust of personality which the Heavens, the earth and the mountains refused to bear :—

> " Verily We proposed to the Heavens and to the earth and to the mountains to receive the ' trust ' but they refused the burden and they feared to receive it. Man undertook to bear it but hath proved unjust, senseless ! " (33 : 72).

Shall we, then, say no or yes to the trust of personality with all its attendant ills ? True manhood, according to the Quran, consists in " patience under ills and hardships." At the present stage of the evolution of self-hood, however, we cannot understand the full import of the discipline which the driving power of pain brings. Perhaps it hardens the self against a possible dissolution. But in asking the above question we are passing the boundaries of pure thought. This is the point where faith in the eventual triumph of goodness emerges as a religious doctrine. " God is equal to His purpose, but most men know it not." (12: 21).

I have now explained to you how it is possible philosophically to justify the Islamic conception of God. But, as I have said before, religious ambition soars higher than the ambition of philosophy. Religion is not satisfied with mere conception; it seeks a more intimate knowledge of and association with the object of its pursuits. The agencies through which this association is achieved is the act of worship or prayer ending in spiritual illumination. The act of worship, however, affects different varieties of consciousness differently. In the case of the prophetic consciousness it is in the main creative; *i.e.* it tends to create a fresh ethical world wherein the Prophet, so to speak, applies the pragmatic test to his revelations. I shall further develop this point in my lecture on the meaning of Muslim culture. In the case of the mystic consciousness it is in the main cognitive. It is from this cognitive point of view that I will try to discover the meaning of prayer. And this point of view is perfectly justifiable in view of the ultimate motive of prayer. I would draw your attention to the following passage from the great American psychologist, Prof. William James:

" It seems probable that in spite of all that science may do to the contrary, men will continue to pray to the end of time, unless their mental nature changes in a manner which nothing we know should lead us to expect. The impulse to pray is a necessary consequence of the fact that whilst the innermost of the empirical selves of a man is a self of the social sort it yet can find its only adequate socius (its ' great companion ') in an ideal world. . . . Most men, either continually or occasionally, carry a reference to it in their breasts. The humblest outcast on this earth can feel himself to be real and valid by means of this higher recognition. And, on the other hand, for most of us, a world with no such inner refuge when the outer social self failed and dropped from us would be the abyss of horror. I say ' for most of us,' because it is probable that men differ a good deal in the degree in which they are haunted by this sense of an ideal spectator. It is a much more essential part of the consciousness of some men than of others. Those who have the most of it are possibly the most religious men. But I am sure that even those who say they are altogether without it deceive themselves, and really have it in some degree."

Thus you will see that, psychologically speaking, prayer is instinctive in its origin. The act of prayer as aiming at knowledge resembles reflection. Yet prayer at its highest is much more than abstract reflection. Like reflection it too is a process of assimilation, but the assimilative process in the case of prayer draws itself closely together and thereby acquires a power unknown to pure thought. In thought the mind observes and follows the working of Reality; in the act of prayer it gives up its career as a seeker of slow-footed universality and rises higher than thought to capture Reality itself with a view to become a conscious participator in its life. There is nothing mystical about it. Prayer as a means of spiritual illumination is a normal vital act by which the little island of our personality suddenly discovers its situation in a larger whole of life. Do not think I am talking of auto-suggestion. Auto-suggestion has nothing to do with the opening up of the sources of life that lie in the depths of the human ego. Unlike spiritual illumination which brings fresh power by shaping human personality, it leaves no permanent life-effects behind. Nor am I speaking of some occult and special way of knowledge. All that I mean is to fix your attention on a real human experience which has a history behind it and a future before it. Mysticism has, no doubt, revealed fresh regions of the self by making a special study of this experience. Its literature is illuminating; yet its set phraseology shaped by the thought-forms of a worn-out metaphysics has rather a deadening effect on the modern mind. The quest after a nameless nothing, as disclosed in Neo-Platonic mysticism—be it Christian or Muslim—cannot satisfy the modern mind which, with its habits of concrete thinking, demands a concrete living experience of God. And the history of the race shows that the attitude of the mind embodied in the act of worship is a condition for such an experience. In fact, prayer must be regarded as a necessary complement to the intellectual activity of the observer of Nature. The scientific observation of Nature keeps us in close contact with the behaviour of Reality, and thus sharpens our inner perception for a deeper vision of it. I cannot help quoting here a beautiful passage from the mystic poet Rumi in which he describes the mystic quest after Reality:

(" The Sufi's book is not composed of ink and letters: it is not but a heart white as snow. The scholar's possession is pen-marks. What is the Sufi's possession?—foot-marks. The Sufi stalks the game like a hunter: he sees the musk-deer's track and follows the footprints. For some while the track of the deer is the proper clue for him, but afterwards it is the musk-gland of the deer that is his guide. To go one stage guided by the scent of the musk-gland is better than a hundred stages of following the track and roaming about.") The truth is that all search of knowledge is essentially a form of prayer. The scientific observer of Nature is a kind of mystic seeker in the act of prayer. Although at present he follows only the footprints of the musk-deer, and thus modestly limits the method of its quest, his thirst for knowledge is eventually sure to lead him to the point where the scent of the musk-gland is a better guide than the footprints of the deer. This alone will add to his power over Nature and give him that vision of the total-infinite which philosophy seeks but cannot find. Vision without power does bring moral elevation but cannot give a lasting culture. Power without vision tends to become destructive and inhuman. Both must combine for the spiritual expansion of humanity.

The real object of prayer, however, is better achieved when the act of prayer becomes congregational. The spirit of all true prayer is social. Even the hermit abandons the society of men in the hope of finding, in a solitary

264 abode, the fellowship of God. A congregation is an association of men who, animated by the same aspiration, concentrate themselves on a single object and open up their inner selves to the working of single impulse. It is a psychological truth that association multiplies the normal man's power of perception, deepens his emotion, and dynamizes his will to a degree unknown to him in the privacy of his individuality. Indeed, regarded as a psychological phenomenon, prayer is still a mystery; for psychology has not yet discovered the laws relating to the enhancement of human sensibility in a state of association. With Islam, however, this socialization of spiritual illumination through associative prayer is a special point of interest. As we pass from the daily congregational prayer to the annual ceremony round the central mosque of Mecca, you can easily see how the Islamic institution of worship gradually enlarges the sphere of human association.

Prayer, then, whether individual or associative, is an expression of man's inner yearning for a response in the awful silence of the universe. It is a unique process of discovery whereby the searching ego affirms itself in the very moment of self-negation, and thus discovers its own worth and justification as a dynamic factor in the life of the universe. True to the psychology of mental attitude in prayer, the form of worship in Islam symbolizes both affirmation and negation. Yet, in view of the fact borne out by the experience of the race that prayer, as an inner act, has found expression in a variety of forms, the Quran says:

" To every people have We appointed ways of worship which they observe. Therefore let them not dispute this matter with thee, but bid them to thy Lord for thou art on the right way: but if they debate with thee, then say: God best knoweth ye what ye do! He will judge between you on the Day of Resurrection, to the matters wherein ye differ." (22: 66–69).

The form of prayer ought not to become a matter of dispute. Which side you turn your face is certainly not essential to the spirit of prayer. The Quran is perfectly clear on this point:

" The East and West is God's: therefore whichever way ye turn, there is the face of God." (2: 109).

" There is no piety in turning your faces towards the East or the West, but he is pious who believeth in God, and the Last Day, and the angels, and the scriptures, and the prophets; who for the love of God disburseth his wealth to his kindred, and to the orphans, and the needy, and the wayfarer, and those who ask, and for ransoming; who observeth prayer, and payeth the legal alms, and who is of those who are faithful to their engagements when they have engaged in them; and patient under ills and hardships, in time of trouble: those are they who are just, and those are they who fear the Lord." (2: 172).

Yet we cannot ignore the important consideration that the posture of the body is a real factor in determining the attitude of the mind. The choice of one particular direction in Islamic worship is meant to secure the unity of feeling in the congregation, and its form in general creates and fosters the sense of social equality inasmuch as it tends to destroy the feeling of rank or race-superiority in the worshippers. What a tremendous spiritual revolution will take place, practically in no time, if the proud aristocratic Brahman of South India is daily made to stand shoulder to shoulder with the untouchable! From the unity of the all-inclusive Ego who creates and sustains all egos follows the essential unity of all mankind. The division of mankind into races, nations and tribes, according to the Quran, is for purposes of identification only. The Islamic form of association in prayer, therefore, besides its cognitive value, is further indicative of the aspiration to realize this essential unity of mankind as a fact in life by demolishing all barriers which stand between man and man.

The following extracts are from Syed Ikbal's *Eastward to Persia*, in which the glory of Eastern poetry is compared with the mystical poems of the English language, constituting a very apt and helpful comparison as seen through Oriental eyes.

MEETING OF THE EAST AND THE WEST

By Syed Ikbal

Quite apart from that wonderful poetry and philosophy which characterized the Semitic mind of the Arabic speaking peoples, the true Oriental thought is recognized to be that which has its origin in Persia. For a critical study of Persian literature I might refer those interested in it to the works exclusively devoted to that subject, because the wisdom of the East has more or less adequately been interpreted by some Western Scholars in the translations of Omar Khyyam, Sadi, Hafiz and others. In the following review, however, I shall concern myself with a new phase of Persian poetry which seeks to establish the fact that in higher aspects of spiritual evolution the Sages of the East have been extremely close to the approved philosophical thought of the West. In drawing attention to this facet of the meeting ground of the East and the West, I am breaking new ground.

" The East is East and the West is West, and never the twain shall meet," sings Kipling with characteristic felicity and force. This assertion, it may be admitted, is, at least, a plausible one, especially in so far as it refers to individual tendencies and experiences. Average Easterners and average Westerners, who come into accidental contact, no doubt find themselves " poles apart," as the English saying goes. Their habits of life are not the same; they appear to have different habits of thought, and a different outlook on the world. Consequently their impressions of each other are, when untinged by fanatical race prejudice, always interesting, sometimes novel, and, perhaps, amusingly odd; but they are rarely, be it borne in mind, based upon intimate knowledge or genuine sympathy in the wide sense of the term. Casual acquaintanceship may not be limited by Time; it may extend over many years and never attain the stage of real or intimate friendship, for mankind is prone to maintain those terrible barriers that separate mind from mind and heart from heart. We are all disposed, more or less, to be tyrannized by preconceptions and first impressions, and to refuse to see more than may be seen at a glance, or, perhaps, to see more than we want to see. Besides, being very human, we are ever inclined to become slaves of such phrases as Kipling has coined simply because they are trenchant and make a marked appeal to our fellows, and it seems not to matter how superficial they may happen to be. This applies to Easterner as well as to Westerner. The clever saying is not necessarily final, or the product of clear thinking and exact knowledge.

R. L. Stevenson's impressions of the Chinamen on the American emigrant train may be cited as an example in this regard. It affords an excellent illustration of the human tendency to paint a word-picture which pleases artist and reader by its sheer novelty and cleverness and finish. "For my own part," wrote R. L. Stevenson in *Across the Plains*, in his charming style, "I could not look but with wonder and respect on the Chinese. Their forefathers watched the stars before mine had begun to keep pigs." (Antiquarians sharply question this statement, I am told.) "Gunpowder and printing, which the other day we imitated, and a school of manners which we never had the delicacy so much as to desire to imitate, were theirs in a long past antiquity. They walk the earth with us, but it seems they must be of different clay. They hear the clock strike the same hour, yet surely of a different epoch. . . . Heaven knows if we had one common thought or fancy all that way, or whether our eyes which yet were formed upon the same design, beheld the same world out of the railway windows." Here the impressionist is carried away by his workable theme. After all, these Chinese, who were not necessarily conscious of racial antiquity, were, like the other emigrants, just pursuing the heart-absorbing quest of wealth, as had done their ancestors who trod out those ancient trade routes of Eastern and Central Asia, greedier for gold than for knowledge. They had at least, therefore, one particular motive in common with the medley of races that crowded the dingy railway carriages, and, among them, there may have been, for all we know, an Oriental Stevenson to whom even his own countrymen seemed strange fellows. The literary Scotsman, it may be noted, regarded the Cornishmen in the same saloon as eccentric aliens.

No greater gulf lies between the Easterner and the Westerner than exists between different classes of society in a single country. There is little in common, for instance, in everyday interests, between slow-witted Hodge in his turnip-field and the alert, calculating speculator on the Stock Exchange, or between the profiteer with an eye for the main chance and the boy-poet musing in his dug-out over a sad last beautiful poem revealing a wonderful soul-history, ere his brief but noble life is brought to an end by a chance bullet. Such men are surely "poles apart." Each would reckon the other, if brought into sudden contact, a strange and, perhaps, a dull fellow.

The average Easterner is not a symbol of the East, nor is the average Westerner necessarily typical of the West. Average men represent commonplace conditions of life and thought; they are puppets of environment. Not average men, but men endowed with a capacity for spiritual and intellectual development are those really capable of representing their race and country and of interpreting the inner life—"the life of life," as Shelley puts it—of which average men in all lands are but pale and sometimes distorted reflections. "All minds," says an Eastern poet, "reflect the Great Mind. Some, like a mirror, reflect the sun and rival it; others have no light to return, but take of it what they can receive, like a stone or a clod of earth." The intellectual life of a country is not reflected by its stones or clods.

National Literature

A first essential for the sympathetic understanding of East by West, or of West by East, is Knowledge. " Wherein lies happiness? " asked the poet Keats and his answer was:

> " *In that which becks*
> *Our ready minds to fellowship divine,*
> *A fellowship with essence.*"

The way to Knowledge is similarly oriented. It is to the Intellectual and not to the labourer, or the man of affairs, the so-called " hard-headed, practical man " who may be, outside his narrow sphere, quite a stupid man, that we look for a solution of the riddle propounded by Kipling.

Are East and West really so far apart as Kipling would have us believe? Do Easterners look on the world so differently from Westerners that it is not possible for them to find a common meeting ground? It is really " begging the question " to set down such queries. In the only real life, the intellectual life, East and West are less far apart than some would apparently care to acknowledge. " The Easterner is a mystic, for one thing," urges some confident theorist. But there are many Western mystics in poetry and prose, for mysticism is, after all, temperamental in essence. What of Blake, Carlyle, Browning, Burke, William Law, Coleridge, Wordsworth, Shelley and a host of others that could be mentioned? Plato was not an Indian, nor was Swedenborg, and the mystical Emerson was an American. The men who have done the thinking for the masses in East and West are not so far apart as are Anglo-Indian trader and native coolie, or as Thackeray's " Jeames " and his lordship whose clothing " Jeames " carefully folds and lays out as if nothing else mattered in life.

Those who would separate East from West forget that it is from the East that Europe has received the essential elements in its religious life. Nor was it merely from the " Near East "—from that wonderful land of Palestine, which " never produced anything of consequence except a great religious literature." For Palestine, as Western scholars have abundantly demonstrated, was itself debtor

270 to Egypt, Babylonia and Persia, and even, as some would have it, to Buddhistic India, for traces of Buddhist ideas are, it would appear, embedded in Isaiah and the Psalms of David. Before Christianity achieved full sway in Europe, it struggled for supremacy with Persian Mithraism which, although overcome in time, has, the scholars assert, left undeniable traces on European religious thought. It was from the East that civilization entered Europe, flowing along trade routes from the cradles of civilization in Egypt and Babylonia. The spiritual and intellectual life of Europe has an Eastern basis; what has flourished with vigour in the West is not necessarily wholly indigenous; from the roots rises the sap which feeds the blossom and the ripe fruit. It is not too much to assume that the influence imported from the area of origin is still flickering amidst the local fuel. Even science which is regarded as essentially Western, is Eastern in origin. Astronomy has emerged from the débris of Babylonian astrology, and the débris was not wholly cast off even in Shakespeare's day and still clings in odd quarters. Western clocks tick out Babylonian echoes, for time is measured on the Babylonian system. The very world is measured by Babylonian degrees. Europeans use the Egyptian calendar as adjusted and re-adjusted in Rome. Geometry was invented by Pharaoh's pyramid builders. The Brahmanic Indians gave the world Algebra, and the Arabs carried it westward. What ancient traders established the gold standard of currency? Was it the Egyptians or Babylonians? Who introduced the agricultural mode of life? What set of Easterners? And who but the Easterners first formed settled communities and built great cities with temples and palaces and villas and even slums? And who were the earliest seafarers and the earliest sculptors and philosophers and writers and publishers? Who would be so bold as to assert that East and West are so far apart when all that the West cherishes is rooted in the East? East and West met ages ago and still meet, and Time has made the East in our own day the heavy debtor of the West.

The gulf that separates the peoples with skins differently

pigmented is, in a sense, wholly mythical. Men in all parts of the world are prone to imagine that gulfs really exist. In the British Isles a gulf is set between Saxon and Celt, which takes much searching to perceive, and between Englishmen and Irishmen, and between Scotsmen and Englishmen and in Scotland between Highlanders and Lowlanders, and even in the Highlands, as the summer tourist discovers, between west coast men and east coast men. Among the Easterners there are many similar gulfs; there are Parsees, Hindus, Mussulmans, and so on, and numerous sub-divisions, and there are lands in which racial gulfs are bridged by the idea of nationality, as is the case in Europe. Between the Easterner and Westerner there is often found more in common than between two groups of Easterners. And in Europe East and West are sometimes more intimately associated than is one part of the West with another.

The Easterner who sojourns for a period in the West, with the purpose of devoting himself to the acquirement of a meed of Western knowledge, invariably looks for enlightenment, during his leisure hours, regarding the intellectual life of the British Isles, not by questioning " the hewers of wood and the drawers of water," but by perusing the works of great men—the real representatives of the West. English literature reveals to him the soul of the English-speaking peoples. When he begins to peruse English literature, he does so with a mind stored with a heritage of ideas, fashions and leanings that have come down through countless generations; and, ere he happens on the light that shines here as elsewhere, he has to accustom himself to local modes of expression and to individual idiosyncrasies. He must master the language to appreciate not only the sense of the metrical line—for he will inevitably begin with the poet—but also its music and verbal beauty. His first impressions depend very much on which poet, or group of poets, chance or a friend's guidance may place in his way. He may choose to begin with the very latest, and find himself startled by the materialism of Masefield:

" ' *Splash water on him, chaps. I only meant*
To hit him just a chip. . . '
' *God send; he looks damn bad,*' *the blacksmith said.*"

He may turn from the " Widow in the Bye Street " and
set himself to get through " Dauber " till an Eastern ray
suddenly breaks through the squalor and brutality of a
rough sea life in the lines:

" *Then in the sunset's flush they went aloft*
And unbent sails in that most lovely hour,
When the light gentles and the wind is soft,
And beauty in the heart breaks like a flower."

An Oriental may find himself in " Comus," from which
I quote, in a veritable Eastern atmosphere, especially when
reading Milton's lines on a song—that since first perusal
have haunted the writer's mind with a sense of mystery
and beauty; they are not surpassed even by Hafiz for
their imaginative and spiritual qualities. The lines I refer
to are:

" *At last a soft and solemn breathing sound*
Rose like a stream of rich distilled perfumes,
And stole upon the air, that even Silence
Was took ere she was 'ware, and wished she might
Deny her nature, and be never more,
Still to be so displaced. I was all ear,
And took in strains that might create a soul
Under the ribs of Death."

Those Himalayan heights of poetry, " Paradise Lost "
and " Paradise Regained " may be found too vast for
pleasurable appreciation without prolonged study, but
" Comus," " Lycidas," and the shorter poems readily
reveal a mind which appeals to the East as profoundly as
to the West.

If, by chance, the reader selects Swinburne, he may be
puzzled by numerous splashing and glimmering obscurities,
and rendered blind or breathless by long, dazzling lines
such as:

> " *Are thy feet on the ways of the limitless waters, thy wings*
> *on the winds of the waste north sea?*
> *Are the fires of the false north dawn over heavens where*
> *summer is stormful and strong like thee?* "

With relief he turns to the jungle of beauty in Keats with
its vivid word-pictures, sharply and swiftly outlined as in
Eastern poetry:

> " *Clear rills*
> *That for themselves a cooling covert make*
> *'Gainst the hot season.*"

> .   .   .   .   .

> *The rocks were silent, the wide sea did weave*
> *An untumultuous fringe of silver foam,*
> *Along the flat, brown sands.*"

In Keats the " Eastern atmosphere " is often evident. He
was a mystic whose religion was Beauty:

> " *Beauty is truth, truth Beauty, that is all*
> *Ye know on earth, and all ye need to know.*"

The introductory sketch to my volume of Keats' poems
is touched with a feeling of regret because the poet lived
among the flowers and ignored the English reservoirs of
learning,—because he was merely a " sensuous poet." An
Eastern perceives that Keats was one of the most intellectual of English poets. To him Truth, which is God,
was revealed by divine beauty. He enters into this Beauty
and becomes a part of it. In his " Endymion," so strangely
neglected, he exclaims:

> " *Behold*
> *The clear religion of heaven!* *Fold*
> *A rose-leaf round thy finger's taperness.*
> *And soothe thy lips; hist, when the airy stress*
> *Of music's Kiss impregnates the free winds. . . .*
> *Feel we these things?*—that moment have we stept
> Into a sort of oneness and our state
> Is like a floating spirit's.*"

S

Keats was no mere sensuous writer. Like the Eastern poets, he realized that Beauty is the essence of the Creator, to whom he really calls in these exquisite lines in "Endymion":

> " *Thou wast the deep glen;*
> *Thou wast the mountain top, the sage's pen,*
> *The poet's harp, the voice of friends, the sun;*
> *Thou wast the river, thou wast glory won;*
> *Thou wast the clarion's blast, thou wast my steed,*
> *My goblet full of wine, my topmost deed:*
> *Thou wast the charm of women, lovely Moon!* "

A deep sense of what may justly be called religious fervour of great poetic intensity pulsated in the soul of this mystical singer. His love of Beauty was adoration of God.

But of all the English poets with whom the Easterner makes early acquaintance, none impresses so readily, so intimately and so permanently as the saintly Shelley, over whom some writers still shake their heads, because of an offence committed against a social convention, despite all the sorrow it brought him. An Easterner can understand this point of view, but he cannot understand what is meant by "Shelley's atheism." In the East the religious sage may be found speculating with even more freedom than did Shelley regarding the mysteries of life and death. Speculation was in the old days encouraged, in the East, and it is still regarded as an attribute of an independent mind. Who can understand the truth if he has never had a cloud of doubt overshadowing his mind? All of us have been loitering in the shadows. The honest man admits his doubts, the impulsive man is no less honest if he insists on them at some period in his life, and declares that the shadow is the only reality. Shelley did this, and it has not yet been forgotten by the orthodox who are "less forgiving than God and therefore somewhat ungodly," as an Eastern sage puts it.

"I never read Shelley because I detest atheistical writings," declared one of my English friends; another, a

Scot, asserted, " There is nothing in Shelley but winds and waters and birds and clouds." Yet Shelley was in the real sense a prophet and a teacher of humanity, one of the greatest minds England has produced, as well as one of its greatest singers, if not its very greatest, not excepting Shakespeare. For Shakespeare never wrote such lyrics as did Shelley and never revealed himself as a solitary pilgrim-thinker in the spiritual world, as did the author of " The Hymn to Intellectual Beauty." Shakespeare was concerned about human character. Shelley was more concerned about human destiny. It is necessary to draw this distinction because there are those who would deny to Shelley, as to Keats, those intellectual qualities which are necessary for the production of great poetry. Both were profound, spiritually-minded thinkers; they were also seers in the real sense; at any rate, in the sense understood in the East. A Persian critic would be inclined to place Shelley and Keats above Shakespeare and yet not fail to admire Shakespeare as much as does the English critic.

Shelley, far from being an atheist, believed that God pervaded all things. He saw the Divine Spirit in Nature, in the tree instinct with life, in the moving river, in the " still, snowy and serene " Mont Blanc, in the cloud, in the skylark, in man. Life was but an episode in the history of man, and Eternity was to him an enduring reality; he sings in the " Adonais ":

> " *The One remains, the many change and pass;*
> *Heaven's light forever shines, Earth's shadows fly;*
> *Life, like a dome of many-coloured glass,*
> *Stains the white radiance of Eternity,*
> *Until Death tramples it to fragments.—Die*
> *If thou wouldst be with that which thou dost seek!*
> *Follow where all is fled! . . .*
> *Why linger, why turn back, why shrink, my Heart?*
> *Thy hopes are gone before . . .*
> *No more let Life divide what Death can join together.*"

Light and Beauty were to Shelley manifestations of divine truth, and Love was God's beauty gleaming in the

276 heart of man. His was a lovely and inspiring creed—
" pleasant if one consider it ":

> " *That Light whose smile kindles the Universe,*
> *That beauty in which all things work and move,*
> *That Benediction which the eclipsing Curse*
> *Of birth can quench not, that sustaining Love*
> *Which through the web of being blindly wove*
> *By man and beast and earth and air and sea,*
> *Burns bright or dim, as each are mirrors of*
> *The fire for which all thirst; now beams on me*
> *Consuming the last clouds of cold mortality.*"

Shelley believed in the immortality of the soul, which, as he held, existed before birth and will endure after death. In that wonderful poem, " Ginevra," he pictures the horrors of death:

> " *When there is felt around*
> *A smell of clay, a pale and icy glare,*
> *And silence.*"

Death comes suddenly to his heroine:

> " *The dark arrow fled*
> *In the moon.*"

He contemplates the earthly phenomena of death with horror, not devoid of grandeur.

> " *Ere the sun through heaven once more has rolled,*
> *The rats in her heart*
> *Will have made their nest,*
> *And the worms be alive in her golden hair;*
> While the spirit that guides the sun,
> Sits throned in his flaming chair,
> She shall sleep."

But that is not the whole story of human destiny as felt in the shadows:

> " *In our night*
> *Of thought we know thus much of death—no more*
> *Than the unborn dream of our life before*
> *Their barks are wrecked on its inhospitable shore.*"

Shelley, like the spirit of his own "West Wind," searched the whole world for God and found Him in the mind of man, the greatest of all Divine gifts, for the gift of mind unites all with the One. The poet makes this clear in his strange poem "Julian and Maddalo," in which the Count says to his friend:

> " *The words you spoke last night might well have cast*
> *A darkness on my spirit—if man be*
> *The passive thing you say, I should not see*
> *Much harm in the religious and old saws*
> (*Tho' I may never own such leaden laws*)
> *Which break a teachless nature to the yoke*:
> *Mine is another faith.*"

Then we are given a glimpse of the beautiful faith of this saintly and mystical singer of England:

> " *See*
> *This lovely child, blithe, innocent and free,*
> *She spends a happy time with little care*
> *While we to such sick thoughts subjected are*
> *As came on you last night—it is our will*
> *That thus enchains us to permitted ill—*
> We might be otherwise—we might be all
> We dream of, happy, high, majestical.
> Where is the love, beauty and truth we seek
> But in our mind? and if we were not weak
> Should we be less in deed than in desire? "

Burns is usually referred to as a "love poet," but Shelley was more truly that, for he sang of the Greater Love, the Love which is God. This love, revealed in beauty to the eye in Nature, was similarly revealed to him in the beauty of character and the beauty of the ideals of peace and justice. He dreamed of the return of the Perfect Age when War would cease to be and men would perceive that there are greater victories than can be won on the battlefield, that there are higher ideals than blood-shedding can bring to frail man.

" The world's great age begins anew,
The golden years return.
The earth doth like a snake renew
Her wintry weeds outworn :
Heaven smiles, and faith and empires gleam
Like wrecks of a dissolving dream."

.   .   .   .   .

" Oh write no more the Tale of Troy,
If earth Death's Scroll must be ! "

The difference between Shelley and the Brahmanic
authors of the " Upanishads " is most marked in one
particular respect. In the famous " Forest Books " of
India, the sages are really agnostics. They despair of the
human mind ever being able to solve the riddle of existence.
They cannot tell aught of God except negatively. They
know what God is not, but not what God is. Shelley
is a seer with a positive knowledge of divine truth. To him
Love and Beauty were synonymous with the Divine
Being. He rejoices in the thought of all-pervading Love.
The idea of Divine Love never occurred to the authors of
the coldly speculative " Upanishads " who likewise were
blind to Divine Beauty. The Brahmans realized that they
could not sway the masses with their vague speculations,
and they provided a host of gods and goddesses with as
many attributes as there was need or demand for. But
behind all their pantheons remains the haunting belief that
nothing positively can be known regarding Narayana or
Brahma, or whatever name they choose to apply to the
unknown God. But Shelley had a definite message for
humanity, and it was essentially a poetical message. He
desired men and women to live noble lives which would
reflect divine beauty and divine love, not by the per-
formance of certain rites, not by the organization of creeds
and cults, but by thinking and living in a manner worthy
of their ideals. To be " one with Nature " meant to
Shelley to be " one with God."

Like the Easterner, Shelley had a symbolizing mind. He
thought in symbols. In Greek mythology he found,

ready-made, a host of Deities whom he spiritualized and glorified. His " Prometheus " is not, however, the old Greek Prometheus at all. He is Shelley's symbol of the human intelligence struggling with the chains that bind him, and the poet's " Asia " is his ideal of Eternal Love. This Love, married to intelligence, produces a new and better world.

Shelley's tendency to deify Nature, which puzzled his critics, including his wife, is manifested in that beautiful poem, " The Witch of Atlas," which, had it been composed by an Indian Brahman, would have added another deity to the Hindu Pantheon. In his lines " To Mary," written because she objected to the " Witch " " upon the score of its containing no human interest," he compares the poem to Wordsworth's " Peter Bell," and says:

> " *If you unveil my Witch, no priest nor primate*
> *Can shrive you of that sin—if sin there be*
> *In Love*, when it becomes idolatry."

Here we have the keynote of the poem, which is no mere fantasy, and something more even than " one of the most ' poetic poems ' in the English language," I never weary of studying the " Witch ":

> " *So fair a creature, as she lay enfolden*
> *In the warm shadow of her loveliness*."

> " *A lovely lady garmented in light*
> *From her own beauty—deep her eyes, as are*
> *Two openings of unfathomable night*
> *Seen through a Temple's cloven roof—her hair*
> *Dark—the dim brain whirls dizzy with delight,*
> *Picturing her form: her soft smiles shone afar,*
> *And her low voice was heard like love, and drew*
> *All living things towards this wonder new*."

One reads with feelings of reverence, perceiving that the lady is the symbol of that Love which to Shelley was the Eternal Good. The beauty of the metrical music and the abundant imagery intensify the spell of the poet's dream:

> " *The deep recesses of her odorous dwelling*
> *Were stored with magic treasures—sounds of air,*
> *Which had the power all spirits of compelling,*
> *Folded in cells of crystal silence there;*
> *Such as we hear in youth, and think the feeling*
> *Will never die.*"

This reference is to Shelley's youth, let us remember, when he had visions of Eternal Purpose which are not realized wholly in this life of ours. The Witch of the poet says to mortals:

> " *Oh, ask not me*
> *To love you till your little race is run;*
> *I cannot die as ye must.*"

She revealed herself in all that is beautiful by night and day, in the clear heaven, among the stars, in the ravine with its roaring river and on the summits of lofty and lonely mountains. She hovered over mankind by night. The poet imagines her visions in the wonderful lines:

> " *A pleasure sweet doubtless it was to see*
> *Mortals subdued in all the shapes of sleep.*
> *Here lay two sister twins in infancy;*
> *There, a lone youth who in his dreams did weep;*
> *Within, two lovers linked innocently*
> *In their loose locks which over both did creep*
> *Like ivy from one stem;—and there lay calm*
> *Old age with snow-bright hair and folded palm.*
>
> *But other troubled forms of sleep she saw,*
> *Not to be mirrored in a holy song—*
> *Distortions foul of supernatural awe,*
> *And pale imaginings of visioned wrong;*
> *And all the code of custom's lawless law*
> *Written upon the brows of old and young:*
> ' *This,' said the wizard maiden, ' is the strife*
> *Which stirs the liquid surface of man's life.'* "

She gives dreams to the sleepers, and each dream reveals the character of the dreamer. Those worthy of her love:

> " *She did unite again with visions clear*
> *Of deep affection and of truth sincere.*"

Why this poem should be neglected, or regarded merely as a poet's fantasy, sorely puzzles an Easterner. It has more poetry and more beauty and more truth than can be found in a dozen of the " popular poems " so often reproduced in anthologies. " The Witch of Atlas " is worth more than many " Don Juans," and is more beautiful than a Dauber, more human than an " Everlasting Mercy," more spiritual than many " Idylls of the King." One must go back to half-forgotten Spenser, " the poet's poet," for such a glimpse of:

> " *That soveraine light*
> *From whose pure beams all perfect beauty springs,*
> *That kindled love in every godly spright*
> Even the love of God: *which loathing brings*
> *Of this vile world and these gay-seeming things.*"

There is much in common between Shelley and Spenser, although the latter takes a longer time to tell his story. Compare, for instance, Shelley's " Hymn to Intellectual Beauty " and Spenser's " Hymne of Heavenly Beautie " in which the same message is given:

> " *Him to behold, is on his workes to looke.*"

And yet Spenser is regarded by many as a poet who wrote musical verse mainly about such trifling and archaic things as fairies and ogres met by wandering knights of old romance. But the poets who followed him heard and understood him, and hailed him, as does Wordsworth, in his enchanting " Prelude ":

> " *Sweet Spenser, moving through his clouded heaven*
> *With the moon's beauty and the moon's soft pace.*"

It cannot be said that Wordsworth is neglected. But he does not seem to appeal to his own countrymen in the same manner as he does to an Easterner, that is, as a seer like Shelley, Keats and Spenser. He knew himself to be a seer, and in his " Prelude " and " Excursion," which so many critics regard as " failures " because they forget that the poet's message is of more account than his manner of setting it forth, and that it could not be concentrated in a series of pretty songs. He required space for his great pronouncement to humanity—the memorable inspiring message he was sent into this world to deliver. A poet without a great message is a mere piper of empty tunes, a mere clasher of brazen cymbals, a mere idolator who bows the knee to Baal in the name of Art, or a noisy reveller in the train of Bacchus. The merely " popular poet " is usually the poet with least intelligence and smallest soul, the poet who strikes the right note of mediocrity for business purposes, or who makes pretty phrases out of trite ideas fashionable in his age, or who glorifies the weaknesses and excesses of mere sensual passion which conceal the Divine spark by its formless, exaggerated and obscuring cloudiness. There is no real beauty which is not a manifestation of the Divine—not the Divine who is a god of a cult—but the divine spirit which is revealed in beauty and love in the heart or in nature.

A manly godliness of spirit is apparent in all immortal verse. He who creates even a poem must bear resemblance to the Creator of all that is beautiful and good and true. Let us not have Art for Art's sake, but Art for God's sake—Art which interprets the Divine element in mankind.

That Wordsworth realized all this is abundantly shown in his autobiographical poem " The Prelude " which is, without doubt, the most wonderful autobiography ever written in any country. He gives his account of what Westerners call his " conversion " in the fourth book. It occurred during a " sober hour " on a dewy evening:

> " *Gently did my soul*
> *Put off her veil, and, self-transmuted, stood*
> *Naked, as in the presence of her God.*
> *While on I walked, a comfort seemed to touch*
> *A heart that had not been disconsolate:*
> *I had inward hopes*
> *And swellings of the spirit, was rapt and soothed,*
> *Conversed with promises, had glimmering views*
> *How life pervades the undecaying mind*

> *How the immortal soul with God-like power*
> *Informs, creates, and thaws the deepest sleep*
> *That time can lay upon her."*

Having acquired " clearer knowledge," Wordsworth saw a new world which was the old, for there was divine love in his heart. The artist in him had been awakened by a loving influence sent direct from God who loves all. Then he became godlike as he relates:

> *" I loved,*
> *More deeply all that had been loved before,*
> *More deeply even than ever."*

Addressing Coleridge, he declares that poets had a message for mankind:

> *" Prophets of Nature, we to them will speak*
> *A lasting inspiration, sanctified*
> *By reason, blest by faith; what we have loved*
> *Others will love and we will teach them how."*

These thoughts might well be translated from Persian or Arabic. East and West are more closely akin than some writers and travellers appear to realize, and this is particularly true in reference to intellectual life.

The religious systems may differ, and divergent views may be entertained as to which religion is the true religion. But in the lands " somewhere East of Suez," as in England, the seer-poets who have lived near to God enable all to surmount barriers and reach those green places which form the garden of God. There all may feel as did the Irish poet:

> *" The stars sang in God's garden,*
> *The stars are the birds of God;*
> *The night-time is God's harvest,*
> *Its fruits are the words of God."*

In the " garden of God " are those divinely-inspired singers from whom we have much to learn as Eastern and Western children of the same Creator. In His eyes East and West are one.

PRE-ISLAMIC ARABIC POETRY

In the following extracts from Sir Charles Lyall's translations will be found the gems of pre-Islamic Arabic poetry. " It is a poetry which makes it its main business to depict life and nature as they are, with little addition of phantasy." The authors of the extracts lived at various periods of history, beginning from the fifth century A.D. The warlike atmosphere of practically all of them is noteworthy. Some of these works were hung from the idol-infested Shrine of Mecca as the finest poems of their time.

III

AL-FIND OF THE BANÛ ZIMMÂN

Forgiveness had we for Hind's sons:
*   we said: ' The men our brothers are:*
The Days may bring that yet again
*   they be the folk that once they were.'*

But when the Ill stood clear and plain,
*   and naked Wrong was bare to day,*
And nought was left but bitter Hate—
*   we paid them in the coin they gave.*

We strode as stalks a lion forth
*   at dawn, a lion wrathful-eyed;*
Blows rained we, dealing shame on shame,
*   and humbling pomp and quelling pride.*

Too kind a man may be with fools,
*   and move them but to flout him more;*
And Mischief oft may bring thee peace,
*   when Mildness works not Folly's cure.*

V

JA'FAR SON OF 'ULBAH, OF THE BANU-L-HÂRITH

The poet with two companions went forth to plunder the herds of 'Ukail, a neighbour-tribe, and was beset on his way back by detached parties of that tribe in the valley of Sahbal, whom he overcame and reached home safe.

*That even when under Sahbal's twin peaks upon us drave the
      horsemen troop after troop, and the foemen pressed us
      sore—*
*They said to us—" Two things lie before you: now must ye
      choose—the points of the spears couched at you, or, if ye
      will not, chains."*
*We answered them—" Yea, this thing may fall to you after
      fight, when men shall be left on ground, and none shall
      arise again;*
*But we know not, if we quail before the assault of Death,
      how much may be left of Life: the goal is too dim
      to see."*
*We strode to the strait of battle: there cleared us a space
      around the white swords in our right hands which the
      smiths had furbished fair.*
*To them fell the edge of my blade on that day of Sahbal dale,
      and mine was the share thereof whereover my fingers
      closed.*

VIII

THÂBIT SON OF JÂBIR OF FAHM,
CALLED TA'ABBATA, SHARRAN

He was at feud with the tribe of Lihyân, a branch of Hudhail, of whom he had slain many. One day he went forth to gather wild honey in a cave situated near the top of a steep precipice, into which he was let down by a rope from the edge of the cliff, while his companions kept watch above. But Hudhail had had news of their coming, and laid an ambush for them, which rose against them and put them to flight. Then the men of Lihyân came to the edge of the cliff, and shook the rope, and called upon Ta'abbata to yield himself prisoner. He began to parley with them, and as he did so, poured forth the honey upon the rock from the mouth of the cave; then he bound upon his breast the skin in which he had stored the honey, and spread himself out upon the slide thus prepared. And he did not cease to slide down thus, kept from slipping by the tenacity of the honey, until he reached the level safe. And he returned unharmed to Fahm, and made this poem to tell of his adventure.

A man must be crafty and wise when peril is round his road, or else is his labour vain, he follows a luck that flees.

Yea, his is the wary soul, on whom lights a thing to do and finds him alert, intent, his end straight before his eyes;

Against him the wild Days dash—he meets them with cunning mind: is one of his nostrils stopped? he breathes through the other free!

To Lihyân I said—(they deemed they had me beyond escape, my day trapped in narrow room, no issue but through their throng)

" Ye give me my choice of two—to yield me and beg for life, or die: and a free man's choice of these twain were surely death.

But yet is a third way left: I ponder it deep within; and there lies a road, methinks, where craft may befriend and skill."

I spread forth my breast thereto: there slid down the rock-face smooth a man stout and square of chest, and slender of flank and lean;

And safe did he reach the ground below down the dizzy cliff with never a scratch, while Death looked on at his deed ashamed.

So gained I again my tribe—and well-nigh returned no more: yea, many the like case lies behind me, and here am I.

X

KATARÎ SON OF AL-FUJÂ'ÂH OF MAZIN

I said to her when she fled in amaze and breathless
  before the array of battle—Why dost thou tremble?
Yea, if but a day of Life thou shouldst beg with weeping
  beyond what thy Doom appoints, thou wouldst not gain it.
Be still then, and face the onset of Death, high-hearted,
  for none upon Earth shall win to abide for ever.
No raiment of praise the cloak of old age and weakness:
  none such for the coward who bows like a reed in tempest.
The pathway of Death is set for all men to travel:
  the Crier of Death proclaims through the Earth his empire.
Who dies not when young and sound dies old and weary,
  cut off in his length of days from all love and kindness;
And what for a man is left of delight in living,
  past use, flung away, a worthless and worn-out chattel?

XI

BASHÂMAH SON OF HAZN OF NAHSHAL

We give thee greeting O Salmà: do thou give us greeting
  back; and if thou givest the cup to the noblest reach it
  to us!
And if thou callest one day to a mighty and valiant deed the
  chiefest of noble men, let thy call go forth to us.
Sons of Nahshal are we: no father we claim but him, nor
  would he sell us for any other sons.
When a goal of glory is set and the runners rush forth thereto,
  of us shalt thou find in the race the foremost and the
  next.
And never there comes to die a mighty man of our line, but
  we wean among us a boy to be mighty in his stead.
Cheap do we hold our lives when the day of dread befalls;
  but if we should set them for sale in peace, they would
  cost men dear.

White are our foreheads and worn: for ever our cauldrons boil: we heal with our rich store the wounds our hands have made.

I come of a house whose elders have fallen one by one as they sprang to the cry of the fighters—" Where are the helpers now? "

If there should be among a thousand but one of us, and men should call—" Ho! a knight! " he would think that they meant him.

When the fighters blench and quail before the deadly stroke of the sword-edge, we leap forth and catch it in our hands.

Never shalt thou see them, though their loss be great and sore, weeping among the weepers over him that is dead!

Many a time we bestride the steed of peril and death, but our valour bears us back safe, and the swords that help us well.

XII

'ABD-AL-MALIK SON OF 'ABD-AR-RAHÎM, OF THE BANU-D-DAYYÂN

When a man stains not his honour by doing a deed of shame, whatso be the raiment he wears, fair is it and comely;

And if he takes not on his soul the burden of loss and toil, there lies not before him any road to praise and glory.

She cast blame on us that our number was little to count and few: I answered her—" Yea : the count of noble men is little.

But not few canst thou call those whose remnants are like to us—young men who vie with the old in the quest of glory.

It hurts us nought that we be few, when our friend by us is safe, though the friends of most men beside be trampled;

A mountain we have where dwells he whom we shelter there, lofty, before whose height the eye falls back blunted:

Deep-based is its root below ground, while overhead there soars its peak to the stars of heaven whereto no man reaches.

A folk are we who deem it no shame to be slain in fight, though
    that be the deeming thereof of Salûl and 'Amir;
Our love of death brings near to us our days of doom, but
    there dooms shrink from death and stand far distant.
There dies among us no lord of quiet death in his bed, and
    never is blood of us poured forth without vengeance.
Our souls stream forth in a flood from the edge of the whetted
    swords: no otherwise than so does our spirit leave its
    mansion.
Pure is our stock, unsullied: fair is it kept and bright by
    mothers whose bed bears well, and fathers mighty.
To the best of the Uplands we wend, and when the season
    comes, we travel adown to the best of fruitful valleys.
Like rain of the heaven are we: there is not in all our
    line one blunt of heart, nor among us is counted a
    niggard.
We say nay whenso we will to the words of other men: but
    no man to us says nay when we give sentence.
When passes a lord of our line, in his stead there rises straight
    a lord to say the say and do the deeds of the noble.
Our beacon is never quenched to the wanderer of the night,
    nor has ever a guest blamed us where men meet together.
Our Days are famous among our foemen, of fair report,
    branded and blazed with glory like noble horses.
Our swords have swept throughout all lands both West and
    East, and gathered many a notch from the steel of
    hauberk-wearers;
Not used are they when drawn to be laid back in their
    sheaths before that the folk they meet are spoiled and
    scattered.
If thou knowest not, ask men what they think of us and
    them:—not alike are he that knows and he that knows
    not.
The children of ad-Dayyân are the shaft of their people's
    mill: around them it turns and whirls, while they stand
    midmost."

XVI

HITTÂN SON OF AL-MU'ALLÀ OF TAYYI

Fortune has brought me down—her wonted way—
from station great and high to low estate;
Fortune has rent away my plenteous store:
of all my wealth honour alone is left.
Fortune has turned my joy to tears: how oft
did Fortune make me laugh with what she gave!
But for these girls, the katà's *downy brood,*
unkindly thrust from door to door as hard—
Far would I roam and wide to seek my bread
in Earth that has no lack of breadth and length.
Nay, but our children in our midst, what else
but our hearts are they, walking on the ground?
If but the bree₂e blow harsh on one of them,
mine eye says no to slumber all night long.

XVII

'URWAH SON OF AL-WARD OF 'ABS

God's scorn on the homeless wight who under the pall of
Night goes cowering the shambles through, and gathers
the marrow-bones!
Who comforts his heart, full rich, as oft as at even-tide he
lights on a wealthy friend to yield him his fill of milk.
He lies in the twilight down, and drowsy the morrow wakes,
and shakes from his dust-spread side the gravel where
he has lain!
A help to the women-folk in all that they bid him do, at even
he sinks outworn like camel outstretched to die.
So he: but the homeless wight the breadth of whose valiant
face glows bright as a mighty flame that shines through
the midnight mirk,
A terror to all he hates, besetting their way with fear, while
home-bound they curse him deep, as losers the luckless
shaft:

*Though far from his haunts they dwell, they image his coming
    nigh and watch, as his kinsmen watch when one whom
    they love comes home:*
*Yea, he, if he lights on Death in faring his way, a death of
    glory it is; and if on Riches one day, how due!*

XVIII

SA'D SON OF MÂLIK, OF THE TRIBE OF KAIS
SON OF THA'LABAH, OF BAKR

How evil a thing is War, that bows men to shameful rest!
War burns away in her blaze all glory and boasting of men:
*Nought stands but the valiant heart to face pain, the hard-
    hoofed steed,*
*The ring-mail set close and firm, the nail-crowned helms and
    the spears,*
*And onset again after rout, when men shrink from the serried
    array—*
*Then then, fall away all the vile, the hirelings, and Shame is
    strong!*
War girds up her skirts before them, and Evil unmixed is bare.
*For their hearts were for maidens veiled, not for driving the
    gathered spoil:*
Yea, evil the heirs we leave, sons of Yashkur and al-Lakâh!
*But let flee her fires who will, no flinching for me, son of
    Kais!*
*O children of Kais, stand firm before her, gain peace or
    give:*
*Who seeks flight before her fear, his Doom stands and bars
    the road.*
*Away! Death allows no quitting of place, and brands are
    bare!*
*What is life for us when the Uplands and valleys are ours no
    more?*
*Ah, where are the mighty now, the spears and the generous
    hands?*

XXII

DURAID SON OF AS-SIMMAH OF JUSHAM

He tells how his brother 'Abdallâh met his death and what manner of man he was.

I warned them both 'Arid and the men who went 'Arid's way—the House of the Black Mother: yea all are my witnesses.

I said to them: " Think—even now two thousand are on your track, all laden with sword and spear, their captains in Persian mail."

But when they would hearken not, I followed their road, though I knew well they were fools and that I walked not in Wisdom's way.

For am not I but one of Ghazîyah? and if they err I err with my house; and if Ghazîyah go right, so I.

I read them my rede one day at Mun'araj al-Liwà: the morrow at noon they saw my counsel as I had seen.

A shout rose, and voices cried—" The horsemen have slain a knight! " I said—" Is it 'Abdallâh, the man who ye say is slain? "

I sprang to his side: the spears had riddled his body through as weaver on outstretched web plies deftly the sharp-toothed comb.

I stood as a camel stands with fear in her heart, and seeks the stuffed skin with eager mouth, and thinks — is her youngling slain?

I plied spear above him till the riders had left their prey, and over myself black blood flowed forth in a dusky tide.

I fought as a man who gives his life for his brother's life, who knows that his time is short, that Death's doom above him hangs.

But know ye, if 'Abdallâh be dead, and his place a void, no weakling unsure of hand, and no holder-back was he!

Alert, keen, his loins well girt, his leg to the middle bare, unblemished and clean of limb, a climber to all things high:

No wailer before ill luck: one mindful in all he did to think
how his work to-day would live in to-morrow's tale:
Content to bear hunger's pain though meat lay beneath his
hand—to labour in ragged shirt that those whom he
served might rest.
If Dearth laid her hand on him, and Famine devoured his
store, he gave but the gladlier what little to him they
spared.
He dealt as a youth with Youth, until, when his head grew
hoar and age gathered o'er his brow, to Lightness he
said—Begone!
Yea, somewhat it soothes my soul that never I said to him
" Thou liest," nor grudged him aught of mine that he
sought of me.

XXIV

TA'ABBATA SHARRAN OF FAHM

His mother's brother had been slain by Hudhail, leaving
to him the duty of vengeance. In this poem he tells how
the message found him, of the mighty deeds and great heart
of the slain man, the onslaught which led in the end to his
fall, the many deeds of daring which Hudhail had to
avenge on him, and the stern vengeance taken by himself
for his uncle's death.

In the cleft of the rocks below Sal' is lying
one slain whose blood drips not without vengeance.
He left the burthen to me and departed,
and I take up the load lightly and bear it—
A heritage of bloodshed to me the son of
his sister, one dauntless,—his knot none looses,
Downcast of eyes, dripping poison, like as
the hooded asp that spits venom, the adder.

Fearful the tidings that reach us, heavy—
the heaviest of burthens thereby is nothing!
Fate has cut off from us, Fate the tyrant,
one mighty whose friend none dared to belittle:

294

A sunshine in wintertide, until when
  the Dog-star burned, he was coolness and shadow;
Lean-sided and thin, but not from lacking:
  liberal-handed, keen-hearted, haughty;

He journeyed with Wariness, and where he halted,
  there Wariness halted herself his comrade;
A rushing rainflood when he gave of his fullness:
  when he sprang to the onset, a mighty lion;
In the midst of his kin flowed his long black hair, and
  his skirts trailed: in war a wolf's whelp with lean flanks;
Two savours had he, of honey and gall; and
  one or the other all men have tasted:
He rode Fear alone without a fellow
  but only his deep-notched blade of al-Yaman.

Many of the warriors, noon-journeying, who when
  night fell, journeyed on, and halted at dawning—
Keen each one of them, girt with a keen blade,
  that when one drew it flashed forth like the lightning—
They were tasting of sleep by sips, when as
  they nodded, thou didst fright them, and they were scattered!
Vengeance we did on them: there escaped us
  of the two houses none save the fewest.

And if Hudhail broke the edge of his sword-blade—
  many the notch that Hudhail gained from him!
Many the time that he made them kneel down on
  jagged rocks where the hoof is worn with running!
Many the morning he fell on their shelter,
  and after slaughter came plunder and spoiling!
Hudhail has been burned by me, one valiant
  whom Evil tires not though they be wearied—
Whose spear drinks deep the first draught, and thereon
  drinks deep again of the blood of foemen.
Forbidden was wine, but now is it lawful:
  hard was the toil that made it lawful!
Reach me the cup, O Sawâd son of 'Amir:
  spent is my body with grief for mine uncle.

To Hudhail we gave to drink Death's goblet,
  whose dregs are disgrace and shame and dishonour.
The hyena laughs over the slain of Hudhail, and
  the wolf—see thou—grins by their corpses,
And the vultures flap their wings, full-bellied
  treading their dead, too gorged to leave them.

XXXII

SŪLMÎ SON OF RABÎ'AH, OF DABBAH

Roast flesh, the glow of fiery wine,
  to speed on camel fleet and sure
As thy soul lists to urge her on
  through all the hollow's breadth and length;
White women statue-like that trail
  rich robes of price with golden hem,
Wealth, easy lot, no dread of ill,
  to hear the lute's complaining string—
These are Life's joys. For man is set
  the prey of Time, and Time is change.
Life strait or large, great store or nought,
  all's one to Time, all men to Death.

XLIX

FROM THE MU'ALLAKAH OF IMRA-AL-KAIS

O Friend—see the lightning there! it flickered, and now is
  gone, as though flashed a pair of hands in the pillar of
  crowned cloud.
Nay, was it its blaze, or the lamps of a hermit that dwells
  alone, and pours o'er the twisted wicks the oil from his
  slender cruse?
We sat there, my fellows and I, twixt Dârij and al-'Udhaib,
  and gazed as the distance gloomed, and waited its
  oncoming.
The right of its mighty rain advanced over Katan's ridge:
  the left of its trailing skirt swept Yadhbul and as-Sitâr;

Then over Kutaifah's steep the flood of its onset drave, and headlong before its storm the tall trees were borne to ground;

And the drift of its waters passed o'er the crags of al-Kanân, and drave forth the white-legged deer from the refuge they sought therein.

And Taimà—it left not there the stem of a palm aloft, nor ever a tower, save one firm built on the living rock.

And when first its misty shroud bore down upon Mount Thabîr, he stood like an ancient man in a gray-streaked mantle wrapt.

The clouds cast their burden down on the broad plain of al-Ghabît, as a trader from al-Yaman unfolds from the bales his store;

And the topmost crest on the morrow of al-Mujaimir's cairn was heaped with the flood-borne wrack like wool on a distaff wound.

At earliest dawn on the morrow the birds were chirping blithe, as though they had drunken draughts of riot in fiery wine;

And at even the drowned beasts lay where the torrent had borne them, dead, high up on the valley sides, like earth-stained roots of squills.

L

THE MU'ALLAKAH OF ZUHAIR

Are they of Umm Aufà's tents—these black lines that speak no word in the stony plain of al-Mutathallam and ad-Darrâj?

Yea, and the place where her camp stood in ar-Rakmatân is now like the tracery drawn afresh by the veins of the inner wrist.

The wild kine roam there large-eyed, and the deer pass to and fro, and their younglings rise up to suck from the spots where they lie all round.

I stood there and gazed: since I saw it last twenty years had flown, and much I pondered thereon: hard was it to know again—

The black stones in order laid in the place where the pot was set, and the trench like a cistern's root with its sides unbroken still.

And when I knew it at last for her resting-place, I cried— " Good greeting to thee, O House—fair peace in the morn to thee! "

Look forth, O Friend—canst thou see aught of ladies camel-borne that journey along the upland there above Jurthum well?

Their litters are hung with precious stuffs, and thin veils thereon cast loosely, their borders rose, as though they were dyed in blood.

Sideways they sat as their beasts clomb the ridge of as-Sûbân—in them were the sweetness and grace of one nourished in wealth and ease.

They went on their way at dawn—they started before sunrise: straight did they make for the vale of ar-Rass as hand for mouth.

Dainty and playful their mood to one who should try its worth, and faces fair to an eye skilled to trace out loveliness.

And the tassels of scarlet wool in the spots where they gat them down glowed red like to 'ishrik seeds, fresh-fallen, unbroken, bright.

And when they reached the wells where the deep blue water lies, they cast down their staves and set them to pitch the tents for rest.

On their right-hand rose al-Kanân and the rugged skirts thereof—and in al-Kanân how many are foes and friends of mine!

At eve they left as-Sûbân: then they crossed its ridge again, borne on the fair-fashioned litters, all new and builded broad.

I swear by the Holy House which worshippers circle round— the men by whose hands it rose, of Jurhum and of Kuraish—

How goodly are ye, our Lords, ye twain who are found by men good helpers in every case, be it easy to loose or hard!

Busily wrought they for peace, those two of Ghaidh, Murrah's
    son, when the kin had been rent in twain and its friend-
    ship sunk in blood.

Ye healed Ab's and Dhubyân's breach when the twain were
    well-nigh spent, and between them the deadly perfume of
    Manshim was working hate.

Ye said—" If we set our hands to Peace, base it broad and
    firm by the giving of gifts and fair words of friendship,
    all will be well."

And ye steadfastly took your stand thereon in the best of
    steads, far away from unbrotherliness and the bitter
    result of wrong.

Yea, glory ye gained in Ma'add, the highest—God guide you
    right! who gains without blame a treasure of glory,
    how great is he!

The wounds of the kindred were healed with hundreds of
    camels good: he paid them forth troop by troop who had
    no part in the crime;

Kin paid them forth to kin as a debt due from friend to friend,
    and they spilt not between them so much as a cupper's
    cup full of blood.

Among them went forth, your gift, of the best of your fathers'
    store, fair spoils, young camels a many, slit-eared, of
    goodly breed.

Ho! carry my message true to the tribesmen together leagued
    and Dhubyân—Have ye sworn all that ye took upon
    you to swear?

It boots not to hide from God aught evil within your breasts:
    it will not be hid—what men would hold back from
    God, He knows.

It may be its meed comes late: in the Book is the wrong set
    down for the Reckoning Day; it may be that vengeance
    is swift and stern.

And War is not aught but what ye know well and have tasted oft:
    not of her are the tales ye tell a doubtful or idle thing.

When ye set her on foot, ye start her with words of little
    praise; but the mind for her grows with her growth, till
    she burst into blazing flame.

*She will grind you as grist of the mill that falls on the skin
    beneath; year by year shall her womb conceive, and the
    fruit thereof shall be twins;*

*Yea, boys shall she bear you, all of ill omen, eviller than
    Ahmar of 'Ad: then suckling and weaning shall bring
    their gain;*

*Such harvest of bitter grain shall spring as their lords reap
    not from acres in al-'Irâk of bushels of corn and gold.*

*Yea, verily good is the kin, and unmeet the deed of wrong
    Husain son of Damdam wrought against them, a murder
    foul!*

*He hid deep within his heart his bloody intent, nor told to any
    his purpose, till the moment to do was come.*

*He said—"I will work my will, and then shall there gird me
    round and shield me from those I hate a thousand stout
    cavalry."*

*So he slew: no alarm he raised where the tents stood peace-
    fully, though there in the midst the Vulture-mother had
    entered in*

*To dwell with a lion fierce, a bulwark for men in fight,
    a lion with angry mane upbristled, sharp tooth and
    claw,*

*Fearless: when one him wrongs, he sets him to vengeance
    straight, unfaltering: when no wrong lights on him, 'tis
    he that wrongs.*

*They pastured their camels athirst, until when the time was
    ripe they drove them to pools all cloven with weapons and
    plashed with blood;*

*They led through their midst the Dooms: then they drove
    them forth again to the pasture rank and heavy, till
    their thirst should grow anew.*

*But their lances—by thy life! were guilty of none that fell:
    Nahîk's son died not by them, nor by them al-Muthallam's
    slain;*

*Nor had they in Naufal's death part or share, nor by their
    hand did Wahab lie slain, nor by them fell al-Mukhaẓ-
    ẓam's son.*

300 *Yet for each of those that died did they pay the price of blood—
good camels unblemished that climb in a row by the
upland road*

*To where dwells a kin great of heart, whose word is enough
to shield whom they shelter when peril comes in a night
of fierce strife and storm;*

*Yea, noble are they! the seeker of vengeance gains not from
them the blood of his foe, nor is he that wrongs them left
without help.*

*Aweary am I of life's toil and travail: he who like me has
seen pass of years fourscore, well may he be sick of life!*

*I know what To-day unfolds, what before it was Yesterday;
but blind do I stand before the knowledge To-morrow
brings*

*I have seen the Dooms trample men as a blind beast at random
treads—whom they smote, he died: whom they missed,
he lived on to strengthless eld.*

*Who gathers not friends by help in many case of need is torn
by the blind beast's teeth, or trodden beneath its foot.*

*And he who his honour shields by the doing of kindly deed
grows richer: who shuts not the mouth of reviling, it
lights on him.*

*And he who is lord of wealth and is niggardly with his hoard
alone is he left by his kin: nought have they for him
but blame.*

*Who keeps faith, no blame he earns: and that man whose
heart is led to goodness unmixed with guile gains freedom
and peace of soul.*

*Who trembles before the Dooms, yea, him shall they surely
seize, albeit he set in his dread a ladder to climb the sky.*

*Who spends on unworthy men his kindness with lavish hand,
no praise does he earn, but blame, and repentance the
end thereof.*

*Who will not yield to the spears when their feet turn to him
in peace, shall yield to the points thereof, and the long
flashing blades of steel.*

*Who holds not his foe away from his cistern with sword and
spear, it is broken and spoiled: who uses not roughness,
him shall men wrong.*

*Who seeks far away from kin for housing, takes foe for friend:
who honours himself not well, no honour gains he from
men.*

*Who makes of his soul a beast of burden to bear men's loads,
nor shields it one day from shame, yea, sorrow shall
be his lot.*

*Whatso be the shaping of mind that a man is born withal,
though he think it lies hid from men, it shall surely one
day be known.*

*How many a man seemed goodly to thee while he held his
peace, whereof thou didst learn the more or less when he
turned to speech!*

*The tongue is a man's one half, the other the heart within:
besides these two nought is left but a semblance of flesh
and blood.*

*If a man be old and a fool, his folly is past all cure: but a
young man may yet grow wise and cast off his foolishness.*

*We asked, and ye gave: we asked again, and ye gave again;
but the end of much asking must be that no giving shall
follow it.*

THE DESERT BORN

By Sheik Feizi

*Day fades amidst the mighty solitude,
    The sun goes down and leaves no hope behind;
Afar is heard the ravening cry, for food,
    Of savage monsters; and the sultry wind
Sears with its furnace-breath, but freshens not
With one reviving sigh, the dismal spot
Where three devoted beings panting lie,
Prone on the scorching ground,—as if to die
Were all of good could reach their helpless state,
Abandoned, 'midst the brackless sands, to Fate!
And does young Aiass yield to fortune's frown?
    Are all his high aspirings come to this?
His haughty bearing to the dust bowed down,
    His glorious visions of success and bliss—*

The dreams that led him from his Tartar home,
　　To seek, in golden Hindostan, renown—
Is this the end of all!—Lost, overcome,
By famine and fatigue subdued, at last—
Patience and firmness—hope and valour—past!
He cried—" Oh, Allah! when the Patriarch's child
　　Forlorn beside his fainting mother lay,
Amidst the howling desert dark and wild,
　　When not a star arose to cheer her way,
Heard she not Zemzem's murmuring waters nigh,
And the blest angel's voice that said they should not die?
But I—look on my new-born child—look there!
On my young wife—what can I but despair!
She left her tents for me—abandoned all
　　The wealth, the state her beauty well might claim:
Alas! the guerdon of her truth, how small—
　　Alas! what had I, but a soldier's name,
A sword—a steed, my faithful, fainting one,
Whose course is, like his master's, almost done.
I led her here to die—to die!—when earth
　　Has lands so beautiful, and scenes so fair,
Cities and realms, and mines of countless worth;
　　Monarchs—with proud sultanas all their care,
　　And none with Zarah worthy to compare!
Yet here she lies—a broken cloud!—this gem,
Fit for the first in India's diadem!

Oh, she was like that tree, all purity,
　　Which, ere the hand of man approach the bough,
No bird or creeping insect suffers nigh,
　　Nor shelter to ought evil will allow;
But once the fruit is plucked, there ends the charm—
Dark birds and baneful creatures round it swarm.
Thou, selfish Aiass, hast destroyed the tree,
Behold its lovely blossoms scathed by thee!

Is there no hope!—revive, my noble steed,
Fail not thy master at his utmost need;
Thou canst, thou wilt support her gentle weight?
Courage!—thou wert not wont to deem it great.

A little further—yet one effort more—
And, if we perish then, our miseries are o'er."

" But, oh!—my child! " the fainting mother cried,
  " My arms are feeble, and support her not.
And thou, lost Aiass, death is in thy face:
Why should we strive to quit this hideous place?
My babe and I can perish by thy side—
  Oh! let our graves be in this fatal spot."
She spoke, and prostrate fell. With nerveless hands
  Her form sad Aiass on his steed has cast,
Which, trembling with that lifeless being, stands—
  His struggling breath comes heavily and fast.

A task, a fearful task, must yet be done,
  Ere he the Desert's path shall dare explore,
His babe must sleep beneath yon tree—alone!
  No parent's kiss shall ever wake her more.
Some leaves he plucked, the only leaves that grew
  Upon that mound, so parched and desolate,
These o'er the sleeping innocent he threw—
  Looked not—nor turned—and left her to her fate.

" My babe! thou wert a pearl too bright
For pitiless earth's unfriendly slight.
He who first called thee forth again,
  Shall place thee in thy parent shell:
There shalt thou slumber, free from pain,
  While guardian Peris watch thee well.
Within our hearts, two living urns,
  Shall live thy memory—blessed one!
As the white water-lily turns
  Her silver petals to the moon;
Though distance must their loves divide,
And but his image gilds the tide."

The following prose-poems are from IBIN-AMJED PAGHMANI

THE MARBLE TEMPLE

O my Goddess of Peace! O my Beautiful One! I seek sanctuary in thy garden from the lurid flashes and turmoil of war. But thy roses are withered and the fountain leaps no more with joy of life. Art thou in thy white marble Niche? O my Idol of Idols!

Or has desolation come upon thy shrine and the dust of the arena powdered thy tresses? Ah! sorrow hangs on thy brow and low! I perceive a mark impressioned on thy cheek, as though by the fangs of a dragon of Conflict. O my Idol of Idols, why art thou forlorn?—Or is it only mine eye that painteth this dismal view?

Do I not remember the lofty crest of thy Temple which rose in splendour? Its glittering pinnacles touched the skies—O my Idol of Magnificence! O my Sublime! Why art thou so changed? Why dost thy glory—which once was enthroned by adoring hands—totter under the veil of oblivion?

Be this the mirror of mankind, reflecting their vanity and showing all life as a farce, and time a masquerade. But, O my Idol of Idols! the sun of thy grandeur will pierce the darkest clouds of human vice, and what is noble will for ever remain: so shall thy torch of happiness glow, till existence furl its wings, O my Beautiful One! O my Supreme One!

" YES," CAME A " VOICE "

The night was dark and furious —the rain fell in torrents —vivid flashes of electric fire lashed their forked blazes across the gloom, for a moment illuminated the surrounding objects, and partially revealed the awful horror of the scene. The deep-toned thunder rolled in long and terrifying

peals through vaulted concave of heaven—as dying man
fumbled in his lonely chamber, and lit a candle. Taking
a pen he wrote:

" MY FRIEND,—Death seizes my throat, but my heart
still survives, and I send you my present thoughts.
While you may be reading these lines I shall be groaning
under the agonies of absolute despair, for my past life
earned me nothing more.

" I see the vast gulf of uncertainty yawning; who
can express the anxiety of my soul? It flutters im-
patiently in its earthly cage. No words can paint my
dread, as it wears a face appallingly fearsome. Looking
back, the pages of life are dark and vacant, though the
blanks are filled in by disgrace and ill doings.

" But yet I have a faint beam of hope, which darts
across the tremendous obscurity and may be called a
faith in the mercy of my Creator. I . . . I wish to
write more, but my hand fails me, so good-bye."

" What, I! " said the amazed soul, " I doubled with the
burden of sins and defiled with the black stains; I in this
celestial light! "

" Yes," came a voice. " Forgiveness knows no bounds.
Go, Mercy calls thee to rest."

A TEAR IN A SAPPHIRE VESSEL

The night was beginning to unfold her ebony wings,
and I in the glow of the fire sat reflecting in my silent
chamber. There was a humble apartment across the road,
lit by the feeble beams of a candle, where sat a poor old
woman at her work. Her hair was white as snow, her face
wrinkled and full of care.

From her movements, from her dress, from a mere
nothing I imagined her mournful story; and any human
heart will melt and weep on its recitation. Presently
someone handed her a letter; her hands trembled as she

opened it. She read, she fell back, she fainted—and people rushed to her aid.

One day the black carriages drew up at the door where I had seen the old woman, and carried their burden. The rain pattered on my window panes, and I gazed in my fire. All was dark, all was still and sad around: my thoughts rose high, and I was dreaming.

I was led to the first gate of the heaven. I saw many sights and heard sweet sounds, like the voices of angels hymning to their lyres. And Seraph Gabriel was with me, as he was conducting me in the paths of infinite. The light of heaven dazzled my eyes on our approach to the second portal; and would have sunk me beneath its insufferable splendour had not the angel shaded me with his ambrosial wings, and touched my eyes with balm of amaranth, which grows only in heaven.

And lo! at the gate of heaven stood a pedestal of Jasper, and on this a vessel of pure Sapphire, encircled with gold—in this vessel lay a tear, which did not evaporate in the celestial lights, but remained the same for ever.

" This tear that you see," said the angel on my inquiry, " dropped from the eye of an earth-born, virtuous old woman. It was shed in her affliction for her son's mutilation by a horde of blood-shedders."

Thence we advanced to the cities of diamonds. The spires looked as if they met and touched each other up above, and passing through an emerald glade I saw two human forms—an old woman and a youth: both were dressed in white, and sat talking on the bank of a rivulet. I hid myself behind trees, and crawled as near as I could, and I heard them speak.

" Do you see," said the old woman, " that small smoky speck far below?—it is the earth."

" Is it the earth, where once we lived? Can it be so?" asked the youth in utter amazement.

" Yes, it is earth, my son," said his mother, " where, as you wonder, we once were—and can you not see the piteous pageant of human beings treading upon the skeleton hands of nations, still holding gore-stained swords?"

" Yes, I can yet recall in the faint distance of time that there was something which was called suffering, but I can no longer remember what it was."

The vision disappeared, I awoke, and was sitting in the red glow of the fire in my lonely chamber.

THE GARDEN

Shall I soon behold thee again, O my garden of gardens, where the bamboo twigs frolic with one another all day long in the sunshine, and the lagging kine wind endlessly upwards the liquid river of life?

And the honey-birds dart between the flowerets, and breath of the winds passes onward, sweetened with the perfume of thy verdure?

Or is thy beauty made desolate for ever?

And the labour of the oxen all in vain?

And the pleadings of the birds, and the sighing of the wind?

Wilt thou nevermore delight the heart with the colours of thy raiment and the perfume of thy tresses, O my garden of gardens?

II

Why art thou wilted, O my garden of contentment? Dost thou miss the loving hands that told thine every petal, and fed thee with the nurture of love, and tended thee ever in the joy of creation?

Or dost thou pine away in longing for the liquid music that the winds once wafted across thy bosom, till thy raiment shone as the noonday sun in the glory of it, and the honeybirds forgot their thirst and the oxen their weariness?

Shall thy ruined cisterns never more echo with the ripple of laughter?

Nor thy groves watch the healing of the sick and sorrowful?

My heart is sore for the anguish of thy passing, O my garden of contentment.

III

But though thou art passed away and withered, O my garden of gardens, O my Beautiful One, yet shall the seed of love that was planted in thee flourish in the hearts of those who know thy glories, and shall spread its branches of compassion till the world be sheltered in the shadow of it.

And thy memory shall live for ever, and the perfume of thee shall be wafted throughout the whole earth, and at the presence of it all evil shall be dried up.

For what good has been, is for ever, O my Beautiful One. So is thy loveliness everlasting, O my garden of gardens.

TWO PHASES OF THE MOON

The moon one night descended her staircase of white clouds, and passed through my window panes. Her phosphoric rays stared in my eyes, and I awoke from my sleep.

O, what a heavenly night!

The silvery scene charmed me out of my chamber. The garden swooned under the Lady Moon, as might a youth in love. Unlike the humans, the ecstasy was expressed by a sublime stillness; and the very water in the marble-bottomed pond seemed in slumber.

The tea-rose petals sang a song without a voice, and the beautiful pansies vainly tried to borrow the variegated effect from the starry sky. Bunches of daffodils in a corner blew their trumpets in rapture, while vapours arose from the mignonette to offer the gift of their perfumes to the Lady Moon.

But ah, what a change!

The air ruffled my hair, the moon hid her fair face behind a shroud of black clouds. The wind rose high; it became distinctly chilly, and I hurried in. Drops followed drops; rain, mingled with lightning, lashed my window.

The blue flashes were fearsome, and presently the thunder crashed at the top of the lofty temple.

The interior was lit as if by a thousand candles, and all was again silent, but it was the grim silence of Death.

IN FADING RAYS

In my sleep I saw a vision, and on waking found myself more able to battle with the difficulties of life: for I had heard the last of the Adamic family converse with the sun.

The rays of the sun were feeble, the earth was worn out with age. The bones of the manhood of nations still held the rusted swords in their skeleton hands, while other humbler remains of those who had died of famine or disease could also be seen scattered here and there.

No echoes resounded in the mighty cities of the world; ships loaded with the dead glided mysteriously towards silent shores. Still in the midst of it all stood the lonely man. His words shook the autumn leaves from the trees, just as though a wind had passed through them.

" Proud sun," said he, " you and I are now left alone, but your race is run, and mercy calls you to rest. Your eyes now dimmed have witnessed the mournful flow of human tears—for ten thousand years or more—but you have seen the last.

" For ages, O sun, you were privileged to participate in the greatness of man. Nations rose and fell beneath you, all glory was yours; but your sway had its limits: for did you ever heal an aching heart or add balm to a wounded soul? "

" Go, then, and let the dark curtain of forgetfulness fall on the stage of human existence, lest your rising light may recall the pitiful pageant of mankind and establish life's tragedies once again.

" Even I long to see the last of your fading rays, and you, who have for long been spectator of the world's agonizing phases, must not wait till my breath escapes. You will not boast to perceive the death of this tongue

OC-L*

that speaks, but the sympathetic night will receive my spirit, and I shall return to the realms of light. When your beams will be no more, I shall glow in the celestial radiance.

"Lose your lustre and go, O sun, while I have but a little time yet in my worldly exile, and gladly await the death which will free me from earth's cruel bondage.

"Go—go, and tell the night, who covered your face every evening with her black wings, that you saw the last of Adam's race standing on worldly ruins, and nothing shook his unflinching faith in immortality.

VISIONS OF A RECLUSE

Earthly pleasures I had all, but none opened my heart. Wine, gold, and kingdom are chimerical, and nothing more than illusions devoid of reality.

Here, look my heart! you have all for nothing. The lordly deodars your roof, the velvety grass your carpet, the majestic Jumna to play music, and the gorgeous lamps of nature your light. What more do you desire? Though once a king of men, yet now I have a domain over the guileless jungle, and reign in happiness of solitude. Here I stay, and perchance my blackened disc of mind may yet get bright in contemplation.

The world's reminiscences are repugnant to my soul, and here I shall recall nothing of life's bitterness. Peace and joy will now abide with me, and I shall be alone, yet not lonesome.

Days go, and shadows of night fall; I listen to the sweet music of Jumna, and roam unhurt amongst my wild friends. No human voice penetrated the wall of mighty hills, no man floated his barge on the river, and I gloried in my lonely splendour.

One divine summer evening the perfumes of wild flowers filled the air, all was calm, all was lovely and peaceful, and I was kneeling at my prayer. Soon a stupor came upon me, and I knew not where I was.

But lo! the scene had changed. It was cold; the Jumna, the jungle, and the hills were all gone, the very shape of my hermitage was altered, and I was in a strange land. The stream was small and leaped furiously from stone to stone, the forest was thick, and black clouds threatened a shower.

I wondered, however, not long on my environment, but I heard a sound as if lightning had struck a building and shaken the very foundation of the earth. It was not, as I thought, thunder, but some phenomenon which I had never before seen or heard. A huge tree fell with a crash, and a few pieces of metal, after striking the rock, rebounded and whizzed past my face.

" What a forcible power! " said I, " that can rend asunder big trees, and can throw metal in this fashion. What can it be? Where am I? . . ."

Not long had I waited when I heard horses in full gallop, and in the distance thunder booming. O Lord and Master! which planet is this? I muttered my prayers. Am I thrown in the pits of demons? Is it not the destination of all sinners after death? A shriek from a thousand voices interrupted my prayer, and horsemen drove down the valley like a hurricane. " Ah, cruel monsters! spare our lives. . . ." A deep moan and a death-like silence once again. The noise startled me, and presently an old man stumbled over stones on my right.

" Protect me! hide me! " uttered the old man in agonizing tones. " They are killing us. Here is my gold, and hide me."

" Come, father! " said I. " I seek neither gold nor silver, but am in quest for the peace of the soul. Your age demands respect; come and hide here; none will disturb the tranquillity of your pious years. He hid himself under my straw bed, as would an ostrich in a desert sand.

He could not speak, his arms were bleeding, and he bore a wound on his face, but after a while he said, " Good hermit, fly for your life; they have drained the wells of brutality to a drop, and the nails of their heels have ejected fountains of blood from the panting necks of the vanquished." My blood boiled with rage. "Where are they?" I asked. "What are they?"

"They are," said the old man, "dancing with mirth and glee in the red glow of their blood-stained swords yonder up that hill." "But who are they?" interrupted I. "Tell me, tell me, what kind of animals are they?"

"They are a race of men called the Dragons of War, and come from the North." "A race of men; surely, reverend friend, not men!" "Yes, men," replied he, "in shape and form—and heaven help us if we are discovered."

"Ay, ay," said I. "I understand you now, and all is clear to me. This place—I wondered if it were an abode of demons; it is not, it is earth, and I have heard of these hordes of whom you speak. Wait here, father, and rest your limbs. To kill may be theirs, yet wrong shall be avenged and. . . ."

I had not finished talking, when lo, two men clad in a peculiar garb approached us, and interrogated me whether I had concealed an old man. "Concealed!" said I, "no! Besides what brings evil messengers to the resting-place of a hermit?"

"A priest! Ha, ha!" laughed one. "A priest? A coward—to dress in the guise of a hermit to escape punishment. Feel the edge of this weapon."

"My order," said I, "prohibits shedding human blood, and I am no coward, but have fought and won, and do not hide behind a priestly cloak. The old man whom you seek is here, but you will cross my corpse to pollute his worthy person. I have said that my order prohibits killing human beings, but you are no humans; so villains, come and let us measure swords. My fingers have not as yet lost their touch of the sword." They spoke no more, and hurriedly retraced their steps. The old man sat in tears, and at last fell dead with wounds, and I knelt over him. Then I awoke.

The water of Jumna was like a sheet of melted gold, and its flow was serene. The evening breeze, loaded with fragrance, produced a music as it glided through the deodar leaves, and the sun was just disappearing behind the mountain chains. The sky was painted red, as I sat on the bank of Jumna meditating over my vision, and thought whether the colour in the sky was not the particles of innocent blood agglomerating up above to supplicate and invoke the wrath of heaven on the offenders in the land of my vision. But visions are visions; there are no such people on God's earth, and I was again at my prayer in my peaceful hermitage.

THE HERMITAGE OF SANKARA

On the sacred banks of the Gomtee, in a solitary part of the jungle containing fruits of every kind, continually resounding with the songs of innumerable birds and the light step of the stag or the timid gazelle, far away from the habitation of man, the hermitage of Sankara was situated.

In this delightful retreat the holy person was entirely devoted to fasting, praying, privation, and many painful duties. When summer reigned in all its terrors he surrounded himself with fires and sat bareheaded in the scorching sun; in the rainy season he lay down in the water; and in the depth of winter he enveloped himself in wet garments, when he was already benumbed with cold.

The Devas, the Gandharvas, and other divinities of India, were struck with admiration. " Oh," they cried, " what an astonishing firmness; what an endurance of pain! " These were witnesses to the appalling rigours capable of ensuring Sankara the conquest of the three worlds.

Their admiration being of a jealous kind, it yielded to fear that the will-power thus acquired would make him greater than themselves. They wished to make the pious hermit lose the reward of his long penance, and with this intention they went to their master to seek advice. Indra, the god of the elements, had also noticed the virtuous character of Sankara, and acceding to the request of the others, he addressed the nymph Pramotoncha, distinguished for her beauty and youthful grace.

" Go, Pramotoncha," commanded he; " go like lightning to the abode of Sankara; employ all your powers to make him break his penance."

" Powerful Divinity," answered the nymph, " I am ready to obey your orders, but I tremble for my existence; I fear that illustrious solitary whose looks are so terrible, for his countenance is as radiant as the sun. He in his anger may load me with imprecations, if he should know the object of my mission. Why not, oh Mighty Power, choose another for this perilous enterprise? "

" No," replied Indra, " other nymphs will remain with me. On your celestial beauty I place my hopes. I shall, however, give you Love, Spring, and Zephyr for your assistance."

The sweet-smiling nymph, much flattered by these words, immediately traversed the air with her three companions and alighted in the jungle near the hermitage of Sankara. They wandered for a time beneath those immense shades, which recall to one's mind the eternal verdure of the gardens of Indian hills. On every side Nature smiled, and they were surrounded with fruits, flowers, and singing birds. Perched on the swaying branches, the birds, as various in plumage as in song, equally delighted the ear and the eye. Here and there were pools, clear as crystal, the surfaces of which were dotted with graceful swans of snowy whiteness and a flock of aquatic fowls that love shade and coolness. Pramotoncha and the others could not sufficiently admire the scene. She, however, reminded her assistants of the object of their journey, and called upon them to act in concert to achieve the success of the undertaking, while she began to devise plans to alienate the thoughts of the pious man from his devotions.

" Ah, ah! " she exclaimed, " we are to see this intrepid conductor of the car of Brahma, who boasts of having under the yoke the fiery coursers of the passions. Oh! how I pity him, that in this encounter the reins will drop from his hand; yes, were he Brahma himself, his heart will this day feel the power of the mighty shaft of Love!"

As she concluded these words she advanced towards the hermitage, where by the influence of the holy anchorite the most savage beasts were deprived of their ferocity. Withdrawing to a distance on the bank of the river, she mingled her enchanting voice with the sweet songs of the lonely kokila and swelled the air with a rapturous melody. At the same time Spring diffused new charms over all Nature. Kokila sighed with great softness, and by an ineffable harmony threw the soul into a voluptuous languor. The trickling pearly drops of the bloom-shaded brooklet made music. The gentle breezes, laden with the perfume of the wild flowers, moved with dancing steps. Zephyr's craft being now so well established, Love, armed with her burning arrows, approached the priest to infuse into his veins a consuming fire.

Struck with the melodious songs and the sudden change in the freshness of the atmosphere, Sankara hastened to the spot whence the sound of the music was coming. He was confounded; the musician could nowhere be seen, yet the music was everywhere. While he thus still wondered, he saw a majestic banyan tree split in half; a most beautiful feminine figure appeared in the cleft, and in an instant the tree closed again, the form vanished. Sankara rubbed his eyes, thinking he was dreaming, but as he opened them the vision was there. Amazed and bewildered, he fell unconscious to the ground, and on recovering his senses he raised his hands towards the skies in supplication. Pramotoncha, assuming mortal form, drew near him. " Who art thou?" asked he. " What is thy origin, O adorable woman? Thou, whose graceful form, whose eyebrows so delicately arched, whose enchanting smile no longer leave me master of my reason. Tell me, oh, tell me, sweet creature, who art thou?"

He tried to touch her, but as soon as their hands met, Pramotoncha smiled and made herself invisible. She called to her sisters to wind up their magical spell till the next day, explaining that the next stroke would entirely captivate the hermit, and that they should then weave the thread inextricably round him.

Sankara reeled in the dust and was afraid that his reason was gone. Whether he was changed and the whole universe was altered with him, whether he was dead or alive, he did not know. Stupefied and at his wit's end, the hermit sought his retreat. But every thought was centred in the image of her he had seen; he found sensations springing up in his mind that he had never felt before; he became agitated and sought in vain for repose; he believed he had only begun to exist from the moment his eyes had met hers—beyond this all was void. Alas! he dared not think of the future; his destiny was irrevocable.

The day dawned in all its splendour, the nymphs were again at work, the birds sang in Sankara's ears, and aroused him from his trance—for trance it was, as he did not sleep. He placed his hand behind his ear, and the same music vibrated in the air; he ran to the spot where he had seen the woman, the same tree opened, and the very same charmer stepping out, advanced towards him.

"Oh, can I believe mine eyes? Can it be thou, again, fair lady? Have compassion on me and tell me what is thy station?" spoke the bewitched hermit.

"Since you ask," replied Pramotoncha, "I am the most humble of all maids, and make my living out of gathering these wild flowers; my station, holy hermit, is now nothing, though once my father swayed the sceptre of four kingdoms. My story is sad, and ill-suited for a reverend ear like thine, so let me detain thee no more and take thee away from thy godly pursuits."

"I implore thee," said the hermit, "to tell me why thou art reduced to thy present state, and if it may be in the power of a poor man, he may, perhaps, lighten thy care and advocate thy cause."

"My cause is in the cold caress of the grave," replied the nymph. "As to my story, listen: I am the only daughter of Raja Bishn! He elicited the wrath of a witch, and not only paid for his own life, but the wicked witch placed an eternal curse upon me, by converting me into an ever-roaming form. And this is why I had to become invisible to thee yesterday, for the witch called on my soul to change my place, lest I should have the pleasure of cherishing thy affection."

" Then thou dost reciprocate my sentiments. Come with me thou, the light of my heart; I shall evoke all the powers of heaven and earth and relieve thee of the base wiles of the witch."

With these gentle words all the firmness of Sankara forsook him, and taking the young nymph by the hand, he conducted her to his hermitage—a hermitage where no woman had before set her foot. Then Love, Spring, and Zephyr, judging that their ministry was no longer needed, returned to the ethereal regions and related to the delighted gods the success of their strategy.

Meantime, Sankara, by supernatural power, which his austerities had procured him, instantly metamorphosed himself into a young man, endowed with divine beauty; celestial garments, garlands like those with which the gods adorned themselves, heightened the lustre of his charms.

Fastings, ablutions, prayers, sacrifices, profound meditation, duties to the gods, were all neglected. Solely taken up with his passion, by night and by day, the poor hermit never thought of the shock given to his penance. Plunged as he was in pleasure, the days succeeded each other without his perceiving it. He did not leave her an instant.

She was therefore greatly surprised when one evening he suddenly rose from her side and hastened towards the consecrated grove. " What is the matter? " she asked, inquiringly.

" Dost thou not see," answered Sankara, " that the day is drawing towards the close; I hasten to offer my evening prayers for fear of committing the least fault in the accomplishment of my duties."

" Oh, man of consummate wisdom! what does this day signify to thee, in preference to a hundred others? Come! come! " said the nymph, " if this should pass uncelebrated like all those which thou hast allowed to pass away for

317

these many long months, tell me, I pray, who would pay attention to it or take offence?"

"But," replied the anchorite, "it was this very morning, O charming woman, that I first saw thee on the bank of the river; and when this is the first evening that witnesses thy presence in this place, tell me, what dost thou mean by such bold remarks and the derisive smile that I perceive upon thy lips?"

"And how," she said, "can I avoid smiling at thy error and forgetfulness, when, since the morning of which thou dost speak, one revolution of the year is nearly complete?"

"What! can it be truth? Thou seducing nymph! Or is it a mere joke?"

"Oh!" ejaculated the sorceress, "how can you suspect me of such falseness? I will not tell a lie to a venerable Brahmin, to a holy hermit who has made a vow never to deviate an instant from the path followed by the wise; but now know me as Pramotoncha, who was sent by the god of the elements to break thy pious life, and I have done it."

"Oh, woe to me!" cried the unfortunate Brahmin, whose eyes were at length opened. "Oh, lost fruit of my long penance! All those meritorious works! All those actions conformable to the doctrine of the Vedas! Are they, then, altogether annihilated?"

"Nay, nay! The ever-watchful eye of the All-seeing is open upon us, and I make Him witness. Fly! fly far from me! That power of concentration, won by austerities, which made a year of pleasure seem but as a day, that power is still with me. Go, woman! Go! Thy mission is accomplished. Yet even from thee have I learned something. With greater will, because with greater love, I turn once more to Him who is All-power, All-love, and bow my pride unto His feet."

National Literature

RACE CONFLICT

By Sir Rabindranath Tagore

The problem of race conflict has ever been present in the history of mankind. This conflict has been at the basis of all great civilizations. It is like the clash of elements in the material world giving rise to complex combinations and evolutions of higher growth.

It was the concussion of peoples brought up in different surroundings and with different outlook upon life that started the original energy resulting in complicated social organizations. All civilizations are mixed products. Only barbarism is simple, monadic and unalloyed.

When differences have to be taken into account perforce, when there is no possible escape from them, then men are compelled to find out some central bond which can bring into unity all the diverse elements. This is really the seeking after truth, the search for the one in the many, the universal through the individuals.

Naturally, in the commencement its appearance is simple and crude. Some common visible object of worship is held as a symbol of the oneness of the people. It is very often gross and frightful. For when man has to depend upon external standards of life these have to be made as conspicuous as possible, and nothing is so compelling to primitive imagination as fear.

But, as the community grows larger and, by conquest and other means, peoples of different traditions unite, then fetishes multiply and more gods than one have to be recognized. In that case, these symbols lose their power as common bonds, and they have to be replaced by something whose appeal is not so much to the senses and whose significance is more universal.

Thus, gradually, as the problem grows more and more wide and complex, the solution of it becomes deeper and more far-reaching, and human solidarity seeks for its foundation something which is abiding and comprehensive. This is the purpose of all history, man seeking truth through complexities of experience impelled by the impetus of the immensity of evergrowing life.

There was a time when owing to the restricted means of communication different races and nations lived in a state of comparative segregation and consequently their social laws and institutions had an intensely local character. They were narrowly racial and aggressively hostile to the aliens. People did not have frequent occasion to learn how to adjust themselves with outsiders. They had to take to violent measures when they collided with alien people. They simplified the problem to its narrowest limits and either absolutely excluded and exterminated all foreign elements or completely amalgamated them.

Men have not yet outgrown this training of racial or national self-sufficiency. They are still burdened with the age-long inheritance of a suspicion of aliens which is the primitive instinct of animals. They still have a lurking ferocity ready to come out at the slightest provocation when in contact with people outside their social boundaries. They have not yet acquired fairness of mind when judging other races and dealing with them. They have not that power of adjusting their mental vision which would enable them to understand the people who are not nearest to them. They strive their utmost to prove the superiority and originality of their own religion and philosophy and they are reluctant to acknowledge that truth, because it is truth, naturally manifests itself in different countries in different garbs. They are ever prone to put more stress on differences which are external and lose sight of the inner harmony.

This is the result of being brought up in the home training of isolation, which makes one unfit for the citizenship of the world. But this cannot continue for long and with the advent of the new age of science and commerce men have been brought nearer to each other than they ever were before and they are face to face with the highest problem of human history, the problem of race conflict.

This problem has been waiting to be solved by experience, through the expansion of history. It is not a mere matter of sentiment or of intellect. We had prophets who preached equality of man, and philosophy and literature which gave us a broader view of reality than is contained in the limits of racial traditions and habits. But this race problem with its vast complexity was never before us—we were not in living contact with it. Humanity, till now, has played with this sentiment of brotherhood of man as a girl does with her doll. It reveals the truth of the feeling which is innate in the heart of man, still it lacks the reality of life. But the play-time is passed and what was only in the sentiment has grown into our life fraught with immense responsibilities.

Of all the ancient civilizations, I think that of India was compelled to recognize this race problem in all seriousness, and for ages she has been engaged unravelling the most bafflingly complicated tangle of race-differences. Europe was fortunate in having neighbouring races more or less homogeneous, for most of them were of the same origin. So, though in Europe there were bitter feuds between different peoples, there was not that physical antipathy between them which the difference in colour of skin and in feature tends to produce. In England it did not take long for the Norman and Saxon elements to coalesce and lose their distinctions. Not only in colour and features but in their ideals of life the western peoples are so near each other that practically they are acting as one in building up their civilization.

But it has been otherwise with India. At the beginning of Indian history the white-skinned Aryans had encounters with the aboriginal people, who were dark and who were intellectually inferior to them. Then there were the Dravidians who had their own civilization and whose gods and modes of worship and social system were totally different from those of the newcomers, which must have proved a more active barrier between them than full-fledged barbarism.

In tropical countries life is not so strenuous as it is where the climate is cold. There the necessities of life are comparatively small and nature more prodigal in her bounties; therefore in those countries strifes between con-

x

tending parties die away for want of incentives. So, in India, after a period of fierce struggles, men of different colours and creeds, different physical features and mental attitudes settled together side by side. As men are not inert matter but living beings, this juxtaposition of different elements became an ever-present problem for India. But with all its disadvantages this it was that stimulated men's minds to find out the essential unity in diversity of forms, to know that, however different be the symbols and rituals, God, whom they try to represent, is one without a second, and to realize him truly is to realize him in the soul of all beings.

When differences are too jarring, man cannot accept them as final; so, either he wipes them out with blood, or coerces them in some kind of superficial homogeneity, or he finds out a deeper unity which he knows is the highest truth.

India chose the last alternative; and all through the political vicissitudes that tossed her about for centuries, when her sister civilizations of Greece and Rome exhausted their life force, her spiritual vitality still continued, and she still retains her dignity of soul. I do not say for a moment that the difficulties about the race differences have been altogether removed in India. On the contrary, new elements have been added, new complications introduced, and all the great religions of the world have taken their roots in the soil of India. In her attempts at bringing into order this immense mass of heterogeneity India has passed through successive periods of expansion and con-traction of her ideals. And her latest has been that of setting up rigid lines of regulations to keep different sections at arm's length to prevent confusion and clash.

But such a negative attitude cannot last long, and mere mechanical contrivances can never work satisfactorily in human society. If, by any chance, men are brought together who are not products of the same history and not moulded in the same traditions, they never can rest till they can find out some broad basis of union which is positive in its nature and which makes for love. And I am sure in India we have that spiritual ideal, if dormant but still living, which can tolerate all differences in the exterior while recognizing the inner unity. I feel sure in India we have that golden key forged by ancient wisdom and love which will one day open the barred gates to bring together to the feast of good fellowship men who have lived separated for generations.

From a very remote period of her history till now all the great personalities of India have been working in the same direction. The Gospel of universal love that Buddha preached was the outcome of a movement long preceding him, which endeavoured to get at the kernel of spiritual unity, breaking through all divergence of symbols and ceremonies and individual preferences.

With the advent of the Mohamedan power not only a new political situation was created in India but new ideas in religion and social customs were brought before the people with a violent force. Nevertheless, it had not the effect of generating an antagonistic fanatical movement among Hindus. On the contrary, all the great religious geniuses that were born during this period in India sought a reconciliation of the old with the new ideals in a deeper synthesis, which was possible because of the inherited spirit of toleration and accumulated wisdom of ages. In all these movements there was the repeated call to the people to forget all distinctions of castes and creeds and accept the highest privileges of brotherhood of man by uniting in love of God.

The same thing has occurred again when India has been closely brought in contact with the Christian civilization with the coming of the English. The Brahmo Samaj movement in India is the movement for the spiritual reconciliation of the East and West, the reconciliation resting upon the broad basis of spiritual wisdom laid in the Upanishads. There is again the same call to the people to rise above all artificial barriers of caste and recognize the common bond of brotherhood in the name of God.

In no other country in the world is the conflux of races different in every respect so great as in India. Therefore it never could have been possible for her to come to such a simple solution of the difficulty as national unity. The fetish of nationalism is powerless to bring her warring elements into a harmony; she must appeal to the highest power in man, the spiritual power, she must come to her God. There has been going on in India a long-continued contention between rigid forms of exclusiveness which is mechanical and a recognition of the unity of mankind which is spiritual. Here, as in every land, the social convention is on the side of the pride of caste, and the higher nature and the deeper wisdom of the people assert in the lives of its greatest personalities the validity of the claims of all men to justice and love. On the one hand there is the regulation which forbids eating and drinking at the same board for men of different castes and on the other hand there comes the voice from the ancient past which preaches that he who realizes his own self in the self of all individuals realizes truly. And I have not the least doubt in my mind that it is the urging of this spiritual impulse in man which will win in the end, and will mould all the social forms in such a way that they may not hinder its purpose but become its instrument.

I bring before you this instance of Indian history to show that a problem must be a living one to rouse man's mind for its solution. It has become so in the present age. Races widely separated in their geographical position and historical growth, in their modes of thought and manners of expression have been brought near each other in closer relations. To each man the human world has been enlarged to an extent never dreamt of in former days. That we are not ready for these changed circumstances is becoming painfully evident every day. The caste feeling is running fearfully high. The western people are cultivating an arrogant exclusiveness against all other races. While keeping for themselves their prerogatives of exploiting weaker nations by threat of force they securely bar their own gates against them in a manner cruelly barbarous and inhospitable. Sentiments of humanity are openly discredited and poets of world-wide reputation are exulting in the triumph of brute force. Nations wakened from a lethargy of centuries and bravely struggling for a larger life are held back by others more fortunate, waiting to turn to their own advantage the situation created by the breaking up of old order. Want of consideration for people held to be inferior to themselves, rising into in-human atrocities where privacy is secured, is not uncommon with the people proud of their colour and the impunity of their position.

Yet, in spite of these untoward aspects of the case I assert strongly that the solution is most assured when difficulties are greatest. It is a matter for congratulation that to-day the civilized man is seriously confronted with this problem of race conflict. And the greatest thing that this age can be proud of is the birth of Man in the con-sciousness of men. Its bed has not been provided for, it is born in poverty, its infancy is lying neglected in a way-side stall, spurned by wealth and power. But its day of triumph is approaching. It is waiting for its poets and prophets and host of humble workers and they will not tarry for long. When the call of humanity is poignantly insistent then the higher nature of man cannot but respond. In the darkest periods of his drunken orgies of power and national pride man may flout and jeer at it, daub it as an expression of weakness and sentimentalism, but in that very paroxysm of arrogance, when his attitude is most hostile and his attacks most reckless against it, he is suddenly reminded that it is the direst form of suicide to kill the highest truth that is in him. When organized national selfishness, racial antipathy and commercial self-seeking begin to display their ugly deformities in all their naked-ness, then comes the time for man to know that his salvation is not in political organizations and extended trade relations, not in any mechanical rearrangement of social system, but in a deeper transformation of life, in the liberation of consciousness in love, in the realization of God in man.

JEWELS OF JEWISH THOUGHT

THE EXPULSION FROM SPAIN, 1492

By L. A. Frankl

" *Look, they move! No comrades near, but curses;*
Tears gleam in beards of men sore with reverses;
Flowers from fields abandoned, loving nurses,
Fondly deck the women's raven hair.

" *Faded, scentless flowers that shall remind them*
Of their precious homes and graves behind them;
Old men, clasping Torah-scrolls, unbind them,
Lift the parchment flags and silent lead.

" *Mock not with thy light, O sun, our morrow;*
Cease not, cease not, O ye songs of sorrow;
From what land a refuge can we borrow,
Weary, thrust-out, God-forsaken we?

" *Could ye, suff'ring souls, peer through the Future,*
From despair ye would awake to rapture;
Lo! The Genoese boldly steers to capture
Freedom's realm beyond an unsailed sea! "

(*Translated by M. D. Louis*)

WHAT IS CULTURE?

By the Very Rev. Dr J. H. Hertz

" Not what a man has—knowledge, skill, or goods of
life—determines his culture, but what a man *is*: Culture
is not so much mastery of things as mastery of self. And
only that nation can be called cultured which adds to or,
at least, broadens and deepens the spiritual assets of man-

kind; which introduces some distinctive note into the soul-life of the world; which teaches humanity a new angle of vision towards the Infinite; and by its living and, if need be, by its dying, vindicates the eternal values of life—conscience, honour, liberty.

" Judged by this test, some of the littlest of peoples— Judea, Greece, Elizabethan England, yea, modern Belgium —and not their mighty enemies and oppressors, are cultured nations, champions of the sacred heritage of man. Judged by this test, many a poor Jew, though he be devoid of the graces, amenities, and comforts of life, is yet possessed of culture. An ancient language, a classical language, a holy language, is as familiar to him as his mother-tongue; saturated is he with the sublimest of literatures, which hallows his life, and endows him with high faith and invincible courage.

" Sympathetic appreciation of this indomitable type, this harmonious albeit rugged personality, might well be taken as a touchstone of a man's mentality, culture, and humanity."

THE POGROM

By Ossip Dymov

" It had already lasted two days. But as nobody dined, nobody exchanged greetings, and nobody thought of winding up the clock for the night (for people slept dressed, anywhere, on lofts, in sheds, or in empty railway-carriages), all notion of time had disappeared. People only heard the incessant jingling of broken glass-panes. At this terrible sound the arms stiffened and the eyes became distended with fright.

" Some distant houses were burning. Along the red-tinted street with the red pavement there ran by a red man, whilst another red man stretched his arm, and from the tips of his fingers there broke forth quickly a sharp snapping, cracking sound—and the running man dropped down.

" A strange, sharp cry, ' They are shoo-ooting ! ' passed along the street.

" Invisible and inexorable demons made their appearance. People were perishing by torture. Houses and nurseries were broken in. Old men had their arms fractured; women's white bosoms were trampled upon by heavy, dirty heels. Many were burnt alive.

" Two persons were hiding in a dark cellar, an old man with his son, a schoolboy. The old man went up and opened the outer door again, to make the place look deserted by the owners. A merchant had run in. He wept, not from fear, but from feeling himself in security.

" ' I have a son like you,' he said, tearfully.

" He then breathed heavily and nervously, and added, reflectively, ' Like you, my boy, yes ! '

" The master of the house caught the merchant by his elbow, pulled him close to himself, and whispered into his ear :

" ' Hush ! . . . They might hear us ! '

" There they stood, expectant. Now and then, a rustling; an even sleepless breathing could be heard. The brain cannot familiarize itself with these sounds in the darkness and silence. Perhaps they were asleep, none could tell.

" At night—it must have been late at night—another two stole in quietly.

" ' Is it you ? ' asked one of them, without seeing anybody, and the sudden sound of his voice seemed to light up the darkness for a moment.

" ' Yes,' answered the schoolboy; ' it's all right ! '

" ' Hush ! . . . They might hear you,' said the owner of the cellar, catching each of them by the arm and pulling them down.

" The newcomers placed themselves by the wall, while one of them was rubbing his forehead with his hand.

" ' What is the matter ? ' asked the schoolboy in a whisper.

" ' It is blood.'

" Then they grew silent. The injured man applied a handkerchief to his wound and became quiet. There followed again a thick silence, untroubled by time. Again a sleepless breathing.

" On the top, underneath the ceiling, a very faint whiteness appeared. The schoolboy was asleep, but the other four raised their heads and looked up. They looked long, for about half an hour, so that their muscles were aching through the protracted craning of their necks. At last it became clear that it was a tiny little window through which dawn peeped in.

" Then hasty, frightened steps were heard, and there appeared a tall, coatless man, followed by a woman with a baby in her arms. The dawn was advancing, and one could read the expression of wild fear that stamped itself within upon their faces.

" ' This way! This way! ' whispered the man.

" ' They are running after us, they are looking out for us,' said the woman. Her shoes were put on her bare feet, and her young body displayed strange, white, malignant spots, reminding one of a corpse.

" ' They won't find us; but, for God's sake, be quiet! '

" ' They are close by in the courtyard. Oh, be quiet, be quiet . . . ! '

" The wounded man got hold of the merchant and the owner by the hand, while the merchant seized the man who had no coat. There they stood, forming a live chain, looking on at the mother with her baby.

" All of a sudden there broke out a strange though familiar sound, so close and doomful. What doom it foreboded they felt at once, but their brains were loth to believe it. . . .

" The sound was repeated. It was the cry of the infant. The merchant made a kindly face and said:

" ' Baby is crying. . . . Lull him, my dear,' said he, rushing to the mother. ' You will cause the death of us all.'

" Everybody's chest and throat gasped with faintness. The mother marched up and down the cellar lulling and coaxing.

" ' You must not cry; sleep, my golden one. . . . It is I, your mother . . . my heart. . . .'

" But the child cried on obstinately, wildly. . . . There must have been something in the mother's face that was not calculated to produce a tranquillizing effect.

" And now, in this warm and strange underground atmosphere, the woman's brain wrenched out a wild, mad idea. It seemed to her that she had read it in the eyes, in the suffering silence of these unknown people. And these unhappy, frightened men understood that she was thinking of them. They understood it by the unutterably mournful tenderness with which she chanted, while drinking in the infant's eyes with her own.

" ' He will soon fall asleep. I know. It is always like that; he cries for a moment, then he falls asleep at once. He is a very quiet boy.' She addressed the tall man with a painful, insinuating smile. From outside there broke in a distant noise. Then came a thud and a crack shaking the air.

" ' They are searching,' whispered the schoolboy.

" But the infant went on crying hopelessly.

" ' He will undo us all,' blurted out the tall man.

" ' I shall not give him away . . . no, never ! ' ejaculated the distracted mother.

" ' Oh, God,' whispered the merchant, and covered his face with his hands. His hair was unkempt after a sleepless night. The tall man stared at the infant with fixed, pro-truding eyes. . . .

" ' I don't know you,' the woman uttered, low and crossly, on catching that fixed look. ' Who are you ? What do you want of me ? '

" She rushed to the other men, but everybody drew back from her with fear. The infant was crying on, piercing the brain with its shouting.

" ' Give it to me,' said the merchant, his right eyebrow trembling. ' Children like me.'

" All of a sudden it grew dark in the cellar; somebody had approached the little window and was listening. At this shadow, breaking in so suddenly, they all grew quiet. They felt that it was coming, it was near, and that not another second must be lost.

" The mother turned round. She stood up on her toes, and with high, uplifted arms she handed over her child to the merchant. It seemed to her that by this gesture she was committing a terrible crime . . . that hissing voices were cursing her, rejecting her from heaven for ever and ever. . . .

" Strange to say, finding itself in the thick, clumsy, but loving hands of the merchant, the child grew silent.

" But the mother interpreted this silence differently. In sight of everybody the woman grew grey in a single moment, as if they had poured some acid over her hair. And as soon as the child's cry died away, there resounded another cry, more awful, more shattering and heartrending.

" The mother rose up on her toes; and grey, terrible, like the goddess of justice herself, she howled in a desperate, inhuman voice that brought destruction with it. . . . Nobody had expected that sudden madness. The schoolboy fell in a swoon.

.　　　.　　　.　　　.　　　.

" Afterwards the newspapers reported details of the killing of six men and an infant by the mob, for none had dared to touch the mad old woman of twenty-six."